Instructor's Resource Manual
for Ahrens's

Essentials of
Meteorology

An Invitation to the Atmosphere

THIRD EDITION

CHARLES D. WEIDMAN
University of Arizona

BROOKS/COLE

THOMSON LEARNING™

Australia • Canada • Mexico • Singapore • Spain • United Kingdom • United States

BROOKS/COLE

THOMSON LEARNING ™

Cover Design: *Irene Morris*
Cover Photo: *Allan Davey/Masterfile*

For more information about this or any other Brooks/Cole product, contact:
BROOKS/COLE
511 Forest Lodge Road
Pacific Grove, CA 93950 USA
www.brookscole.com
1-800-423-0563 (Thomson Learning Academic Resource Center)

Printed in the United States of America

5 4 3 2 1

ISBN 0-534-37524-3

Contents

Chapter 1
The Earth's Atmosphere

Summary

This introductory chapter presents a broad overview of the physical and chemical structure of the atmosphere and weather. The chapter begins with a discussion of the present composition of the earth's atmosphere. Special attention is given to the importance of water vapor, which is both a source of latent heat energy and also the most abundant of the greenhouse gases. Current concern over increasing concentrations of another constituent, carbon dioxide, and its role in global warming are also examined. The principle atmospheric pollutants, including ozone, are listed but are covered in additional detail in a later chapter.

The concepts of air density and air pressure are introduced and students should understand why both decrease with increasing altitude. A vertical profile of temperature, which does not decrease steadily with increasing altitude, provides a basis for separating the atmosphere into several layers with distinct properties. The ozone layer and the ozone hole are mentioned briefly.

Finally, the student is introduced to the elements that constitute weather and will see how weather conditions and a variety of different types of storms might appear on a surface weather map or a photograph from a meteorological satellite. The chapter ends with discussions of the historical development of meteorology and the many ways that weather and climate can affect our lives and interests, and provides information on sources of detailed weather information.

Key Terms

(Listed in approximately the same order they appear in the text. Terms in boldface are emphasized and appear at the end of the chapter in the text.)

radiant energy
atmosphere
nitrogen (N_2)
oxygen (O_2)
water vapor (H_2O)
parts per million (ppm)
condensation
evaporation
latent heat
greenhouse gas
carbon dioxide (CO_2)
photosynthesis
global warming
methane (CH_4)
nitrous oxide (N_2O)
chlorofluorocarbons (CFCs)
ozone (O_3)
photochemical smog

ozone hole
aerosols
pollutants
nitrogen dioxide (NO_2)
carbon monoxide (CO)
hydrocarbons
sulfur dioxide (SO_2)
acid rain
hydrogen and helium
   (early atmosphere)
outgassing
gravity
air density
weight
mass
air pressure
barometer
millibar (mb)

hectopascal (hPa)
inches of mercury (Hg)
lapse rate
temperature inversion
radiosonde
dropsonde
rawinsonde
sounding
troposphere
isothermal zone
stratosphere
tropopause
jet streams
mesosphere
hypoxia
thermosphere
exosphere
homosphere

2

heteorosphere	low (pressure center)	wind chill
ionosphere	high (pressure center)	frostbite
ions	anticyclone	hypothermia
weather	**wind**	heat exhaustion
weather elements	**wind direction**	heat stroke
climate	Coriolis force	heat waves
geostationary satellite	**front**	severe thunderstorms
meridians of longitude	cold front	flash floods
parallels of latitude	warm front	downburst
middle latitudes	occluded front	wind shear
middle latitude cyclonic	**meteorology**	American Meteorological
storm	Meteorologica	Society (AMS)
extratropical cyclone	Book of Signs	National Weather
hurricane	isobars	Service (NWS)
eye	Doppler radar	The Weather Channel
thunderstorm	Tiros I	NOAA weather radio
tornado		

Teaching Suggestions, Demonstrations, and Visual Aids

1.　A large classroom demonstration vacuum chamber can be used to show that sound does not travel through a vacuum (place an alarm clock or buzzer in the vacuum chamber). Heat can't be transported via conduction and convection through a vacuum either. The rates of cooling of a warm object inside and outside the vacuum chamber could be compared to reinforce this fact (a third object could be placed in a large container of water at room temperature to illustrate the higher thermal conductivity of water). Students might become more aware of the importance of radiant energy transport between the earth and sun.

2.　Chapter 1 in Hands-On Meteorology by Zbigniew Sorbjan (publ. by American Meteorological Society, 1996, ISBN 1-878220-20-9) discusses some of the early theories about air and early determinations of the chemical composition of air.

3.　Place a candle in the center of a dish and partially fill the dish with water. Light the candle and then cover it with a large jar or beaker. The flame will consume the oxygen inside the jar and reduce the pressure. Water will slowly flow into the jar to re-establish pressure balance. The change in volume should be close to 20%, the volume originally occupied by the oxygen in the air. This demonstration can be used to illustrate the concept of partial pressure, which is later used in the chapter on humidity. The students should also be asked what they think the products of the combustion might be and why these gases do not replace the oxygen and maintain the original pressure in jar. One of the combustion products is water vapor, which condenses as the air in the jar cools. Another combustion product is carbon dioxide, which presumably goes into solution. Students should be asked what effect the heat generated by the burning candle might have on the results of the experiment.

4.　Students often confuse water vapor with liquid water. Students should understand that water vapor is an invisible gas. Haze, fog, clouds, and the steam from a boiling pot all become visible when water vapor condenses and forms small drops of liquid water.

5.　Some of the atmospheric pressure demonstrations described in Chapter 6 could be performed here also.

6.　Fill a wine glass completely with water and cover it with a piece of plastic (such as the lid from a tub of margarine), being careful to remove any air. Invert the glass. The water remains in the glass because the upward force on the cover due to the pressure of the air is much stronger than the downward gravitational force on the water. The demonstration can be made much more convincing if a 4000 mL flask is used instead of the wine glass. When full of water, the flask weighs approximately 10 pounds.

7.   Photographs showing the flat tops of thunderstorms taken from the ground or an airplane often mark the top of the troposphere. Shadows will often be apparent on visible satellite photographs taken when the sun is at a low angle in the sky. This creates the appearance of depth reinforces the fact that the earth's atmosphere is thin.

8.   The discussion of surface air motions in Chapter 1 is a good place to introduce satellite photographs, loops, and surface weather maps. Many students have occasion to watch television weather broadcasts. Being able to observe and understand weather phenomena on their own may heighten interest in the subject.

Student Projects

1.   Students could attempt to repeat some of the experiments in Hands-On Meteorology.

2.   "A General Chemistry Experiment for the Determination of the Oxygen Content of Air" by James P. Birk, Larry McGrath, and S. Kay Gunter (*J. Chem. Educ., 58*, 804-805, 1981) describes a simple experiment that can be used to determine atmospheric oxygen concentrations (see also: "Percent Oxygen in Air," George F. Martins, *J. Chem. Educ., 64*, 809-810, 1987).

3.   The sensitive manometer described in Chapter 6 of this manual can be used to monitor daily and longer term variations in atmospheric pressure. If we assume that the pressure in the flask remains constant (the air temperature in the flask remains constant) the pressure difference, ΔP, between the air inside and outside the flask can be computed using the hydrostatic equation:

$$\Delta P = \rho_{liquid}\, g\, \Delta h$$

where ρ_{liquid} is the density of the liquid in the manometer (gm/cm^3), g is the acceleration of gravity (980 cm/sec^2), and Δh is the difference in the heights of the two columns (cm). ΔP will have units of dynes/cm^2 (1000 dynes/cm^2 = 1 mb). The sketch at right shows a case where the ambient air pressure is less than the flask pressure.

4.   Have the students mark the positions of fronts and pressure systems for each day on an outline map of the United States. (This information can be obtained from the daily newspaper, television news and weather programs, or from NOAA weather radio broadcasts.) Have students do this for a week at a time, noting the general movement of these systems.

5.   Have students compose a one-week journal, including daily newspaper weather maps and weather forecasts. Ask them to write a commentary for each day as to the coincidence of actual and predicted weather.

6.   Have students keep a daily record of weather conditions that they actually observe. Then, periodically, the instructor can supply mean daily data such as high and low temperatures, pressure, dew point, wind speed, cloud cover, and precipitation amounts. The students should plot this data and annotate the graph with their observations. Students can use their graphs to experimentally test concepts developed in class. After studying Chapter 1, for example, students might try to determine whether periods of stormy weather really are associated with lower-than-average surface pressure.

4

Multiple Choice Exam Questions

1.   Almost 99% of the atmosphere lies within ____ of the earth's surface.
   a. 3 km
   * b. 30 km
   c. 300 km
   d. 3000 km

2.   The most abundant gases in the earth's atmosphere by volume are
   a. carbon dioxide and nitrogen.
   b. oxygen and water vapor.
   * c. nitrogen and oxygen.
   d. oxygen and helium.
   e. oxygen and ozone.

3.   Which of the following gases could be found in the atmosphere with a concentration greater than 1%?
   a. hydrogen (H)
   * b. water vapor (H_2O)
   c. carbon dioxide (CO_2)
   d. ozone (O_3)

4.   The primary gases found in the homosphere.
   * a. nitrogen and oxygen
   b. oxygen and ozone
   c. oxygen and helium
   d. nitrogen and helium

5.   In a volume of air near the earth's surface, ____ occupies 78% and ____ nearly 21%.
   * a. nitrogen, oxygen
   b. hydrogen, oxygen
   c. oxygen, hydrogen
   d. nitrogen, water vapor
   e. hydrogen, helium

6.   Water vapor
   * a. is invisible.
   b. colors the sky blue.
   c. makes clouds white.
   d. is very small drops of liquid water.

7.   Water vapor is
   * a. a gas.
   b. a cloud of small water droplets.
   c. a cloud of small ice crystals.
   d. another name for fog.

8.   The only substance near the earth's surface that is found naturally in the atmosphere as a solid, liquid, and a gas.
   a. carbon dioxide
   * b. water
   c. molecular oxygen
   d. ozone
   e. methane

9. Which of the following is considered a variable gas in the earth's atmosphere?
* a. water vapor
   b. nitrogen
   c. oxygen
   d. argon
   e. all of the above

10. The gas that shows the most variation in concentration from place to place and from time to time in the lower atmosphere.
   a. ozone (O_3)
   b. carbon dioxide (CO_2)
* c. water vapor (H_2O)
   d. methane (CH_4)
   e. argon (Ar)

11. The concentration of this gas in the atmosphere can range from about 0% to near 3 or 4%.
   a. oxygen (O_2)
   b. ozone (O_3)
   c. carbon dioxide (CO_2)
* d. water vapor (H_2O)

12. Typically, water vapor occupies about what percentage of the air's volume near the earth's surface?
   a. about 90%
   b. about 78%
   c. about 21%
   d. close to 10%
* e. less than 4%

13. In the atmosphere, tiny solid or liquid suspended particles of various composition are called
* a. aerosols.
   b. carcinogens.
   c. greenhouse gases.
   d. fog.

14. Since the turn of this century, CO_2 in the atmosphere has
   a. disappeared entirely.
   b. been decreasing in concentration.
   c. remained at about the same concentration from year to year.
* d. been increasing in concentration.

15. The concentration of carbon dioxide (CO_2) in the atmosphere is relatively low compared to some of the other constituents. CO_2 is important none the less because
   a. it dissolves in water to form acid rain.
* b. it is a greenhouse gas.
   c. it is the main ingredient in photochemical smog.
   d. it is toxic.

16. Carbon dioxide (CO_2) levels are currently about 368 ppm; "ppm" are units of
* a. concentration.
   b. weight.
   c. volume.
   d. pressure.

6

17. Which of the following processes acts to remove carbon dioxide from the atmosphere?
    a. lightning
    b. deforestation
*   c. photosynthesis
    d. burning fossil fuels

18. The combustion of methane (burning of natural gas) could be written in the form of a chemical equation as follows: $CH_4 + O_2$ ---> product gases. The product gases would most likely include which of the following?
*   a. carbon dioxide (CO_2) and water vapor (H_2O)
    b. sulfur dioxide (SO_2) and carbon dioxide (CO_2)
    c. ozone (O_3) and oxygen (O_2)
    d. water vapor (H_2O) and ozone (O_3)

19. The greenhouse gas that has been increasing in concentration, at least partly due to deforestation.
*   a. carbon dioxide (CO_2)
    b. chlorofluorocarbons (CFCs)
    c. water vapor (H_2O)
    d. ozone (O_3)

20. This greenhouse gas is used as a refrigerant, a solvent, and during the manufacture of foam.
    a. water vapor (H_2O)
    b. carbon dioxide (CO_2)
    c. methane (CH_4)
    d. nitrous oxide (N_2O)
*   e. chlorofluorocarbons (CFCs)

21. The most abundant greenhouse gas in the earth's atmosphere is
    a. carbon dioxide (CO_2).
    b. nitrous oxide (N_2O).
*   c. water vapor (H_2O).
    d. methane (CH_4).
    e. chlorofluorocarbons (CFCs).

22. Which below is not considered a greenhouse gas?
    a. carbon dioxide (CO_2)
    b. nitrous oxide (N_2O)
    c. water vapor (H_2O)
    d. methane (CH_4)
*   e. oxygen (O_2)

23. Which of the following is considered a greenhouse gas?
    a. oxygen (O_2)
*   b. water vapor (H_2O)
    d. carbon monoxide (CO)
    e. nitrogen (N_2)
    f. sulfur dioxide (SO_2)

24. Which of the following ingredients are needed for ozone formation in the stratosphere?
    a. carbon dioxide (CO_2) and water vapor (H_2O)
    b. nitrogen (N_2) and oxygen (O_2)
    c. water vapor (H_2O) and oxygen (O_2)
*   d. oxygen molecules (O_2) and oxygen atoms (O)
    e. hydrogen (H) and helium (He)

25. When chlorofluorocarbons are subjected to ultraviolet radiation, ozone-destroying _____ is released.
    *
    a. chlorine
    b. nitrogen
    c. carbon dioxide
    d. carbon
    e. water vapor

26. About 97% of the _____ in the atmosphere is found in the stratosphere where it absorbs harmful ultraviolet radiation.
    a. water vapor
    b. nitrous oxide
    c. carbon dioxide
    * d. ozone
    e. chlorofluorocarbons

27. What gas is produced naturally in the stratosphere and is also a primary component of photochemical smog in polluted air at the surface?
    a. carbon dioxide
    b. carbon monoxide
    * c. ozone
    d. nitrogen dioxide
    e. hydrocarbons

28. Which of the following greenhouse gases is also capable of destroying ozone in the stratosphere?
    a. water vapor (H_2O)
    b. carbon dioxide (CO_2)
    c. methane (CH_4)
    * d. chlorofluorocarbons (CFCs)
    e. all of the above

29. The so-called "ozone hole" is observed above
    a. the equator.
    b. the continent of Australia.
    * c. the continent of Antarctica.
    d. the continent of Asia.

30. The earth's first atmosphere was composed primarily of
    a. carbon dioxide and water vapor.
    * b. hydrogen and helium.
    c. oxygen and water vapor.
    d. argon and nitrogen.

31. The outpouring of gases from the earth's hot interior is called
    a. evaporation.
    * b. outgassing.
    c. photodissociation.
    d. the hydrologic cycle.

32. The most abundant gas emitted from volcanoes is
    a. nitrogen.
    b. sulfur dioxide.
    c. oxygen.
    d. carbon dioxide.
    * e. water vapor.

33. The primary source of the oxygen in the earth's atmosphere during the past half billion years or so appears to be
    a. volcanic eruptions.
  * b. photosynthesis.
    c. photodissociation.
    d. exhalations of animal life.
    e. transpiration.

34. Which of the following statements is true?
    a. the earth is approximately 4.6 million years old
  * b. the earth's first atmosphere is thought to have escaped into space
    c. oxygen concentrations decreased rapidly once plant life had evolved on the earth
    d. carbon dioxide and water vapor are the two most abundant gases in the universe

35. The amount of force exerted over an area of surface is called
    a. density.
    b. weight.
    c. temperature.
  * d. pressure.

36. This holds a planet's atmosphere close to its surface.
    a. solar radiation
  * b. gravity
    c. cloud cover
    d. moisture
    e. temperature

37. Much of Tibet lies at altitudes over 18,000 feet where the pressure is about 500 mb. At such altitudes, the Tibetans live above roughly
    a. 10% of the air molecules in the atmosphere.
    b. 25% of the air molecules in the atmosphere.
  * c. 50% of the air molecules in the atmosphere.
    d. 75% of the air molecules in the atmosphere.

38. Based on the pressures shown in the figure at right, 30% of the weight of the atmosphere lies
    a. above point C.
    b. between points B and C.
  * c. between points A and C.
    d. between points A and B.

39. Inches of mercury (Hg) are commonly used units of
    a. mass
  * b. atmospheric pressure
    c. altitude
    d. air density

40. Which of the following weather elements <u>always</u> decreases as we climb upward in the atmosphere?
    a. wind
    b. temperature
  * c. pressure
    d. moisture
    e. all of the above

41. The number of air molecules in a given space or volume is called
*   a. density.
    b. pressure.
    c. temperature.
    d. weight.

42. The ozone hole is found in this atmospheric layer.
    a. thermosphere
    b. troposphere
*   c. stratosphere
    d. ionosphere

43. At jet aircraft cruising altitude (33,000 ft. or about 10 km) you are
    a. near the top of the stratosphere.
*   b. near the top of the troposphere.
    c. above the ozone layer.
    d. in the ionosphere.

44. Almost all of the earth's weather occurs in the
    a. exosphere.
    b. stratosphere.
    c. mesosphere.
    d. thermosphere.
*   e. troposphere.

45. In the stratosphere, the air temperature normally
    a. decreases with increasing height.
*   b. increases with increasing height.
    c. both increases and decreases depending on the season.
    d. cannot be measured.

46. The order of the layers of the atmosphere from lowest to highest is
*   a. troposphere, stratosphere, mesosphere, thermosphere.
    b. stratosphere, troposphere, thermosphere, mesosphere.
    c. mesosphere, stratosphere, troposphere, thermosphere.
    d. thermosphere, stratosphere, mesosphere, troposphere.

47. The flat top of a thunderstorm about 30,000 or 10 km high would mark the top of the
    a. atmosphere.
*   b. troposphere.
    c. stratosphere.
    d. ozone layer.

48. The earth's atmosphere is divided into layers based on changes in the vertical profile of
*   a. air temperature.
    b. air pressure.
    c. air density.
    d. wind speed.

49. The most abundant gas in the <u>stratosphere</u> is
    a. oxygen (O_2).
*   b. nitrogen (N_2).
    c. carbon dioxide (CO_2).
    d. ozone (O_3).

50. The hottest atmospheric layer is the
    a. stratosphere.
    b. mesosphere.
* c. thermosphere.
    d. troposphere.

51. Which of the following would remain constant if you travelled up through the troposphere?
    a. air density
* b. percentage oxygen concentration
    c. air temperature
    d. air pressure

52. Warming in the stratosphere is mainly caused by
* a. absorption of ultraviolet radiation by ozone.
    b. release of latent heat energy during condensation.
    c. chemical reactions between ozone and chlorofluorocarbons.
    d. frictional heating caused by meteorites.

53. In a temperature inversion
* a. air temperature increases with increasing height.
    b. air temperature decreases with increasing height.
    c. air temperature remain constant with increasing height.
    d. it is warmer at night than during the day.

54. The rate at which temperature decreases with increasing altitude is known as the
    a. temperature slope.
* b. lapse rate.
    c. sounding.
    d. thermocline.

55. About 97% of all ozone in the atmosphere is found in the
* a. stratosphere.
    b. troposphere.
    c. exosphere.
    d. thermosphere.

56. Air temperature increases with increasing altitude
* a. in the stratosphere.
    b. over the oceans.
    c. in the troposphere.
    d. everywhere.
    e. nowhere.

57. The atmospheric layer in which we live is called the
* a. troposphere.
    b. stratosphere.
    c. thermosphere.
    d. exosphere.

58. Which of the following is found at the highest altitude?
    a. the top of the troposphere
    b. the ozone layer
* c. the top of the stratosphere
    d. the top of Mt. Everest (30,000 ft)

59. The temperature of the tropopause
    a. is close to the temperature at the earth's surface.
*   b. is much colder than the temperature at the earth's surface.
    c. has never been measured.
    d. is much warmer than the temperature at the earth's surface.

60. The instrument that measures temperature, pressure, and humidity in the vertical is the
    a. barograph.
*   b. radiosonde.
    c. aneroid barometer.
    d. altimeter.

61. A radiosonde
    a. is used to monitor surface weather conditions in remote areas.
    b. uses radiowaves to determine the height of the ionosphere.
*   c. is carried aloft by balloon and measures weather conditions above the ground.
    d. measures water flow in stream beds during flash floods.

62. The electrified region of the upper atmosphere is called the
    a. thermosphere.
    b. mesosphere.
    c. stratosphere.
*   d. ionosphere.

63. ____ has a major effect on radio communications.
    a. Air pressure
    b. The ozone layer
*   c. The ionosphere
    d. Air density

64. The ionosphere is an atmospheric layer that contains a high concentration of ions. An ion is
    a. another term for ozone.
*   b. an atom or molecule that has lost or gained an electron.
    c. atomic oxygen.
    d. a radioactive element.

65. The horizontal movement of air is the weather element
    a. temperature.
    b. pressure.
*   c. wind.
    d. humidity.

66. The word "weather" is defined as
    a. the average of the weather elements.
    b. the climate of a region.
*   c. the condition of the atmosphere at a particular time and place.
    d. any type of falling precipitation.

67. Which of the following best determines the weather?
    a. air temperature
    b. humidity
    c. wind
    d. air pressure
*   e. all of the above

68. The wind direction is
*   a. the direction from which the wind is blowing.
     b. the direction to which the wind is blowing.
     c. always directly from high toward low pressure.
     d. always directly from low toward high pressure.

69. Knots are units of
*   a. wind speed.
     b. altitude.
     c. air pressure.
     d. wind direction.

70. Meteorology is the study of
     a. landforms.
     b. the oceans.
*   c. the atmosphere.
     d. outer space.
     e. extraterrestrial meteoroids that enter the atmosphere.

71. A south wind
     a. blows from the north.
     b. is any warm wind.
*   c. blows from the south.
     d. is any moist wind.

72. Storms vary in size (diameter). Which list below arranges storms from largest to smallest?
     a. hurricane, tornado, middle latitude cyclone, thunderstorm
     b. hurricane, middle latitude cyclone, thunderstor, tornado
     c. middle latitude cyclone, tornado, hurricane, thunderstorm
*   d. middle latitude cyclone, hurricane, thunderstorm, tornado

73. A tropical storm system whose winds are in excess of 74 mi/hr is called a(n)
     a. anticyclone.
     b. tornado.
     c. extratropical cyclone.
*   d. hurricane.

74. Middle latitude storms are also known as
     a. anticyclones.
     b. hurricanes.
*   c. extratropical cyclones.
     d. tornadoes.

75. A towering cloud, or cluster of clouds, accompanied by thunder, lightning, and strong gusty winds.
     a. hurricane
     b. trough
*   c. thunderstorm
     d. tornado

76. A relatively small, rotating funnel that extends downward from the base of a thunderstorm is called a(n)
*   a. tornado.
     b. middle latitude storm.
     c. hurricane.
     d. extratropical cyclone.

77.   In the middle latitudes of the Northern Hemisphere, surface winds tend to
       blow ___ and ___ around an area of surface low pressure.
       a. clockwise, inward
       b. clockwise, outward
*   c. counterclockwise, inward
       d. counterclockwise, outward

78.   In the middle latitudes of the Northern Hemisphere, surface winds tend to
       blow ___ and ___ around an area of surface high pressure.
       a. clockwise, inward
*   b. clockwise, outward
       c. counterclockwise, inward
       d. counterclockwise, outward

79.   Where cold surface air is replacing warm air, the boundary separating the different bodies of air is
       termed a
       a. parallel of latitude.
       b. tornado.
*   c. cold front.
       d. warm front.

80.   Where warm surface air is replacing cold air, the boundary separating the different bodies of air is
       termed a
       a. high pressure area.
       b. parallel of latitude.
       c. tornado.
       d. cold front.
*   e. warm front.

81.   On a weather map, sharp changes in temperature, humidity, and wind direction are marked by
*   a. a front.
       b. an anticyclone.
       c. a ridge.
       d. blowing dust.

82.   Areas of high atmospheric pressure are also known as
       a. hurricanes.
       b. middle latitude cyclonic storms.
       c. troughs.
       d. tornadoes.
*   e. anticyclones.

83.   The letters H and L on a surface weather map refer to high and low
       a. temperature.
       b. altitude.
*   c. pressure.
       d. latitude.

84.   Which of the following is most likely associated with fair weather?
*   a. high pressure area
       b. low pressure area
       c. a cold front
       d. a warm front

85. Clouds often form in the
*   a. rising air in the center of a low pressure area.
    b. rising air in the center of a high pressure area.
    c. sinking air in the center of a low pressure area.
    d. sinking air in the center of a high pressure area.

86. Meteorology did not become a genuine science until
    a. Aristotle wrote <u>Meteorologica</u>.
*   b. the invention of weather instruments.
    c. scientists discovered weather fronts.
    d. computers were invented.
    e. satellite data became available to the weather forecaster.

87. During the late 1500s Galileo
    a. invented the mercury barometer.
*   b. invented a crude thermometer.
    c. formulated the laws of gravitation.
    d. explained how the earth's rotation affects the wind.

88. The first weather satellite, Tiros I, was launched in
    a. 1940
    b. 1950
*   c. 1960
    d. 1970

True False Exam Questions

1. While the atmosphere absorbs dangerous ultraviolet radiation, it is too thin to protect surface inhabitants from meteors and other solid objects coming from space.
(ans: FALSE)

2. The concentrations of nitrogen, oxygen, and water vapor show very little variation in concentration from place to place and from time to time in the lower atmosphere.
(ans: FALSE)

3. Most of the water vapor in the atmosphere is thought to have come from the earth's hot interior.
(ans: TRUE)

4. Carbon dioxide concentrations have increased nearly 250% since the early 1800s.
(ans: FALSE)

5. While carbon dioxide concentrations are increasing, the concentrations of other greenhouse gases such as methane are decreasing.
(ans: FALSE)

6. Chlorofluorocarbons (CFCs) play a role in stratospheric ozone destruction and are also greenhouse gases.
(ans: TRUE)

7. The atmosphere's first oxygen is thought to have come from the splitting of water vapor molecules by solar radiation.
(ans: TRUE)

8. Sea-level pressure is determined by both the amount of air in the atmosphere and the strength of the earth's gravity.
    (ans: TRUE)

9. Air temperatures in the thermosphere are higher than at the ground because sunlight energy is absorbed and shared by relatively few atoms and molecules.
    (ans: TRUE)

10. Extratropical cyclone is another word for hurricane.
    (ans: FALSE)

Word Choice Exam Questions

1. 99% of the air in the atmosphere is found in a layer that is much THICKER than, much THINNER than, about the SAME thickness as the diameter of the earth. (circle one answer)
    (ans: THINNER)

2. Are the highest water vapor concentrations found in TROPICAL or POLAR regions? (circle one answer)
    (ans: TROPICAL)

3. Does photosynthesis increase OXYGEN(O_2) or CARBON DIOXIDE(CO_2) concentrations in the atmosphere? (circle one answer)
    (ans: OXYGEN)

4. You would expect atmospheric CO_2 concentrations to be lowest in the WINTER SUMMER when photosythesis activity is HIGHEST LOWEST. (choose one word from each pair)
    (ans: SUMMER, HIGHEST)

5. It is the observed steady INCREASE DECREASE in OZONE CARBON DIOXIDE concentrations that has lead to concern over global warming. (choose one word from each pair).
    (ans: INCREASE, CARBON DIOXIDE)

6. There is currently concern about INCREASING DECREASING ozone concentrations in the troposphere and INCREASING DECREASING concentrations of ozone in the stratosphere. (choose one word from each pair).
    (ans: INCREASING, DECREASING)

7. Peak ozone (O_3) concentrations are found in the stratosphere near 25 km altitude. Would you expect to find the highest molecular oxygen (O_2) concentrations at HIGHER, LOWER, or the SAME altitude? (circle one answer)
    (ans: LOWER)

8. Sea level pressure is determined by the COMPOSITION WEIGHT THICKNESS of the atmosphere. (circle one answer)
    (ans: WEIGHT)

9. Would you expect to find the strongest vertical air motions in the TROPOSPHERE or in the STRATOSPHERE? (circle one answer)
    (ans: TROPOSPHERE)

10. Lines of LATITUDE LONGITUDE on a map or globe are parallel to the equator. (circle one answer)
    (ans: LATITUDE)

11. AM radio waves are able to propagate a LONGER SHORTER distance at night than they do during the day because of WEAKENING STRENGTHENING of the lower D layer in the ionosphere. (choose one word from each pair)
(ans: LONGER, WEAKENING)

12. Clear skies occurs in regions where the surface pressure is HIGH LOW and the air is RISING SINKING. (choose one word from each pair)
(ans: HIGH, SINKING)

Short Answer Exam Questions

1. Without _____ in the atmosphere we would only survive for a few minutes.
(ans: OXYGEN)

2. Measurements begun in 1958 at the Mauna Loa observatory in Hawaii indicate a steady increase in the concentration of what greenhouse gas?
(ans: CARBON DIOXIDE (CO_2))

3. Match one of the gases listed at right with   argon (Ar)
the appropriate atmospheric concentration below.   carbon dioxide (CO_2)
a. ranges from near 0 to 3 or 4% _____   nitrogen (N_2)
b. currently about 0.037% _____   oxygen (O_2)
c. in dry air, _____ has a concentration of 1%.   water vapor (H_2O)
d. about 78% _____
(ans: a. H_2O, b. CO_2, c. Ar, d. N_2)

4. The breakdown of plant material by bacteria in rice paddies and biochemical reactions in the stomachs of cows are important sources of atmospheric _____.
(ans: METHANE (CH_4))

5. Because these atmospheric consituents absorb a portion of the earth's outgoing radiant energy, _____ play a significant role in the earth's heat-energy budget.
(ans: GREENHOUSE GASES)

6. The most abundant greenhouse gas in the earth's atmosphere is _____.
(ans: WATER VAPOR)

7. The white clouds that form over active volcanoes indicate that they release large amounts of this common atmospheric constituent.
(ans: WATER VAPOR)

8. Match the description below with one of the gases in the list at right
a. greenhouse gas   sulfur dioxide (SO_2)
b. acid rain   ozone (O_3)
c. pollutant   carbon dioxide (CO_2)
d. photochemical smog   carbon monoxide (CO)
(ans: a. CO_2, b. SO_2, c. CO, d. O_3)

9. Outside an airplane at 30,000 feet altitude (about 10 km), the air temperature would be _____, the air pressure would be _____, and the air density would be _____ than(as) at sea level. (fill in each blank with HIGHER, LOWER, or the SAME)
(ans: LOWER, LOWER, LOWER)

10. _____ is defined as the mass of an object multiplied by the acceleration of gravity.
(ans: WEIGHT)

11. A _____ is a region in the atmosphere where temperature increases with increasing altitude.
(ans: TEMPERATURE INVERSION)

12. The vertical distribution of temperature, humidity, and pressure can be measured with an instrument called a(n) _____, that is carried upward with a balloon.
(ans: RADIOSONDE)

13. The basis for dividing the earth's atmosphere into layers is the change of _____ with altitude.
(ans: TEMPERATURE)

14. The name of the layer in the atmosphere that can have a strong effect on radio communications.
(ans: IONOSPHERE)

15. The word _____ refers to the "average weather" observed over a period of many years.
(ans: CLIMATE)

16. _____ has the ability to peer into severe thunderstorms and unveil their winds.
(ans: DOPPLER RADAR)

Essay Exam Questions

1. Explain how ozone might be thought to have both a beneficial and a detrimental role in the earth's atmosphere.

2. Describe the various types of storms found in the earth's atmosphere. Can you find any correlation between storm size and storm duration? What factors might determine a storm's severity?

3. What instruments are used in meteorology? What role did the discovery of instruments play in the emergence of the science of meteorology?

4. Briefly describe some of the historical events that helped meteorology progress as a natural science from Aristotle to the present day.

5. What role does deforestation play in the current concern over global warming?

6. What causes air pressure? Why does air pressure decrease with increasing altitude?

7. Describe some of the processes that release and remove carbon dioxide from the atmosphere. Is there any evidence that suggests that these processes are not in balance?

8. There is currently concern that the amount of ozone in the stratosphere may be decreasing. Why would a decrease in ozone concentration be important?

9. Draw a diagram showing how air temperature normally changes with height. Begin at the ground and end in the upper thermosphere. Be sure to label the four main layers. Give one important characteristic of each layer. Where on your diagram would the top of Mt. Everest, the ozone layer, and the ionosphere be found?

10. What are the principal gaseous components of the earth's atmosphere? Where do scientists believe these gases came from?

11.	What information might you find on a surface weather map that is not readily apparent on a satellite photograph? What information could a satellite photograph provide that a surface chart could not?

12.	Explain why the invention of the telegraph should have resulted in more accurate weather predictions.

Chapter 2
Warming the Earth and the Atmosphere

Summary

This chapter begins with definitions of temperature and heat, and compares the Kelvin (absolute), Celcius, and Fahrenheit temperature scales. Heat is the flow of energy between objects with different temperatures and can occur by the processes of conduction, convection, latent heat transport, and radiation. Air is a relatively poor conductor of heat but can transport energy efficiently over large distances by the process of convection. The latent heat energy associated with changes of phase of water is also a very important energy transport mechanism in the atmosphere. A physical explanation of why rising air cools and sinking air warms is given.

The electromagnetic spectrum and the rules which govern the emission of electromagnetic radiation are reviewed next. This provides sufficient background for a detailed study of the atmospheric greenhouse effect and the exchange of energy between the earth's surface, the atmosphere, and space. Students will see that, because the amounts of energy absorbed and emitted by the earth are in balance, the earth's average radiative equilibrium temperature varies little from year to year. Students should understand that the energy the earth absorbs from the sun consists primarily of short-wave radiation. Essentially all of the energy emitted by the earth is in the form of infrared radiation. Selective absorbers in the atmosphere, such as water vapor and carbon dioxide, absorb some of the earth's infrared radiation and then radiate a portion of it back to the surface. Because of this effect, the earth's average surface temperature is appreciably higher than would otherwise be the case. Results from recent research relating to the effect of increasing concentrations of carbon dioxide and other greenhouse gases and the effects of clouds on the earth's energy balance are reviewed.

The final portion of this chapter demonstrates that variations in the intensity of sunlight reaching the ground and the length of the day caused by the changing tilt of the earth relative to the plane of its orbit around the sun that are the main causes of seasonal variations on the earth. We follow seasonal changes for a full year in the Northern Hemisphere. By comparison, seasons in the Southern Hemisphere are six months out of phase and moderated somewhat by the larger surface coverage by oceans.

Key Terms
(Listed in approximately the same order they appear in the text. Terms in boldface are emphasized and appear at the end of the chapter in the text.)

kinetic energy	**latent heat**	watt
temperature	evaporation	joule
absolute zero	**sensible heat**	**convection**
heat	condensation	**thermals**
absolute scale	melting	convective circulation
Kelvin scale	sublimation	(thermal cell)
Fahrenheit scale	freezing	**advection**
Celcius scale	deposition	parcel
change of state	calorie	**radiant energy**
(phase change)	**conduction**	(radiation)

19

electromagnetic waves
wavelength (λ)
micrometer
photons
UV-A
UV-B
UV-C
sun protection factor
   (SPF)
Experimental Ultraviolet
   Index
Wien's law
Stefan-Boltzmann law
electromagnetic spectrum
visible region
ultraviolet (UV) radiation
infrared (IR) radiation
shortwave radiation
longwave (terrestrial)
   radiation

blackbody
radiative equilibrium
   temperature
selective absorbers
greenhouse effect
atmospheric greenhouse
   effect
atmospheric window
general circulation
   models (GCMs)
global warming
positive feedback
Earth Radiation Budget
   Experiment (ERBE)
negative feedback
free convection cells
solar constant
scattering
diffuse light
reflected (light)

albedo
aurora
solar wind
perihelion
aphelion
aurora borealis
aurora australis
Tropic of Cancer
summer solstice
Arctic Circle
insolation
autumnal equinox
Indian Summer
winter solstice
Tropic of Capricorn
cold wave
vernal equinox

Teaching Suggestions, Demonstrations, and Visual Aids

Heat Transport

1.   Heat a thin iron bar in a flame (from a bunsen burner or a propane torch). Begin by holding the bar fairly close to the end of the bar. Students will see that heat is quickly conducted through the metal when the instructor is forced to move his or her grip down the bar. Repeat the demonstration with a piece of glass tubing or glass rod. Glass is a poor conductor and the instructor will be able to comfortably hold the glass just 2 or 3 inches from the tip. Ask the students if they believe energy is being transported away from the hot glass and if so, how? Without heat loss by conduction, the glass will get hotter than the iron bar and the tip should begin to glow red - a good demonstration of energy transport by radiation. Faint convection currents in the air can be made visible if the hot piece of glass is held in the light beam between an overhead projector and a projection screen. Ask the students what they would do to quickly cool a hot object. Many will suggest blowing on it, an example of forced convection. Someone might suggest plunging the hot object into water. This makes for a satisfying end to the demonstration. Evaporating water can be seen and heard when the hot iron rod is put into the water (caution: the glass may shatter if suddenly cooled in water). The speed with which the rod is cooled is proof of the large latent heat energy transfer associated with changes of phase.

2.   Ask the students whether they believe water could be brought to a boil most rapidly in a covered or an uncovered pot. The question can be answered experimentally by filling two beakers with equal amounts of water and placing them on a single hot plate (to insure that energy is supplied to both at equal rates). It is a good idea to place boiling stones in the beakers to promote gentle boiling. Cover one of the beakers with a piece of foil. The covered pot should boil first.   A portion of the energy added to the uncovered pot is used to evaporate water, not to increase the water's temperature. Weigh the uncovered beaker after the experiment to determine how much water is lost by evaporation.

3.   Newton's law of cooling states that the rate at which an object cools is proportional to the temperature difference between the object and its surroundings. This useful concept is easily demonstrated during the course of a 50 minute lecture. See, for example, "Newton's Law of Cooling or is Ten Minutes Enough Time for a Coffee Break" (ref: C.M. Dennis, Jr., *Phys. Teacher*, 532-533, Oct. 1980) or "A Murder in Ceylon" (ref: C.F. Bohren, *Weatherwise, 35*, 184-187, Aug. 1982)

4.   The concept of energy equilibrium is sometimes difficult for students to grasp. Place a glass of water on a table top and ask the students whether they think the temperature of the water in the glass is warmer, cooler

or the same as the surroundings. Many will say it is the same. Ask the students whether they think there is any energy flowing into or out of the glass. With some encouragement, they will recognize that the water is slowly evaporating and that this represents energy flow out of the glass. Energy flowing out of the glass will cause the water's temperature to decrease. Will the water just continue to get colder and colder until it freezes? No. As soon as the water's temperature drops below the temperature of the surroundings, heat will begin to flow into the water. The rate at which heat flows into the glass will depend on the temperature difference between the glass and the surroundings. The water temperature will decrease until energy flowing into the glass balances the loss due to evaporation.

Radiation

5.   Use a lamp with a 150 watt reflector bulb to help explain the concept of radiation intensity. Blindfold a student and hold the lamp at various distances from the student's back. Ask the student to judge the distance of the bulb. Use the same lamp to illustrate the concepts of reflection, albedo, and absorption by measuring the amount of reflected light from various colored surfaces with a sensitive light meter. The reflectivity of natural surfaces outdoors could be measured or form the basis for a student or group project.

6.   A 200 watt clear light bulb connected to a dimmer switch can be used to illustrate how the temperature of an object affects the amount and type of radiation that the object will emit. Explain that passage of electricity through the resisitive filament heats the filament. The filament's temperature will increase until it is able to emit energy at the same rate as it gains energy from the electric current. With the dimmer switch set low, the bulb can be made to faintly glow red. At low temperatures, the bulb emits low-intensity, longwave radiation. As the setting on the dimmer switch is increased, the color of the filament will turn orange, yellow and then white as increasing amounts of shortwave radiation are emitted. The intensity of the radiation will increase dramatically.

7.   Some students may not understand that a colored object appears that way because it reflects or scatters light of that color. The object isn't emitting visible light (ask the student whether they would see the object if all the lights in the room were turned off). Some students have the misconception that a green object reflects all colors but green. Similarly it is important that students understand that a red or green filter transmits red or green light. Put a red and a green (or blue) filter on an overhead projector and draw a hypothetical filter transmission curve. Put the two filters together and show that no light is transmitted. Ask the students what happens to the light that is not transmitted by the filter.

Seasons

8.   Begin the lecture by drawing an ellipse on the blackboard with the sun positioned much closer to one end of the ellipse. On the other end of the ellipse, closest to the sun, make a dot for the earth and label it, "January and winter." Then label the other end "July and summer." Act confused and ask, "Wait a minute, is that correct?" Usually this is enough to start an interesting discussion on what causes the seasons.

9.   Explain the seasons by shining a fairly broad, collimated beam of light onto a globe in a darkened room. Begin by showing the earth with no tilt, then increase the tilt to 23.5°. Finally increase the tilt to 45°. Explain how the change in tilt would influence the average temperature measured in July and January in the Northern Hemisphere.

Using the globe or drawings, the students should understand whether they would need to look to the south or north of overhead to see the sun at noon from different locations on the earth at different times of year. They should also understand whether it is necessary to look east, northeast, or southeast to see the sun rise.

10.   The attenuation of light as is passes through a scattering medium can be demonstrated by placing a photodetector at one end of an aquarium full of water and a light source at the other end. Then begin to add milk in small, but measurable amounts. The signal at the detector will decay exponentially with the amount of milk added. The decay will depart from the exponential law when enough milk is added that appreciable multiple scattering begins to occur. The effect of an absorbing medium can be demonstrated if India ink (diluted with water if necessary) is used in place of milk.

22

11.   A photodetector can be placed on a flat board that is then oriented perpendicularly to light rays coming from a source placed further away. As the detector is tilted with respect to the light source, the signal will decrease. If the tilt angle is measured, the photodetector signal will be seen to obey a cosine law.

Student Projects

1.   Items #2, #3, 10 and #11 above could form the basis of a student project or experiment.

2.   There are several interesting experiments in Chapter 4 (Heat) in <u>Hands-On Meteorology</u> (see reference on p. 2 of this manual).

3.   The solar irradiance (calories/cm² min) at the ground can be measured relatively easily using a rectangular piece of aluminum. One side of the block should be painted black to make it a good absorber of sunlight. Drill a hole in the side of the block so that a thermometer can be inserted. The block is positioned in a piece of styrofoam so that only the blackened surface is exposed. Position the block in full sunlight and orient it so that a dowel stuck into the styrofoam does not cast a shadow; this will insure that the block is pointing directly at the sun. Record the temperature of the block at 30 to 60 second intervals for 15 to 20 minutes.

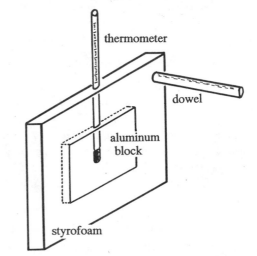

        The solar irradiance, S, can be determined using the following formula:

$$S = (\text{mass} \times \text{specific heat} \times \Delta T/\Delta t)/\text{area}$$

The area is the cross sectional area of the surface exposed to the sun. The time rate of change of temperature, $\Delta T/\Delta t$, can be determined from a graph of temperature and time. The block's temperature should increase fairly linearly early in the experiment before the block becomes too hot and begins to lose significant amounts of heat to the surroundings (the plot of temperature versus time should show this).

4.   A rough estimate of the latent heat of vaporization of liquid nitrogen (or alternatively the latent heat of fusion of ice or latent heat of sublimation of dry ice) can be determined relatively easily. Pour 100 to 200 grams of warm tap water into a 16 oz styrofoam cup. Measure the exact mass and temperature of the water. Measure about 30 grams of liquid nitrogen into a smaller cup. Pour the liquid nitrogen into the warm water (carefully to avoid splashing). Once the nitrogen has evaporated remeasure the temperature of the water. If we assume that all of the heat removed from the warm water is used to evaporate the liquid nitrogen we can use the measured drop in water temperature, ΔT, to determine the latent heat of vaporization:

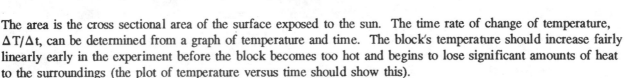

Heat lost by warm water = Heat used to evaporate nitrogen
(mass water) x specific heat x ΔT = latent heat x (mass N$_2$ evaporated)

        By varying the initial temperature of the warm water, students can investigate an important source of error in this experiment. Students could also perform the experiment with a cover on the cup or in a dewar flask to try to reduce heat loss to the surroundings.

Multiple Choice Exam Questions

1.   Which of the following provides a measure of the average speed of air molecules?
        a. pressure
*   b. temperature
        c. density
        d. heat

2.   A change of one degree on the Celcius scale is ___ a change of one degree on the Fahrenheit scale.
        a. equal to
*   b. larger than
        c. smaller than
        d. is in the opposite direction of

3.   Which of the following is <u>not</u> considered a temperature scale?
        a. Fahrenheit
        b. Kelvin
*   c. Calorie
        d. Celcius

4.   The temperature scale where 0° represents the freezing point and 100° the boiling point of water.
        a. Fahrenheit
*   b. Celcius
        c. Kelvin
        d. absolute

5.   If the temperature of the air is said to be at absolute zero, one might conclude that
        a. the motion of the molecules is at a maximum.
        b. the molecules are occupying a large volume.
*   c. the molecules contain a minimum amount of energy.
        d. the temperature is 0° F.
        e. the air temperature is 0° C.

6.   The temperature scale that sets freezing of pure water at 32°.
        a. Kelvin
*   b. Fahrenheit
        c. Celcius
        d. British

7.   If the radio announces that it is 32 degrees outside on a warm summer day, they are probably using the ___ temperature scale.
*   a. Celcius
        b. Fahrenheit
        c. Kelvin
        d. Absolute

8.   Room temperature is about 300 degrees on the ___ temperature scale.
        a. Fahrenheit
        b. British
        c. Celcius
*   d. Kelvin

9. A temperature of 27° C would be equal to what temperature on the Kelvin scale?
*   a. 300 K
    b. 270 K
    c. 100 K
    d. 27 K
    e. 0 K

10. Energy of motion is also known as
    a. dynamic energy.
*   b. kinetic energy.
    c. sensible heat energy.
    d. static energy.
    e. latent heat energy.

11. The transfer of heat by molecule-to-molecule contact is
*   a. conduction.
    b. convection.
    c. radiation.
    d. ultrasonic.

12. Which of the following is the poorest conductor of heat?
*   a. still air
    b. water
    c. ice
    d. snow
    e. soil

13. Heat is energy in the process of being transferred from
*   a. hot objects to cold objects.
    b. low pressure to high pressure.
    c. cold objects to hot objects.
    d. high pressure to low pressure.
    e. regions of low density toward regions of high density.

14. The horizontal transport of any atmospheric property by the wind is called
*   a. advection.
    b. radiation.
    c. conduction.
    d. latent heat.
    e. reflection.

15. Heat transferred upward from the surface of the <u>moon</u> can take place by
    a. convection.
    b. conduction.
    c. latent heat.
*   d. radiation.

16. Which of the following is <u>not</u> a heat-transport process in the atmosphere?
    a. conduction
    b. radiation
*   c. convergence
    d. convection

17. A heat transfer process in the atmosphere that depends upon the movement of air is
    a. conduction.
    b. reflection.
  * c. convection.
    d. radiation.

18. Snow will usually <u>melt</u> on the roof of a home that is a
    a. good radiator of heat.
  * b. good conductor of heat.
    c. poor radiator of heat.
    d. poor conductor of heat.

19. The heat energy released when water vapor changes to a liquid is called
    a. latent heat of evaporation.
    b. latent heat of fusion.
    c. latent heat of fission.
  * d. latent heat of condensation.

20. When water changes from a liquid to a vapor, we call this process
    a. freezing.
    b. condensation.
    c. sublimation.
    d. deposition.
  * e. evaporation.

21. This is released as sensible heat during the formation of clouds.
    a. potential energy
    b. longwave radiation
  * c. latent heat
    d. kinetic energy

22. The term "latent" means
    a. late.
    b. hot.
  * c. hidden.
    d. dense.

23. The processes of condensation and freezing
  * a. both release sensible heat into the environment.
    b. both absorb sensible heat from the environment.
    c. do not affect the temperature of their surroundings.
    d. do not involve energy transport.

24. This process causes rising air to cool.
  * a. expansion
    b. evaporation
    c. compression
    d. condensation

25. The cold feeling that you experience after leaving a swimming pool on a hot, dry, summer day is
    a. heat transport by conduction.
    b. heat transport by convection.
    c. heat transport by radiation.
  * d. heat transport by latent heat.

26

26. ___ of the phase changes shown at right release(s) energy to the surroundings.
    a. none
*   b. one
    c. two
    d. all

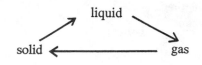

27. The temperature of a rising air parcel
*   a. always cools due to expansion.
    b. always warms due to expansion.
    c. always cools due to compression.
    d. always warms due to compression.
    e. remains constant.

28. Sinking air warms by this process.
*   a. compression
    b. expansion
    c. condensation
    d. friction

29. Which of the following carries the least amount of energy?
    a. a photon of ultraviolet light
    b. a photon of red light
    c. a photon of blue light
    d. a photon of green light
*   e. a photon of infrared light

30. Energy transferred by electromagnetic waves is called
    a. magnetism.
    b. convection.
    c. conduction.
*   d. radiation.

31. Micrometers (μm) are units of
    a. intensity.
*   b. distance.
    c. frequency.
    d. speed.

32. The proper order from shortest to longest wavelength is
    a. visible, infrared, ultraviolet.
    b. infrared, visible, ultraviolet.
*   c. ultraviolet, visible, infrared.
    d. visible, ultraviolet, infrared.
    e. ultraviolet, infrared, visible.

33. Which of the following has a wavelength shorter than that of violet light?
    a. green light
    b. blue light
    c. infrared radiation
    d. red light
*   e. ultraviolet radiation

34.   Points A and C are ___ wavelength apart.
        a. 1
*   b. 1/2
        c. 1/3
        d. 1/4

35.   One micrometer is a unit of length equal to
        a. one million meters.
*   b. one millionth of a meter.
        c. one tenth of a millimeter.
        d. one thousandth of a meter.

36.   Electromagnetic radiation with wavelengths between 0.4 and 0.7 micrometers is called
        a. ultraviolet light.
*   b. visible light.
        c. infrared light.
        d. microwaves.

37.   Which of the following represents the smallest unit of length?
        a. mile
        b. centimeter
        c. meter
*   d. micrometer
        e. inch

38.   Solar radiation reaches the earth's surface as
        a. visible radiation only.
        b. ultraviolet radiation only.
        c. infrared radiation only.
        d. visible and infrared radiation only.
*   e. ultraviolet, visible, and infrared radiation.

39.   Which of the following is <u>not</u> found in the infrared (IR) portion of the electromagnetic spectrum?
*   a. 0.4 to 0.7 μm interval
        b. the atmospheric window
        c. selective absorption by water vapor (H_2O) and carbon dioxide (CO_2)
        d. peak emission from the earth

40.   The earth's radiation is often referred to as ___ radiation, while the sun's radiation is often referred to as ___ radiation.
        a. shortwave, longwave
        b. shortwave, shortwave
*   c. longwave, shortwave
        d. longwave, longwave

41.   The sun emits a maximum amount of radiation at wavelengths near ___, while the earth emits maximum radiation near wavelengths of ___.
        a. 0.5 micrometers, 30 micrometers
*   b. 0.5 micrometers, 10 micrometers
        c. 10 micrometers, 30 micrometers
        d. 1 micrometer, 10 micrometers
        e. 0.3 micrometers, 50 micrometers

42. The earth emits radiation with greatest intensity at
  * a. infrared wavelengths.
   b. radio wavelengths.
   c. visible wavelengths.
   d. ultraviolet wavelengths.

43. When we see the moon at night, we are seeing
   a. visible light emitted by the moon.
   b. infrared light emitted by the moon.
  * c. visible light reflected by the moon.
   d. infrared light reflected by the moon.

44. Most of the radiation emitted by a human body is in the form of
   a. ultraviolet radiation and is invisible.
   b. visible radiation but is too weak to be visible.
  * c. infrared radiation and is invisible.
   d. humans do not emit electromagnetic radiation.

45. The sun emits its greatest intensity of radiation in
  * a. the visible portion of the spectrum.
   b. the infrared portion of the spectrum.
   c. the ultraviolet portion of the spectrum.
   d. the x-ray portion of the spectrum.

46. Which of the following has the highest energy and is potentially the most dangerous kind of radiation?
   a. UVA radiation
   b. UVB radiation
  * c. UVC radiation
   d. IR radiation

47. About 90% of all skin cancers are linked to exposure to
   a. UVA radiation.
  * b. UVB radiation.
   c. UVC radiation.
   d. IR radiation.

48. If a careful series of measurements reveals that the wavelength of peak emission from the sun
   (λ_{max}) is slowly increasing (shifting to longer wavelength), you might conclude that the sun is getting
   a. hotter.
   b. bigger.
  * c. colder.
   d. closer.

49. If the average temperature of the sun increased, the wavelength of peak solar emission would
  * a. shift to a shorter wavelength.
   b. shift to a longer wavelength.
   c. remain the same.
   d. impossible to tell from given information

50. Which of the following determine the kind (wavelength) and amount of radiation that an object emits?
  * a. temperature
   b. thermal conductivity
   c. density
   d. latent heat

51. At which temperature would the earth be radiating energy at the greatest rate or intensity?
    a. -5° F
    b. -40° F
    c. 60° F
    d. 32° F
    * e. 105° F

52. The rate at which radiant energy is emitted by a body
    * a. increases with increasing temperature.
    b. increases with decreasing temperature.
    c. does not depend on the temperature.
    d. depends on the chemical composition of the body.

53. This property of electromagnetic radiation is inversely proportional to temperature; if temperature increases ___ will decrease.
    a. propagation speed
    b. intensity
    c. rate of emission
    * d. wavelength of peak emission

54. The earth's atmospheric window is in the
    a. ultraviolet region.
    b. visible region.
    * c. infrared region.
    d. polar regions.

55. Which of the following is known primarily as a selective absorber of ultraviolet radiation?
    a. carbon dioxide
    * b. ozone
    c. water vapor
    d. clouds

56. Which of the following statements is not correct?
    a. calm, cloudy nights are usually warmer than calm, clear nights
    b. each year the earth's surface radiates away more energy than it receives from the sun
    c. the horizontal transport of heat by the wind is called advection
    * d. good absorbers of radiation are usually poor emitters of radiation

57. The atmospheric greenhouse effect is due primarily to the fact that
    a. oxygen and ozone absorb ultraviolet radiation.
    b. nitrogen and oxygen transmit visible radiation.
    c. cloud formation releases latent heat energy.
    * d. carbon dioxide and water vapor absorb infrared radiation.

58. The atmospheric greenhouse effect is produced mainly by the
    a. absorption and re-emission of visible light by the atmosphere.
    b. absorption and re-emission of ultraviolet radiation by the atmosphere.
    * c. absorption and re-emission of infrared radiation by the atmosphere.
    d. absorption and re-emission of visible light by clouds.
    e. absorption and re-emission of visible light by the ground.

59. Without the atmospheric greenhouse effect, the average surface temperature would be
   a. higher than at present.
   * b. lower than at present.
   c. the same as it is now.
   d. much more variable than it is now.

60. Imagine going outside at night with an instrument that can detect infrared (IR) radiation. Which of the following would you expect to observe?
   a. IR radiation travelling upward from the ground only
   b. IR radiation propagating downward from the sky only
   * c. IR radiation coming from both the ground and the sky
   d. no IR radiation would be detected at night

61. Which of the following gases are mainly responsible for the atmospheric greenhouse effect in the earth's atmosphere?
   a. oxygen and nitrogen
   b. nitrogen and carbon dioxide
   c. ozone and oxygen
   * d. water vapor and carbon dioxide

62. Clouds ___ infrared radiation and ___ visible radiation.
   a. absorb, absorb
   * b. absorb, reflect
   c. reflect, reflect
   d. reflect, absorb

63. At night, low clouds
   * a. enhance the atmospheric greenhouse effect.
   b. weaken the atmospheric greenhouse effect.
   c. are often caused by the atmospheric greenhouse effect.
   d. have no effect on the atmospheric greenhouse effect.

64. Suppose last night was clear and calm. Tonight low clouds will be present. From this you would conclude that tonight's minimum temperature will be
   * a. higher than last night's minimum temperature.
   b. lower than last night's minimum temperature.
   c. the same as last night's minimum temperature.
   d. above freezing.

65. Of the gases listed below, which is <u>not</u> believed to be responsible for enhancing the earth's greenhouse effect?
   a. chlorofluorocarbons (CFCs)
   * b. molecular oxygen (O_2)
   c. nitrous oxide (N_2O)
   d. carbon dioxide (CO_2)
   e. methane (CH_4)

66. Low clouds retard surface cooling at night better than clear skies because
   * a. the clouds absorb and radiate infrared energy back to earth.
   b. the water droplets in the clouds reflect infrared energy back to earth.
   c. the clouds start convection currents between them.
   d. the clouds are better conductors of heat than is the clear night air.
   e. the formation of the clouds releases latent heat energy.

67. If the present concentration of CO_2 doubles by the end of the 21st century, climate models predict that for the earth's average temperature to rise 2.5° C, what gas must also increase in concentration?
     a. nitrogen
     b. oxygen
     c. methane
*   d. water vapor

68. The combined albedo of the earth and the atmosphere is approximately
     a. 4 percent.
     b. 10 percent.
*   c. 30 percent.
     d. 50 percent.
     e. 90 percent.

69. The albedo of the earth's surface is only about 4%, yet the combined albedo of the earth and the atmosphere is about 30%. Which set of conditions below best explains why this is so?
*   a. high albedo of clouds, low albedo of water
     b. high albedo of clouds, high albedo of water
     c. low albedo of clouds, low albedo of water
     d. low albedo of clouds, high albedo of water

70. The albedo of the moon is 7%. This means that
*   a. 7% of the sunlight striking the moon is reflected.
     b. 7% of the sunlight striking the moon is absorbed.
     c. the moon emits only 7% as much energy as it absorbs from the sun.
     d. 93% of the sunlight striking the moon is reflected.

71. Which of the following is an incorrect identification?
     a. albedo - percent of radiation reflected from a surface
     b. kinetic energy - energy of motion
*   c. black body - selective absorber
     d. long-wave radiation - earth radiation

72. Which of the following has the highest albedo?
*   a. snow
     b. sand
     c. forests
     d. water
     e. grass

73. An increase in albedo would be accompanied by ___ in radiative equilibrium temperature.
     a. an increase
*   b. a decrease
     c. no change
     d. unstable oscillations

74. On the average, about what percentage of the solar energy that strikes the outer atmosphere eventually reaches the earth's surface?
     a. 5%
     b. 15%
     c. 30%
*   d. 50%
     e. 70%

75. The combined albedo of the earth and its atmosphere averages about 30%. This value could effectively be altered by
    a. increasing the amount of cloud cover around the earth.
    b. increasing the amount of snow and ice covering the earth's surface.
    c. increasing the amount of particulate matter in the atmosphere that will reflect incoming solar radiation.
  * d. all of the above are correct

76. About 50% of the sunlight reaching the top of the atmosphere is
    a. absorbed by ozone in the stratosphere.
    b. reflected or scattered by air molecules and clouds.
  * c. absorbed at the ground.
    d. absorbed by greenhouse gases.

77. The major process that warms the lower <u>atmosphere</u> is
    a. the release of latent heat during condensation.
    b. conduction of heat upward from the surface.
    c. convection.
  * d. absorption of infrared radiation.
    e. direct absorption of sunlight by the atmosphere.

78. If the sun suddenly began emitting more energy, the earth's radiative equilibrium temperature would
  * a. increase.
    b. decrease.
    c. remain the same.
    d. begin to oscillate.

79. If the amount of energy lost by the earth to space each year were not approximately equal to that received ,
  * a. the atmosphere's average temperature would change.
    b. the length of the year would change.
    c. the sun's output would change.
    d. the mass of the atmosphere would change.

80. Sunlight that bounces off a surface is said to be ___ from the surface.
    a. radiated
    b. absorbed
    c. emitted
  * d. reflected

81. The earth's surface
  * a. radiates more energy than it receives from the sun.
    b. radiates less energy than it receives from the sun.
    c. radiates the same amount of energy that it receives from the sun.
    d. does not radiate any energy.

82. The atmosphere near the earth's surface is "heated from below." Which of the following contributes the smallest amount of energy?
    a. conduction of heat upward from a hot surface
    b. convection from a hot surface
    c. absorption of infrared energy that has been radiated from the surface
  * d. heat energy from the earth's interior

83. An object is absorbing 3 units of visible light, has a temperature of 300 K, and is in radiative equilibrium. Which of the following is true?
    a. the object is not emitting any radiation
    b. the object is emitting 3 units of visible radiation
 * c. the object is emitting 3 units of infrared radiation
    d. the object is reflecting 3 units of visible radiation

84. The blueness of the sky is mainly due to
 * a. the scattering of sunlight by air molecules.
    b. the presence of water vapor.
    c. absorption of blue light by the air.
    d. emission of blue light by the atmosphere.

85. Which of the following processes transports, on average, the most energy from the ground to the atmosphere?
    a. convection
    b. conduction
 * c. radiation
    d. latent heat

86. Which of the following is true when the earth is in radiative equilibrium?
    a. the earth absorbs 100% of the sunlight reaching it
    b. the earth does not emit any radiant energy into space
    c. the earth does not reflect any of the radiation reaching it
 * d. the earth gains and loses energy at equal rates

87. The earth's radiative equilibrium temperature is
 * a. the temperature at which the earth is absorbing solar radiation and emitting infrared radiation at equal rates.
    b. the temperature at which the earth is radiating energy at maximum intensity.
    c. the average temperature the earth must maintain to prevent the oceans from freezing solid.
    d. the temperature at which rates of evaporation and condensation on the earth are in balance.

88. In the earth's upper atmosphere, visible light given off by excited atoms and molecules produces
    a. flares.
    b. the solar wind.
 * c. the aurora.
    d. prominences.

89. Charged particles from the sun that travel through space at high speeds are called
    a. radiation.
    b. the aurora.
 * c. solar wind.
    d. solar flares.

90. The solar wind is
    a. the strong wind in outer space.
    b. strong surface winds that develop in response to daytime temperature differences
    c. another name of electromagnetic radiation.
    d. another name for a solar flare.
 * e. charged particles streaming through space from the sun.

91. The aurora is produced by
    a. reflections of sunlight by polar ice fields.
  * b. fast-moving charged particles colliding with air molecules.
    c. burning oxygen caused by the intense sunlight at high altitude.
    d. the combination of molecular and atomic oxygen to form ozone.
    e. scattering of sunlight in the upper atmosphere.

92. Incoming solar radiation in middle latitudes is less in winter than in summer because
  * a. the sun's rays slant more and spread their energy over a larger area.
    b. there is a decrease in carbon dioxide levels in the atmosphere.
    c. the cold dense air lowers the intensity of the sun's rays.
    d. the earth is furthest from the sun.

93. The earth is closest to the sun in
  * a. January
    b. March
    c. July
    d. September

94. During an equinox
    a. the days and nights are of equal length except at the poles.
    b. at noon the sun is overhead at the equator.
    c. the earth is not tilted toward nor away from the sun.
  * d. all of the above.

95. On a clear day, the sun's rays are most intense at
    a. 10 am
  * b. 12 pm (noon)
    c. 2 pm
    d. 4 pm

96. The main reason for warm summers in middle latitudes is that
    a. the earth is closer to the sun in summer.
  * b. the sun is higher in the sky and we receive more direct solar radiation.
    c. oceans currents transport heat from the tropics to middle latitudes.
    d. growing plants enhance the greenhouse effect.

97. Which of the following is one of the main causes of the seasons?
    a. the changing distance between the earth and the sun
    b. a periodic reveral in global scale air circulation patterns
  * c. the length of the daylight hours
    d. land/ocean temperature contrasts

98. In the Northern Hemisphere, this day has the fewest hours of daylight.
    a. summer solstice
  * b. winter solstice
    c. vernal equinox
    d. autumnal equinox

99. Indian Summer would most likely occur during the month of
  * a. October.
    b. December.
    c. June.
    d. August.

100. Which of the following is correct at the time of the summer solstice in June?
   a. it marks the beginning of astronomical summer in the Northern Hemisphere
   b. it occurs around June 22
   c. the noon sun is overhead at the Tropic of Cancer
* d. all of the above

101. Where are the days and nights of equal length all year long?
   a. at 66.5° latitude
   b. nowhere
   c. at 23.5° latitude
* d. at the Equator

102. Which of the following best describes the weather conditions necessary to bring Indian Summer weather to the eastern half of the United States?
   a. a cold front moving off the New Jersey coast
   b. a strong slow-moving low pressure area just east of Virginia
* c. a strong slow-moving high pressure area off the southeast coast
   d. a strong fast-moving low pressure area over Georgia
   e. a cold front that stretches from South Carolina to Texas

103. During the summer in the Northern Hemisphere, the "land of the midnight sun" would be found
* a. at high latitudes.
   b. at middle latitudes.
   c. near the equator.
   d. in the Southern Hemisphere.

104. During the course of a year the sun will disappear from view at the North Pole on or about what date?
   a. June 21
* b. September 23
   c. December 23
   d. January 1
   e. March 21

105. The first day of spring occurs on or about March 21; March 21 is called the
   a. vernal solstice
* b. equinox
   c. aphelion
   d. parhelion

106. At the time of the winter solstice in the Northern Hemisphere
   a. astronomical winter begins in the Northern Hemisphere.
   b. the noon sun is over latitude 23.5° S.
   c. at middle latitudes in the Northern Hemisphere, this marks the longest night of the year.
* d. all of the above

107. Which of the following helps to explain why even though northern latitudes experience 24 hours of sunlight on June 22, they are not warmer than latitudes further south?
   a. solar energy is spread over a larger area in northern latitudes
   b. some of the sun's energy is reflected by snow and ice in the northern latitudes
   c. increased cloud cover reflects solar energy in the northern latitudes
   d. solar energy is used to melt frozen soil in the northern latitudes
* e. all of the above

108.   The sun is directly overhead at Mexico City (latitude 19°N)
        a. once a year.
*   b. twice a year.
        c. four times a year.
        d. never.

109.   Which of the latitudes below would experience the fewest hours of daylight on December 22?
        a. 60° S
        b. 20° S
        c. Equator
        d. 20° N
*   e. 60° N

110.   On what day would you expect the sun to be overhead at Lima, Peru (latitude 12° S)?
        a. August 15
*   b. February 4
        c. March 10
        d. April 21

111.   In the middle latitudes of the Northern Hemisphere on June 22, the sun
        a. rises in the east and sets in the west.
        b. rises in the southeast and sets in the southwest.
*   c. rises in the northeast and sets in the northwest.
        d. rises in the north east and sets in the southwest.
        e. rises in the southeast and sets in the northwest.

112.   The astronomical beginning of spring occurs around this date in the Northern Hemisphere.
        a. March 1
        b. April 1
*   c. March 21
        d. March 15
        e. April 15

113.   Between Christmas and New Year's, at middle latitudes in the Northern Hemisphere, the length of the
        day
*   a. increases.
        b. decreases.
        c. does not change.
        d. is 12 hours long.

114.   On which date would the sun's rays be closest to being perpendicular to the earth's surface in the middle
        latitudes of the Northern Hemisphere?
        a. March 21
*   b. June 21
        c. July 1
        d. July 21
        e. August 1

115.   The sun will pass directly overhead at noon in Miami, Florida (latitude 26° N)
        a. once a year.
        b. twice a year.
        c. four times a year.
*   d. never.

116. When it is January and winter in the Northern Hemisphere, it is ___ and ___ in the Southern Hemisphere.
*   a. January and summer
     b. January and winter
     c. July and winter
     d. July and summer

117. At middle latitudes in the Northern Hemisphere, we can expect the day with the longest number of daylight hours to occur on or about
*   a. June 22.
     b. December 22.
     c. September 23.
     d. July 4.
     e. August 1.

118. At middle latitudes in the Northern Hemisphere, we can expect the day with the shortest number of daylight hours to occur around
     a. June 22.
*   b. December 22.
     c. September 23.
     d. January 1.
     e. February 15.

119. At the North Pole the sun will rise above the horizon on ___ and set below the horizon on ___.
     a. June 22, September 23
     b. September 23, December 22
*   c. March 21, September 23
     d. June 22, December 22
     e. March 21, December 22

120. In July, at middle latitudes in the Northern Hemisphere, the day is ___ long and is ___ with each passing day.
     a. less than 12 hours, getting longer
     b. less than 12 hours, getting shorter
     c. more than 12 hours, getting longer
*   d. more than 12 hours, getting shorter

121. At noon on June 22, the sun will be directly overhead at
     a. the Arctic circle.
     b. the Equator.
*   c. the Tropic of Cancer.
     d. the North Pole.

122. The sun will be directly overhead at noon at the equator
     a. never
*   b. on March 21
     c. on June 21
     d. always

123. For maximum winter warmth, in the Northern Hemisphere, large windows in a house should face
     a. north.
*   b. south.
     c. east.
     d. west.

38

124. Although the polar regions radiate away more heat energy than they receive by insolation in the course of a year, they are prevented from becoming progressively colder each year by the
   a. conduction of heat through the interior of the earth.
   b. concentration of earth's magnetic field lines at the poles.
 * c. circulation of heat by the atmosphere and oceans.
   d. the insulating properties of snow.
   e. release of latent heat to the atmosphere when polar ice melts.

125. The most important reason why summers in the Southern Hemisphere are not warmer than summers in the Northern Hemisphere is that
   a. the earth is closer to the sun in January.
   b. the earth is farther from the sun in July.
 * c. over 80% of the Southern Hemisphere is covered with water.
   d. the sun's energy is less intense in the Southern Hemisphere.

126. The north-facing side of a hill in a mountainous region tends to
   a. receive less sunlight during a year than the south-facing side.
   b. grow a variety of trees that are typically observed at higher elevation.
   c. be a better location for a ski run than the south-facing side.
   d. have snow on the ground for a longer period of time in winter compared to the south-facing side.
 * e. all of the above

127. Solar panels on a solar home built in the Southern Hemisphere should face
 * a. north.
   b. south.
   c. east.
   d. west.

128. In meteorology, the word insolation refers to
   a. a well-constructed, energy-efficient home.
   b. the solar constant.
 * c. incoming solar radiation.
   d. an increase in solar output.

129. Suppose you drive to and from work on a street that runs east to west. On what day would you most likely have the sun shining directly in your eyes while driving to and from work?
   a. summer solstice
   b. winter solstice
 * c. autumnal equinox
   d. any day at noon

True False Exam Questions

1. There are no negative numbers on the Celcius temperature scale.
   (ans: FALSE)

2. In most of the world, temperature readings are taken in Kelvins (degrees Kelvin).
   (ans: FALSE)

3. As you heat air you would expect its density to decrease.
   (ans: TRUE)

4. The formation of frost (deposition) releases heat and warms the surroundings.
   (ans: TRUE)

5. Microwave radiation has a longer wavelength and is a more energetic form of radiation than visible light.
    (ans: FALSE)

6. Virtually all the UV-C radiation, which is more harmful than UV-A or UV-B, is absorbed by ozone in the stratosphere.
    (ans: TRUE)

7. The atmosphere is essentially completely transparent to electromagnetic radiation.
    (ans: FALSE)

8. If our eyes responded to infrared radiation instead of visible light, clouds would appear black because they are good absorbers of IR.
    (ans: TRUE)

9. Because air molecules are so small, compared to the wavelength of light, air does not scatter or absorb incoming sunlight.
    (ans: FALSE)

10. Satellite data from the *Earth Radiation Budget Experiment (ERBE)* indicate that the overall effect of clouds is to cool the earth's climate.
    (ans: TRUE)

11. The earth's surface receives nearly twice as much longwave IR energy from the atmosphere as it does shortwave radiation from the sun.
    (ans: TRUE)

12. The Southern Hemisphere has warmer summers and colder winters than the Northern Hemisphere.
    (ans: FALSE)

Word Choice Exam Questions

1. If you could somehow see the random motions of the atoms and molecules in air, would they all be moving at the SAME or at DIFFERENT speeds? (circle one answer)
    (ans: DIFFERENT)

2. 50° C is WARMER than, COLDER than, EQUAL to 100° F. (circle one answer)
    (ans: WARMER)

3. Is the energy transport in the figure at right UPWARD, DOWNWARD, or ZERO? (circle one answer)
    (ans: UPWARD)

    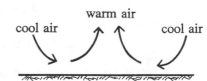

4. About 44% of the energy emitted by the sun is visible light. Most of the remaining radiation falls in the INFRARED ULTRAVIOLET portion of the spectrum. (circle one answer)
    (ans: INFRARED)

5. As the air in the picture at right moves from A to B will its volume INCREASE, DECREASE, or remain the SAME. Will its temperature INCREASE, DECREASE, or remain the SAME? (choose one word from each group)
    (ans: INCREASE, DECREASE)

    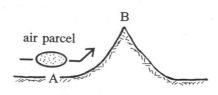

6. If the earth's average surface temperature were to increase, the amount of radiation emitted from the earth's surface would INCREASE DECREASE and the wavelength of peak emission would shift toward LONGER SHORTER wavelengths. (choose one word from each pair)
    (ans: INCREASE, SHORTER)

7. A "window" is a wavelength region where the atmosphere TRANSMITS ABSORBS EMITS radiant energy. (circle one answer)
    (ans: TRANSMITS)

8. Overcast skies usually result in WARMER COOLER daytime temperatures because clouds are good REFLECTORS ABSORBERS of VISIBLE INFRARED light. (choose one word from each pair)
    (ans: COOLER, REFLECTORS, VISIBLE)

9. Generally speaking, to see the aurora you must be located at high ALTITUDE LATITUDE. (circle one answer)
    (ans: LATITUDE)

10. Compared to Pheonix (30° N latitude), Minneapolis (45° N) will have LONGER SHORTER days in the winter and LONGER SHORTER days in the summer. (choose one word from each pair)
    (ans: SHORTER, LONGER)

11. In a positive water vapor-temperature feedback process, warming will result in INCREASED DECREASED atmospheric water vapor concentrations which will STRENGTHEN WEAKEN the greenhouse effect. (choose one word from each pair)
    (ans: INCREASED, STRENGTHEN)

12. High latitudes lose MORE, LESS, the SAME amount of energy to space as(than) they receive from the sun. (circle one answer)
    (ans: MORE)

Short Answer Exam Questions

1. _____ provides a measure of the average speed or kinetic energy of the atoms or molecules in air.
    (ans: TEMPERATURE)

2. Fill in the blanks below using one of the choices at right. (choices at right may be used more than once or not at all).
    a. boiling point of water (sea level)_____   0° F   0° C
    b. hottest temperature_____   100 °F   100° C
    c. coldest temperature_____
    d. melting point of ice_____
    (ans: a. 100°C, b. 100°C, c. 0° F, d. 0°C)

3. Warm rising air has formed a cloud in the figure at right.
    This illustrates which two energy transport processes?
    (ans: CONVECTION and LATENT HEAT ENERGY TRANSPORT)

4. Ocean currents transport energy in the form of warm ocean water from the tropical oceans to higher latitudes. This is an example of which energy transport process?
    (ans: CONVECTION or ADVECTION)

5. One _____ of energy is needed to raise the temperature of 1 gram of water 1° C.
    (ans: CALORIE)

6.   _____ originates from rapidly vibrating electrons which exist in every object.
(ans: ELECTROMAGNETIC RADIATION)

7.   In some situations light behaves as if it were composed of particles rather than having a wavelike nature. What is the name given to light "particles?"
(ans: PHOTONS)

8.   What important ability or property does electromagnetic radiation have that other energy transport processes, such as conduction and convection, do not?
(ans: Radiation can propagate through empty space.)

9.   How can the energy budget at the earth's surface be in balance when the ground loses more energy than it receives from the sun?
(ans: Some of the radiation emitted by the earth is absorbed by the atmosphere. The atmosphere then radiates a portion of this energy back to the ground.)

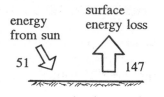

10.   Which of the processes listed at right transports the most energy from the earth to the atmosphere? Which process transports the least amount of energy? What important process is missing from the list?
conduction
convection
radiation
(ans: most - RADIATION, least - CONDUCTION, missing - LATENT HEAT)

11.   What is the name given to the stream of charged particles that travels outward from the sun?
(ans: SOLAR WIND)

12.   A faint glow known as the _____ can be seen at high latitudes when charged particles from the sun collide with atmospheric gases causing them to emit visible light.
(ans: AURORA)

13.   The line drawn at 23.5° S latitude on maps and globes is called the _____.
(ans: TROPIC OF CAPRICORN)

Essay Exam Questions

1.   What is meant by the term "positive feedback?" What role could positive feedback play in the atmospheric greenhouse effect? Would this enhance or reduce global warming? Can you think of any "negative feedback" mechanisms?

2.   In the discussion of the earth's annual energy balance we saw that the earth absorbed approximately 51 units of solar energy but emitted 117 units of infrared energy. What prevents the earth from getting colder and colder?

3.   Will a rising parcel of air always expand? Why? Does this expansion cause the air temperature to increase or decrease? Why?

4.   Describe and give examples of the various ways that heat can be transported in the atmosphere.

5.   Explain how energy in the form of sunlight absorbed at the ground could be transferred upward in the atmosphere in the form of latent heat. How or when is the latent heat energy released in the air above the ground?

6. The moon is located at about the same distance from the sun as the earth. How would you expect surface temperatures on the moon to compare with the earth? (you can assume that the moon has the same average albedo as the earth)

7. Describe the atmospheric greenhouse effect. Is there any difference between the way the atmospheric greenhouse effect works on a clear night and on a cloudy night?

8. Several of the planets in our solar system are further from the sun and cooler than the earth. Do they emit electromagnetic radiation? Why are we able to see the planets in the sky at night?

9. How could increased cloud cover cause an increase in the average surface temperature? How could increased cloudiness cause a decrease in average surface temperatures?

10. When you remove a cold beverage from a refrigerator in a humid room, water vapor will condense on the sides of the container. Would this act to warm or cool the beverage, or would the condensation have no effect on the beverage's temperature?

11. Imagine that the temperature of the sun were to change. Describe or discuss some of the effects that this might have on the earth's energy budget and the earth's climate.

12. Describe the seasons that you would experience at two widely different points on the earth. How do you think seasonal changes can influence a region's culture and traditions?

13. Many automobile engines are cooled by water which flows in a closed circuit through the engine block and the car's radiator. How many different heat transport processes do you find in operation here?

14. Many people will blow on a bowl of hot soup to try to cool it. In your view, what are the two most important heat transport processes cooling the soup?

Chapter 3
Air Temperature

Summary

Daily, seasonal, and geographic variations in temperature have important practical and economic implications and are examined in this chapter. The chapter begins with a discussion of the daily heating and cooling cycle in a thin air layer near the ground. Daily temperature is controlled by incoming energy, primarily from the sun, and outgoing energy from the earth's surface. While energy from the sun is generally most intense at noon, daytime temperatures continue to rise into the afternoon as long as energy input exceeds output. Because most of the incident sunlight is first absorbed at the ground and then transported into the atmosphere, large temperature gradients can develop between the ground and the air just above, especially under calm wind conditions. At night, the ground cools more rapidly than the air above and a radiation inversion will often form. With an understanding of the factors which promote the formation of an inversion layer, it is often possible for farmers and growers to reduce the severity of a nighttime inversion and to protect cold-sensitive plants and trees.

Temperature varies considerably on a global scale and mean and record temperatures observed throughout the world are summarized. The main factors that affect the range of temperatures at different locations around the world are latitude, elevation, and proximity to land, water, or ocean currents. Variables, such as mean daily temperature and normal temperatures, mean annual temperature, and annual range of temperature, can be used to characterize the climate of different regions. Additional parameters such as the number of heating or cooling degree-days can be used to estimate a region's heating or cooling needs.

The chapter concludes with an examination of how the human body's perception of temperature is influenced by atmospheric conditions and discusses the different types of thermometers and instruments that are used to measure temperature.

Key Terms

(Listed in approximately the same order they appear in the text. Terms in boldface are emphasized and appear at the end of the chapter in the text.)

lag-in-temperature
forced convection
radiational cooling
radiation inversion
nocturnal inversion
thermal belt
orchard heater
wind machine
freeze
controls of temperature
isotherm
gradient (of temperature)
**daily (diurnal) range
   of temperature**

specific heat
**mean (average) daily
   temperature**
**annual range of
   temperature**
**mean (average) annual
   temperature**
heating degree-day
cooling degree-day
growing degree-day
base (zero) temperature
sensible temperature
wind-chill factor
frostbite

hypothermia
**liquid-in-glass
   thermometer**
maximum thermometer
minimum thermometer
meniscus
electrical thermometer
infrared sensor
radiometer
Automated Surface
   Observing System (ASOS)
bimetallic thermometer
thermograph
instrument shelter

Teaching Suggestions, Demonstrations, and Visual Aids

1.   Students may not understand why the ground cools more quickly than the air above at night. The soil radiates nearly as a black body. The atmosphere is a selective absorber and also a selective emitter of infrared radiation.

2.   Make an inversion. Fill a container with crushed ice or dry ice. Attach 3 or 4 thermometers to a vertical ringstand such that the thermometers are several inches apart and the lowest thermometer is about 1 inch above (but not touching) the ice. Cover the entire setup with a large glass bell jar.

        Make a graph of the change in temperature with time for each thermometer. At first, the readings will be isothermal, but eventually the coldest air will be observed just above the ice and a strong inversion will have formed.

        This demonstration can be applied to important concepts presented in this chapter. Explain why the air cools faster near the ice and relate this to the formation of a radiation inversion. Ask what ingredients are necessary to maintain the inversion. Explain how the inversion would be destroyed. See also the article "Temperature Inversions Have Cold Bottoms" (ref: C.F. Bohren and G.M. Brown, *Weatherwise, 34*, 273-276, 1981)

3.   Pass around a piece of metal, a piece of wood, and a piece of foam (all three could be attached to a larger piece of plywood perhaps). Explain that all three objects have been sitting in the classroom and have the same temperature. Ask the students whether all three objects <u>feel</u> like they have the same temperature. This is a good demonstration that our perception of temperature is often a better indication of how quickly our body is loosing heat rather than absolute temperature and leads into a discussion of the wind-chill effect.

Student Projects

1.   Have students measure the temperature of a variety of different surfaces on a sunny afternoon. Are there differences in the temperature values? Ask the students to explain what causes the differences.

2.   Have several students, who live in different parts of a city or town, make simultaneous early morning temperature measurements. Are there appreciable differences? Can these differences be attributed to topography? Is there evidence of a "thermal belt" in their city?

3.   Students could design a simple weather station for their school. Where would the instrument shelter be located? What types of temperature instruments would be needed? How would the data be collected? See "Basic Meteorological Observations for Schools: Temperature" by J.T. Snow and S.B. Harley (*Bull. Am. Meteorol. Soc., 68*, 486-496, 1987) for a detailed discussion of temperature measurement, instruments, and activities.

4.   Have the students plot an early morning and late afternoon sounding. Is a radiation inversion visible on the morning sounding? If so, how deep is the inversion layer? Did the students observe any visual evidence of a strong radiation inversion that morning? How has the sounding changed by that afternoon? How much of a change was observed at the ground and at different levels above the ground? (Tabulated data may use pressure as the vertical coordinate; in this case it is probably sufficient to assume a 1 mb decrease per 10 meters)

5.   Students can study radiative cooling at night in a variety of ways. Have the students place a piece of wood and a plate of aluminum outside on the ground on a cold, clear night. The wood will often be covered with frost the next morning while the aluminum is not (ref: C.F. Bohren, "An Essay on Dew," <u>What Light Through Yonder Window Breaks</u>, John Wiley and Sons Inc., New York, 1991). A surface that is insulated from the ground may radiatively cool to well below the air temperature (ref: "The Cold Night Sky," *Phys. Teacher*, 248, April, 1984).

6.   Have students determine the record high and low temperatures for their state or region. Then, review the controls of temperature and have students try to understand why these record values occurred where and when they did.

7.   Plans for simple air and water thermometers are given in Chapter 4 of <u>Hands-On Meteorology</u> (see reference on p. 2 of this manual). The student-made thermometers could be calibrated using a laboratory-grade thermometer.

Multiple Choice Exam Questions

1.   The lag in daily temperature refers to the time lag between
*   a. the time of maximum solar radiation and the time of maximum temperature.
        b. the time of minimum temperature and the time of maximum solar radiation.
        c. the time between the minimum and maximum temperatures for a day.
        d. the time of minimum and maximum solar energy received at the surface for a given day.
        e. sunrise and sunset.

2.   During the afternoon the greatest temperature difference between the surface air and the air several meters above occurs on a
*   a. clear, calm afternoon.
        b. clear, windy afternoon.
        c. cloudy, calm afternoon.
        d. cloudy, windy afternoon.

3.   The greatest variation in daily temperature usually occurs
*   a. at the ground.
        b. about 5 feet above the ground.
        c. at the top of a high-rise apartment complex.
        d. at the level where thermals stop rising.

4.   In summer, humid regions typically have ___ daily temperature ranges
        and ___ maximum temperatures than drier regions.
*   a. smaller, lower
        b. smaller, higher
        c. larger, lower
        d. larger, higher

5.   In most areas the warmest time of the day about 5 feet above the ground occurs
        a. around noon.
*   b. in the afternoon between 2 and 5 pm.
        c. in the early evening after 6 pm.
        d. just before the sun sets.

6.   Everything else being equal, the lowest air temperature on a winter night will occur above a
        a. surface covered with vegetation.
*   b. surface covered with snow.
        c. bare surface.
        d. surface covered with water.

7.   Which of the following is generally true at night?
        a. the earth emits and absorbs energy at equal rates
*   b. the earth emits more energy than it absorbs
        c. the earth does not emit any energy
        d. the earth does not absorb any energy

8.   The lowest temperature is usually observed
        a. at the time of sunset.
        b. near midnight.
        c. several hours before sunrise.
*   d. around sunrise.
        e. several hours after sunrise.

9.   Which of the following is generally true at night?
        a. the earth does not emit any energy
        b. the earth emits and absorbs energy at equal rates
*   c. the earth emits more energy than it absorbs
        d. the earth does not absorb any energy

10.   In clear weather the air next to the ground is usually ___ than the air above during the night,
        and ___ than the air above during the day.
*   a. colder, warmer
        b. colder, colder
        c. warmer, colder
        d. warmer, warmer

11.   One would expect the lowest temperatures to be found next to the ground on a
        a. clear, damp, windy night.
        b. cloudy night.
*   c. clear, dry, calm night.
        d. clear, dry, windy night.
        e. rainy night.

12.   Suppose yesterday morning you noticed ice crystals (frost) on the grass, yet the minimum temperature
        reported in the newspaper was only 35° F. The most likely reason for this apparent discrepancy is that
*   a. temperature readings are taken in instrument shelters more than 5 feet above the ground.
        b. the thermometer was in error.
        c. the newspaper reported the wrong temperature.
        d. the thermometer was read before the minimum temperature was reached for that day.
        e. the thermometer was read incorrectly.

13.   Warmer-than-average overnight temperatures are probably not associated with
        a. humid conditions.
        b. windy conditions.
*   c. a strong radiation inversion.
        d. cloudy conditions.

14.   At what time during a 24-hour day would a radiation temperature inversion best be developed?
        a. at sunset
*   b. near sunrise
        c. at noon
        d. toward the end of the morning
        e. between 2 and 5 pm when the air temperature reaches a maximum

15.   Ideal conditions for a strong radiation inversion are a
*   a. clear, calm, dry, winter night.
        b. clear, calm, moist, summer night.
        c. cloudy, calm, moist, winter night.
        d. cloudy, windy, moist, summer night.
        e. clear, windy, dry, summer night.

16. Assuming that the night will remain clear, calm, and unsaturated, the predicted minimum temperature is 32° F. Suddenly the wind speed increases and remains gusty throughout the night. The minimum temperature will most likely be
    a. about the same as predicted, but will occur earlier in the night.
    b. higher than predicted due to the release of latent heat.
    c. much lower than predicted due to radiational cooling.
*   d. higher than predicted due to mixing.
    e. lower than predicted due to forced convection.

17. The primary cause of a radiation inversion is
*   a. infrared radiation emitted by the earth's surface.
    b. infrared radiation absorbed by the earth's surface.
    c. solar radiation absorbed by the earth's surface.
    d. solar radiation reflected by the earth's surface.
    e. infrared radiation absorbed by the atmosphere and clouds.

18. An important reason for the large daily temperature range over deserts is
*   a. there is little water vapor in the air to absorb and re-radiate infrared radiation.
    b. the light-colored sand radiates heat very rapidly at night.
    c. dry air is a very poor heat conductor.
    d. free convection cells are unable to form above the hot desert ground.
    e. the ozone content of desert air is very low.

19. The deepest radiation inversion would be observed
    a. at the equator any day of the year.
*   b. in polar regions in winter.
    c. at the top of a high mountain in winter.
    d. on a desert in winter.
    e. in a deep valley during the summer.

20. A radiation inversion is most commonly observed
    a. when it is raining.
    b. during the afternoon.
    c. at sunset.
*   d. just above the ground.
    e. in the upper atmosphere.

21. On a clear, calm, night, the ground and air above cool mainly by this process.
    a. evaporation
    b. reflection
    c. convection
    d. conduction
*   e. radiation

22. Orchard heaters and wind machines are most useful in preventing damaging low temperatures from occurring next to the ground on
    a. clear, windy nights.
    b. cloudy, windy nights.
    c. cloudy, snowy nights.
*   d. clear, calm nights.
    e. rainy nights.

23. Thermal belts are
    a. pockets of warm air resting on a valley during the afternoon.
    b. pockets of cold air resting on a valley floor at night.
    * c. warmer hillsides that are less likely to experience freezing conditions.
    d. cold, below-freezing air found at the top of a mountain.

24. Which of the following can be used as a method of protecting an orchard from damaging low
    temperatures during a radiation inversion?
    a. orchard heaters
    b. wind machines
    c. irrigation (cover the area with water)
    * d. all of the above

25. In a hilly region the best place to plant crops that are sensitive to low temperatures is
    a. on the valley floor.
    * b. along the hillsides.
    c. on the top of the highest hill.
    d. in any dry location.

26. Lines connecting points of equal temperature are called
    a. isobars.
    * b. isotherms.
    c. thermals.
    d. thermographs.

27. If tonight's temperature is going to drop into the middle 20s (°F) and a fairly stiff wind is predicted,
    probably the best way to protect an orchard against a hard freeze is to (assume that cost is not a factor)
    a. use helicopters.
    b. use wind machines.
    * c. sprinkle the crops with water.
    d. put orchard heaters to work.
    e. pray for clouds.

28. Wind machines can prevent surface air temperatures from reaching extremely low readings by
    a. blowing smoke over an orchard or field.
    b. increasing the evaporation rate from fruits and vegetables.
    * c. mixing surface air with air directly above.
    d. reducing the rate of cooling by evaporation.
    e. increasing the likelihood of condensation on fruits and vegetables.

29. Two objects A and B have the same mass but the specific heat of A is larger than B. If both objects
    absorb equal amounts of energy
    a. A will become warmer than B.
    * b. B will become warmer than A.
    c. both A and B will warm at the same rate.
    d. A will get warmer, but B will get colder.

30. If energy is added to an object, the smallest temperature change will occur when the object has
    a. large mass, small specific heat.
    * b. large mass, large specific heat.
    c. small mass, small specific heat.
    d. large mass, small specific heat.

31. Which of the following statements is true?
*   a. If you travel from Dallas, Texas to St. Paul, Minnesota in January, you are more likely to experience greater temperature variations than if you make the same trip in July
   b. Annual temperature ranges tend to be much greater near the ocean than in the middle of the continent
   c. If two cities have the same mean annual temperature, then their temperatures throughout the year are quite similar
   d. all of the above are true

32. Which of the following is <u>not</u> a reason why water warms and cools much more slowly than land?
   a. solar energy penetrates more deeply into water
   b. water has a higher heat capacity
   c. a portion of the solar energy that strikes water is used to evaporate it
*   d. it takes more heat to raise the temperature of a given amount of soil 1° C than it does to raise the temperature of water 1° C.

33. When you observe large changes in the temperature of an object even though only small amounts of energy are added or removed, you might conclude the object has low
   a. albedo
   b. thermal conductivity
   c. density
*   d. specific heat

34. Two object have the same temperature. Object A feels colder to the touch than object B. This is probably because the two objects have different
*   a. thermal conductivities.
   b. densities.
   c. specific heats.
   d. latent heats.

35. During the course of a year, the hottest temperatures would probably be observed near
   a. the North Pole.
*   b. 30° latitude.
   c. the Equator.
   d. 45° latitude.

36. The largest annual range of temperatures are found
*   a. at polar latitudes over land.
   b. at polar latitudes over water.
   c. at middle latitudes near large bodies of water.
   d. at the Equator.

37. If you subtract the daily minimum from the daily maximum temperature you have the
   a. daily average temperature
*   b. daily range of temperature
   c. number of heating degree days
   d. number of cooling degree days

38. This is used as a guide to planting and for determining the approximate date for harvesting crops.
*   a. growing degree-days
   b. heating degree-days
   c. cooling degree-days
   d. mean annual temperature

39. This is used as an index for fuel consumption.
    a. growing degree-days
    b. consumer price index
*   c. heating degree-days
    d. mean annual temperature

40. How many heating degree-days would there be for a day with a maximum temperature of 30° F and a minimum temperature of 20° F? (Assume a base temperature of 65° F)
    a. 65
    b. 45
*   c. 40
    d. 35
    e. 10

41. How many cooling degree-days would there be for a day with a maximum temperature of 95° F and a minimum temperature of 65° F? (Assume a base temperature of 65° F)
    b. 30
    c. 20
*   d. 15
    e. 0

42. Suppose peas are planted in Indiana on May 1. If the peas need 1200 growing degree-days before they can be picked, and if the mean temperature for each day during May and June is 70° F, in about how many days will the peas be ready to pick? (Assume a base temperature of 40° F)
    a. 11
    b. 30
*   c. 40
    d. 70
    e. 120

43. The wind-chill factor
*   a. relates body heat loss with wind to an equivalent temperature with no wind.
    b. indicates the temperature at which water freezes on exposed skin.
    c. takes into account humidity and air temperature in expressing the current air
       temperature.
    d. tells farmers when to protect crops from a freeze.
    e. determines how low the air temperaturre will be on any given day.

44. In calm air the air temperature is -10° C, if the wind speed should increase to 30 knots (with no change in air temperature) the thermometer would indicate
    a. a much higher temperature than -10° C.
    b. a much lower temperature than -10° C.
*   c. a temperature of -10° C.
    d. a temperature of -30° C.

45. The air temperature is 45° F, the wind is blowing at 30 MPH, and the wind chill temperature is 15° F. These conditions would be equivalent to
*   a. a 15° F air temperature and 0 MPH winds.
    b. a 30° F air temperature and 45 MPH winds.
    c. a 30° F air temperature and 15 MPH winds.
    d. a 15° F air temperature and 30 MPH winds.

46.   Hypothermia is most common in
        a. hot, humid weather.
*   b. cold, wet weather.
        c. hot, dry weather.
        d. cold, dry weather.

47.   Which of the following is usually a liquid-in-glass thermometer?
        a. radiometer
        b. thermistor
        c. electrical resistance thermometer
*   d. minimum thermometer
        e. thermograph

48.   A thermometer with a small constriction just above the bulb is a
*   a. maximum thermometer.
        b. minimum thermometer.
        c. electrical thermometer.
        d. thermocouple.
        e. bimetallic thermometer.

49.   When would be the best time to reset a minimum thermometer?
        a. just after the time of minimum temperature
*   b. just after the time of maximum temperature
        c. just before sunrise
        d. just before sunrise
        e. around noon

50.   A thermometer that measures temperature and records it on a piece of chart paper is called a
        a. minimum thermometer.
        b. thermistor.
*   c. thermograph.
        d. maximum thermometer.

51.   This instrument obtains air temperature by measuring emitted infrared energy.
*   a. radiometer
        b. bimetallic thermometer
        c. electrical resistance thermometer
        d. thermistor
        e. thermograph

52.   The thermometer that has a small dumbell-shaped glass index marker in the tube is called a
        a. bimetallic thermometer.
        b. maximum thermometer.
        c. electrical thermometer.
        d. thermocouple.
*   e. minimum thermometer.

53.   The thermometer most likely to contain alcohol.
        a. bimetallic thermometer
        b. radiometer
        c. maximum thermometer
        d. thermograph
*   e. minimum thermometer

54.   When a liquid thermometer is held in direct sunlight
       a. it will accurately measure the air temperature.
*   b. it will measure a much higher temperature than that of the air.
       c. it will measure a much lower temperature than that of the air.
       d. it will measure the temperature of the sun rather than the air.

55.   Which of the following true for surface temperature measurements?
       a. made in the sun
*   b. made in the shade
       c. made at ground level
       d. made in a shelter that does not allow inside and outside to mix

True False Exam Questions

1.   Sandy soil has a relatively low thermal conductivity and will reach a higher temperature during the day than other types of soil.
      (ans: TRUE)

2.   On a windy day, you would expect to record warmer daytime and warmer nighttime temperatures than on a day with calm winds.
      (ans: FALSE)

3.   The ground is a better emitter of IR radiation and cools more quickly than air.
      (ans: TRUE)

4.   The thermal conductivity tells you the amount of heat needed to warm 1 gram of a material 1° C.
      (ans: FALSE)

5.   The Great Lakes are large enough to affect the climate of the surrounding area.
      (ans: TRUE)

6.   Two cities can have the same mean annual temperature but different mean annual ranges of temperature.
      (ans: TRUE)

7.   Other conditions being equal, a city at low latitude would probably have a higher mean annual average temperature and a lower annual range of temperature than a city at high latitude.
      (ans: TRUE)

8.   Hypothermia is a serious medical condition brought on by higher than normal human body temperature.
      (ans: FALSE)

9.   In the upper atmosphere a person would feel very cold even though air temperatures are very high (500° C or 900° F).
      (ans: TRUE)

10.   The official temperature reading reported by the Weather Service is an average of two temperature measurements, one made in the sun and the other in the shade.
      (ans: FALSE)

Word Choice Exam Questions

1.   Incoming sunlight energy is usually most intense at noon. Would you expect to record the daytime maximum temperature BEFORE noon, AT noon, or just AFTER noon? (circle one answer)
      (ans: AFTER)

2. Thermals and turbulent eddies will INCREASE DECREASE daytime temperature differences between the ground and the air a few feet above the ground. (circle one answer)
    (ans: DECREASE)

3. The earth emits energy 24 hours per day. Does the peak terrestrial emission normally occur during the DAY or at NIGHT? (circle one answer)
    (ans: DAY)

4. In a radiation inversion is the air next to the ground COLDER or WARMER than the air higher up? (circle one answer)
    (ans: COLDER)

5. The temperature sounding shown at right is probably a DAYTIME NIGHTTIME profile. (circle one answer)
    (ans: NIGHTTIME)

300 ft	13°C
200	13.5
100	14
0	13

6. Farmers will sometimes flood their fields or orchards with water. Are they trying to reduce damage caused by unusually WARM or COLD temperatures? (circle one answer)
    (ans: COLD)

7. It takes MORE LESS energy to warm 1 gram of water 1°C than to warm 1 gram of dry soil the same amount. This is because water has a HIGHER LOWER specific heat than dry soil. (choose one word from each pair)
    (ans: MORE, HIGHER)

8. Would you expect to observe the smallest variation in temperature from day to day at HIGH or LOW latitude and in the middle of a(n) OCEAN or LAND MASS? (choose one word from each pair)
    (ans: LOW, OCEAN)

9. Would you expect to hear cooling degree data when the weather is relatively WARM or COLD? (circle one answer)
    (ans: WARM)

10. The largest diurnal temperature ranges would usually be observed in a RURAL URBAN area. (circle one answer)
    (ans: RURAL)

11. You might expect to find alcohol used in a thermometer to measure unusually WARM COLD temperatures. (circle one answer)
    (ans: COLD)

12. Would point A or B on the drawing of the index marker in a minimum thermometer at right indicate the minimum temperature reading? (circle one answer)
    (ans: B)

Short Answer Exam Questions

1. What is the common name given to the rising bubbles of air that transport heat from the ground to the air above?
    (ans: THERMALS)

2. Water has a relatively high _____ which means that large amounts of energy must be added to or removed from water to cause its temperature to change.
    (ans: SPECIFIC HEAT)

3. The highest temperature ever observed in North America (134° F) was observed in _____, California.
    (ans: DEATH VALLEY)

4. The world cold temperature record (-129° F) was set on July 21, 1983 in Antarctica. In addition to high southern latitude, list two additional factors that probably contributed to this unusually cold reading.
    (ans: LAND MASS, HIGH ALTITUDE)

5. Contour lines on a weather map that connect points with equal temperatures are called _____.
    (ans: ISOTHERMS)

6. The rate of change of some quantity with distance is the _____.
    (ans: GRADIENT)

7. In an automatic surface weather observing station, air temperature would likely be determined by measuring changes in a materials electrical _____.
    (ans: RESISTANCE)

8. By measuring the intensity of radiant energy and also the wavelength of peak emission from a particular gas, radiometers in orbiting satellites can be used to estimate _____ at different levels in the atmosphere.
    (ans: AIR TEMPERATURE)

Essay Exam Questions

1. An air temperature of 70° F feels quite comfortable. If you were in 70° F water, it would feel cold. Explain why.

2. Explain why it is possible for the nighttime minimum to occur as much as 30 minutes after the sun has risen.

3. What is the hottest (coldest) place in the United States (the world)? What factors cause these extreme conditions at this location?

4. Explain why it is possible to see frost on the ground or on the tops of parked automobiles even though the measured nighttime minimum temperature remains above 32° F.

5. What meteorological conditions contribute to the formation of a strong radiation inversion? Why?

6. How is it possible for the ground to become warmer than the air just above during the day and then turn colder than the air above during the night?

7. What are the various methods used to protect sensitive crops from damaging low temperatures? Explain why each method works.

8. Sunlight energy is being added at equal rates, to the soil and water at right. What reasons can you think of to explain the very different temperatures that result?

sunlight

soil 100° F   water 75° F

9.   A city which is located near a large body of water will generally have a milder climate than a city located at the same latitude in the center of a large mass. What factors account for this?

10. Would a strong radiation inversion be more likely to form on a winter night or a summer night? Explain your answer.

11. What types of temperature data might it be appropriate to include in a short description of a city or region's climate?

12. Would you expect dry or wet soil to warm up the most during the day? Explain why.

Chapter 4
Humidity, Condensation, and Clouds

Summary

The transformation of water from the gaseous to the liquid or solid state is an important source of energy in many meteorological processes and also makes weather phenomena visible to us. Some of the ways of measuring and quantifying atmospheric water vapor concentrations are discussed in this chapter.

The chapter begins with a short description of the hydrologic cycle. The important concept of saturation is developed next. Saturation represents an effective upper limit to the amount of water vapor that may be found in air and is a function of air temperature. Several different parameters can be used to express the air's humidity. Students are shown that the dew point temperature provides a better absolute measure of the air's water vapor content than a more commonly used parameter, relative humidity. The heat index is a practical measure of the effect that a combination of hot temperatures and high humidity have on our perception of temperature.

Condensation occurs when moist air is cooled below its dew point temperature. Dew or frost forms when this occurs at ground level. When air above the ground becomes saturated, water vapor will condense onto small condensation nuclei in the air and will form a cloud composed of small droplets of water. Fog is just a cloud that forms at ground level and can be produced either by cooling moist air to saturation or evaporating and mixing water vapor into air.

Finally, students are shown that a seemingly infinite variety of cloud forms may actually be classified into ten basic types according to their appearance and the altitude at which they form. Photographic illustrations of each of the basic cloud types are given and key characteristics that can be used to distinquish different different kinds of clouds are discussed. This should allow students to develop a reasonable proficiency at cloud identification.

Key Words
(Listed in approximately the same order they appear in the text. Terms in boldface are emphasized and appear at the end of the chapter in the text.)

evaporation	mixing ratio	heat exhaustion
condensation	water vapor pressure	heat stroke
precipitation	**actual vapor pressure**	**heat index (HI)**
hydrologic cycle	Dalton's law	**apparent temperature**
transpiration	**saturation vapor pressure**	**psychrometer**
saturated air	**relative humidity**	sling psychrometer
condensation nuclei	**supersaturated air**	aspirated psychrometer
humidity	**dew point temperature**	dry-bulb temperature
parcel	(dew point)	wet-bulb depression
absolute humidity	**wet-bulb temperature**	**hygrometer**
(water vapor density)	hypothalamus gland	hair hygrometer
specific humidity	heat cramps	electrical hygrometer

infrared hygrometer	fog drip	castellanus
dew-point hygrometer	advection-radiation fog	**altostratus clouds**
dew cell	ice fog	**nimbostratus clouds**
dew	**upslope fog**	stratus fractus (scud)
frozen dew	**evaporation (mixing) fog**	**stratocumulus clouds**
frost point	steam fog	**stratus clouds**
hoar frost	steam devils	**cumulus clouds**
white frost	arctic sea smoke	cumulus humilis
frost	precipitation fog	cumulus fractus
freeze	frontal fog	cumulus congestus
black frost	cold fog	(towering cumulus)
hygroscopic (nuclei)	supercooled fog	**cumulonimbus clouds**
haze	warm fog	**lenticular clouds**
fog	**cirrus clouds**	cap cloud
radiation fog	mare's tails	**pileus clouds**
ground fog	cirrocumulus clouds	**mammatus clouds**
valley fog	mackerel sky	**contrail**
high fog	**cirrostratus clouds**	**nacreous clouds**
advection fog	**altocumulus clouds**	**noctilucent clouds**

Teaching Suggestions, Demonstrations, and Visual Aids

1.   The dew point temperature can be determined by filling a metal cup or container with warm tap water (at least 50° F in winter and 75° F in summer). Place a thermometer in the water and begin to slowly add ice while continuously stirring the mixture. Read the temperature when the first sign of condensation begins to appear on the outside of the container. This reading should be within about 3° F of the dew point temperature.

The reading above could be compared with a simultaneous measurement made using a sling psychrometer and with the current dew point temperature announced on the local weather radio broadcast. Students could be asked to measure the dew point temperature and the relative humidity indoors and outdoors and asked to account for any similarities or differences.

2.   Saturation can be illustrated by filling a test tube with a few grams of solid iodine. The iodine will sublimate and fill the air in the test tube with iodine vapor. The iodine vapor has a purple-pink color which should just be visible at normal room temperature when viewed against a white background.

The effect of temperature on the saturation vapor pressure can be demonstrated by immersing the bottom of a second test tube in hot water. The gas in the test tube will have a noticeably darker color indicating a higher vapor concentration. If this warm test tube is cooled, iodine vapor will be deposited on the sides of the test tube. With some care two test tubes (warm and cool) may be passed around a small class for examination. The iodine vapor is also visible when the test tubes are placed on an overhead projector. Another good demonstration of the effect of temperature on vapor pressure has been given by W.S. Richardson and R.F. Jones (ref: "Demonstration of Vapor Pressure," *J. Chem. Educ., 64,* 968-969, 1987).

3.   The strong dependence of saturation water vapor pressure on temperature can be demonstrated using several glass beakers with different volumes. The saturation vapor pressure doubles approximately with every 20° F increase in temperature. For example, 250 mL, 500 mL, 1000 mL and 2000 mL beakers can be used to represent the saturation vapor pressures at 30°, 50°, 70°, and 90° F (the saturation vapor pressures at these temperatures are approximately 6, 12, 25, and 50 mb). The concept of relative humidity can be shown by partially filling one of the beakers with water (meant to represent water vapor). By then transferring the water in the first beaker to another larger (warmer air) or smaller (cooler air) beaker, students can see how air temperature will change the RH even though the actual amount of water vapor in the air remains the same. Cooling the air to the dew point can be demonstrated by progressively transferring the water into smaller and smaller beakers (cooling the air) until a beaker is finally filled to capacity.

4.	A dramatic demonstration of cloud formation in a bottle has been described by C.F. Bohren (ref: Clouds in a Glass of Beer, pps 8-14, John Wiley and Sons, New York, 1987). Place a small amount of water in a large thick-walled bottle or flask. Close the top of the bottle with a rubber stopper. Connect a pump (an ordinary bicycle pump works well) to the bottle with a tube through a hole in the stopper. Pump air into the bottle. If the stopper has not been inserted too firmly, it will suddenly pop as air is being pumped into the bottle and will allow the air to expand outward and cool. A faint cloud should be visible in the bottle.

Repeat the experiment, but this time add hygroscopic smoke particles by dropping a lighted match into the bottle prior to pressurization. This time a cloud will be much thicker and more clearly visible. The visibility is enhanced if a light source is placed behind the bottle so that the students are in a position to see light scattered in the forward direction by the cloud droplets. The cloud will disappear when the air in the bottle is pressurized. The compression warms the air and mixes in drier air from outside the bottle.

This demonstration can be used to explain the formation of haze, fog, and clouds, as well as the role that condensation nuclei play in their development. The chapter by Bohren also includes a good demonstration of cloud droplet formation on grains of salt.

5.	Dry ice offers a convenient way of producing thick clouds. Ask the students why a thicker cloud is formed when one blows on the piece of dry ice. Students should also understand why the cloud sinks.

6.	Photographic slides greatly enhance a discussion of clouds and cloud identification. Use a portion of the cloud slide collection to illustrate the common cloud types and their characteristics. Then show additional cloud slides and ask the students to identify the cloud type. If possible, include photographs of cloud patterns from the local area. This will give the students some experience identifying clouds they are likely to see outside during the course. In some areas, students should be made aware of local topography that can be used to judge low cloud base heights. In many cities it is possible to have slides processed overnight. In this way, interesting weather features or events can be photographed and then shown and discussed in a timely manner in class.

Student Projects

1.	Have students plot daily high and low temperatures together with average dew point temperature and an estimate of cloud cover for a period of a week or two. Were the coldest nighttime temperatures observed with clear or cloudy skies, dry or humid conditions? Have students plot the daily temperature range against one of the moisture variables. How much variation is there in the dew point temperature from day to day? Can students explain sudden changes in the daily average dew point? Is there any correlation between apparent visibility and dew point temperature?

2.	Students could build and test one of the simple hygrometers described in Chapter 4 (Moisture) of Hands-On Meteorology (see reference on p. 2 of this manual).

3.	During certain times of the year, students can observe the formation of dew, frost or fog. Have the students record weather data on these days as well as days on which dew, frost and fog did not form.

Is frost ever observed when the measured overnight minimum temperature remains above freezing? Is the layer of dew or frost thicker on some objects than other objects? Does the color or composition of the object have any effect on the formation of dew or frost? Is the formation of dew or frost thicker at ground level or on objects above ground level? An excellent discussion of how environmental factors affect the formation of dew and frost can be found in What Light Through Yonder Window Breaks by C.F. Bohren (see reference on p. 44 of this manual). Many of Bohren's experiments and observations could serve as the foundation of a student project.

4.	Students should be encouraged to observe, photograph, and try to identify different types of clouds. Students could observe and record the sequence of different types of clouds that are associated with the approach and passage of a low pressure center or front.

Multiple Choice Exam Questions

1.   ____ occupy or cover approximately 70% of the earth's surface.
   a. Forests
   b. Cities
 * c. Oceans
   d. Clouds

2.   The total mass of water vapor stored in the atmosphere represents about one ____ supply of the world's precipitation.
   a. day's
 * b. week's
   c. month's
   d. year's

3.   When the air is saturated, which of the following statements is <u>not</u> correct?
   a. the air temperature equals the wet-bulb temperature
   b. the relative humidity is 100%
   c. the air temperature equals the dew point temperature
 * d. an increase in temperature will cause condensation to occur
   e. the wet bulb temperature equals the dew point temperature

4.   As the air temperature increases, the air's capacity for water vapor
 * a. increases.
   b. decreases.
   c. remains constant.
   d. is unrelated to air temperature and can either increase or decrease.

5.   When the air temperature increases, the saturation vapor pressure will
 * a. increase.
   b. decrease.
   c. remain the same.
   d. vary over an increasingly broad range of values.

6.   If water vapor comprises 3.5% of an air parcel whose total pressure is 1000 mb, the water vapor pressure would be
   a. 1035 mb.
 * b. 35 mb.
   c. 350 mb.
   d. 965 mb.

7.   The density of water vapor in a given parcel of air is expressed by the
 * a. absolute humidity.
   b. relative humidity.
   c. mixing ratio.
   d. specific humidity.
   e. saturation vapor pressure.

8.   A rough rule of thumb is that ____ will double if you warm the air 10° C.
   a. relative humidity
 * b. saturation water vapor pressure
   c. dew point
   d. air density

9.   The ratio of the mass of water vapor in a given volume (parcel) of air to the mass of the remaining dry air describes the
      a. absolute humidity.
*   b. mixing ratio.
      c. relative humidity.
      d. dew point.

10.   If the air temperature in a room is 70° F, the saturation vapor pressure is 25 mb, the dew point temperature is 45° F, and the actual vapor pressure is 10 mb, then the relative humidity must be ____ percent.
      a. 15
      b. 20
      c. 35
*   d. 40

Questions 11 through 14 refer to the temperature and dew point data in the following cities

City	Air Temperature (° F)	Dew Point (°F)
City A	95	76
City B	10	10
City C	30	21
City D	50	42

11.   Which city has the highest relative humidity?
      a. City A
*   b. City B
      c. City C
      d. City D

12.   Which city has the least amount of water vapor in the air?
      a. City A
*   b. City B
      c. City C
      d. City D

13.   Which city has the greatest amount of water vapor in the air?
*   a. City A
      b. City B
      c. City C
      d. City D

14.   Which city has the highest saturation vapor pressure?
*   a. City A
      b. City B
      c. City C
      d. City D

15.   The percentage of water vapor present in the air compared to that required for saturation is the
      a. mixing ratio.
      b. absolute humidity.
      c. dew point.
*   d. relative humidity.
      e. specific humidity.

16.
* a. a relatively large number of water vapor molecules in the air.
A high water vapor pressure indicates
a. a relatively large number of water vapor molecules in the air.
b. a relatively small number of water vapor molecules in the air.
c. a relatively high rate of evaporation.
d. an abundant supply of condensation nuclei in the air.

17.   Which of the following is the best indicator of the actual amount of water vapor in the air?
a. air temperature
b. saturation vapor pressure
c. relative humidity
* d. dew point temperature

18.   Relative humidity changes with
a. addition of water vapor to the air.
b. decreases in temperature.
c. increases in temperature.
d. removal of water vapor from the air.
* e. all of the above

19.   Which of the following would cause relative humidity to decrease?
a. cooling the air
* b. warming the air
c. increasing the actual water vapor pressure
d. decreasing the saturation water vapor pressure

20.   If very cold air is brought indoors and warmed with no change in its moisture content, the saturation vapor pressure of this air will ___ and the relative humidity of this air will ___.
a. increase, increase
b. decrease, decrease
* c. increase, decrease
d. decrease, increase

21.   With which set of conditions below would you expect wet laundry hanging outdoors on a clothesline to dry most quickly?

	Air Temperature (° F)	Relative Humidity	Wind Speed
a.	60	75%	20 MPH
b.	40	75%	20
* c.	60	50%	20
d.	40	50%	10
e.	60	75%	10

22.   At what time of day is the relative humidity normally at a minimum?
* a. when the air temperature is highest
b. just before sunrise
c. about midnight
d. when the air temperature is lowest

23.   Evaporative coolers are primarily used in climates where the summers are
a. hot and humid.
* b. hot and dry.
c. cold and humid.
d. cold and dry.

24.   If the air temperature remains constant, evaporating water into the air
       will ___ the dew point and ___ the relative humidity.
*   a. increase, increase
       b. increase, decrease
       c. decrease, increase
       d. decrease, decrease

25.   The temperature to which air must be cooled in order to become saturated is the
       a. minimum temperature.
*   b. dew point temperature.
       c. wet-bulb temperature.
       d. freezing point.

26.   As the air temperature increases, with no addition of water vapor to the air, the dew point will
*   a. remain the same.
       b. increase.
       c. decrease.
       d. increase and become equal to the air temperature.

27.   As the difference between the air temperature and the dew point increases, the relative humidity
       a. increases.
*   b. decreases.
       c. remains constant at a value less than 100%.
       d. remains constant and equal to 100%.

28.   The Heat Index (HI) is based on the apparent temperature which is a combination of air temperature and
       a. wind speed.
*   b. relative humidity.
       c. solar intensity.
       d. cloud cover.

29.   Suppose saturated polar air has an air temperature and dew point of -10° C, and unsaturated desert air
       has an air temperature of 35° C and a dew point of 10° C. The desert air contains ___ water vapor and
       has a ___ relative humidity than the polar air.
*   a. more, lower
       b. more, higher
       c. less, lower
       d. less, higher

30.   During a blinding snowstorm in Vermont the air temperature and dew-point temperature are both 30° F.
       Meanwhile, under clear skies in Arizona, the air temperature is 85° F and the dew point temperature is
       38° F. From this information you could conclude
*   a. there is more water vapor in the air in Arizona.
       b. there is more water vapor in the Vermont snowstorm.
       c. the same amount of water vapor is found in the air in Vermont and Arizona.
       d. Vermont and Arizona are both located next to the ocean.

31.   At 40° F, the atmosphere is saturated with water vapor. If the air temperature increases to 60° F, with
       no addition or removal of water vapor, one may conclude that the dew point is about
       a. 20° F.
*   b. 40° F.
       c. 60° F.
       d. 100° F.

32.   This instrument uses wet-bulb and dry-bulb temperatures to obtain relative humidity.
      a. infrared hygrometer
*   b. sling psychrometer
      c. hair hygrometer
      d. electrical hygrometer

33.   A large difference between the dry- and wet-bulb readings on a sling psychrometer indicates
*   a. dry conditions.
      b. hot conditions.
      c. cold conditions.
      d. moist conditions.

34.   Which of the following statements is not correct?
      a. The length of human hair changes as the relative humidity changes.
      b. During the winter, low relative humidities can irritate the mucus membranes
         in the nose and throat.
*   c. The relative humidity is a measure of the air's actual water vapor content.
      d. A change in the air temperature can change the relative humidity.

35.   On a hot, humid day a measure of how cool the human skin can become is the
      a. air temperature.
      b. relative humidity.
      c. dew point temperature.
*   d. wet-bulb temperature.

36.   Dew is most likely to form on
*   a. clear, calm nights.
      b. cloudy, calm nights.
      c. clear, windy nights.
      d. cloudy, windy nights.
      e. rainy nights.

37.   The name given to a liquid drop of dew that freezes when the air temperature drops below freezing is
      a. frost.
      b. black frost.
      c. hoarfrost.
      d. white frost.
*   e. frozen dew.

38.   The cooling of the ground to produce dew is mainly the result of
      a. conduction.
*   b. radiational cooling.
      c. cooling due to the release of latent heat.
      d. advection.

39.   Which of the following statements is(are) correct?
      a. the largest concentration of condensation nuclei are usually observed near the
         earth's surface
      b. wet haze restricts visibility more than dry haze
      c. fog is actually a cloud resting on the ground
      d. with the same water vapor content, fog that forms in dirty air is usually thicker
         than fog that forms in cleaner air
*   e. all of the above are correct

40. For frozen dew to form
    a. the dew point must be above freezing.
    b. the minimum temperature must fall to freezing or below.
    c. dew must form and then freeze.
*   d. all of the above

41. Frost forms when
    a. objects on the ground cool below the dew point temperature.
    b. the dew point is 32° F or below.
    c. water vapor changes into ice without first becoming a liquid.
*   d. all of the above

42. Particles that serve as surfaces on which water vapor may condense are called
    a. hydrophobic nuclei.
    b. nacreous nuclei.
*   c. condensation nuclei.
    d. scud.

43. Foggy weather conditions outside would indicate a
    a. high dew point temperature.
    b. high water vapor pressure.
    c. high saturation water vapor pressure.
*   d. high relative humidity.

44. Fog that most often forms as warm rain falls into a cold layer of surface air is called
    a. radiation fog.
*   b. evaporation (mixing) fog.
    c. advection fog.
    d. upslope fog.

45. Which of the following identifications is not correct?
    a. hydrophobic - water producing
    b. radiation fog - ground fog
*   c. steam devils - advection fog
    d. hygroscopic - water seeking nuclei
    e. steam fog - arctic sea smoke

46. "Arctic sea smoke" and "steam devils" are forms of this type of fog.
    a. radiational fog
    b. advection fog
*   c. evaporation (mixing) fog
    d. upslope fog

47. Wet haze forms when the relative humidity is
    a. equal to 100%.
    b. above 100%.
*   c. less than 100%.
    d. equal to the dew point temperature.

48. Radiation fog forms when
    a. air pressure at the ground drops suddenly.
*   b. air next to the ground is cooled.
    c. water vapor is added to air next to the ground.
    d. there is a increase in condensation nuclei in air at the ground.

66

49. If fog is forming at Denver, Colorado, and the wind is blowing from the east, then the fog is most likely
     a. advection fog.
     b. frontal fog.
     c. evaporation fog.
*   d. upslope fog.
     e. radiation fog.

50. Which statement(s) below is(are) correct?
     a. valleys are more susceptible to radiation fog than hill tops
     b. without the summer fog along the coast of California, redwoods would not
        grow well there
     c. fog can be composed of ice crystals
*   d. all of the above are correct

51. Radiation fog forms best on a
*   a. clear winter night with a slight breeze.
     b. cloudy winter night with a strong breeze.
     c. clear summer night with a strong breeze.
     d. cloudy summer night with a slight breeze.
     e. cloudy winter night with a slight breeze.

52. Exhaled breath from your mouth in cold weather produces
     a. radiation fog.
     b. frontal fog.
     c. advection fog.
     d. upslope fog.
*   e. evaporation (mixing) fog.

53. When fog "burns off" it
     a. absorbs sunlight and warms up.
*   b. evaporates.
     c. thickens from the ground up.
     d. settles to the ground in the form of rain.

54. The fog that forms along the Pacific coastline of North America is mainly this type.
     a. radiation fog
     b. upslope fog
     c. frontal fog
*   d. advection fog
     e. steam fog

55. Fog that forms off the coast of Newfoundland is mainly a form of
*   a. advection fog.
     b. frontal fog.
     c. steam fog.
     d. radiation fog.
     e. upslope fog.

56. Steam fog is actually a form of
     a. advection fog.
     b. radiation fog.
*   c. evaporation (mixing) fog.
     d. upslope fog.
     e. frontal fog.

57. Frontal fog most commonly forms as ___ raindrops fall into a layer of ___ air.
    a. cold, warmer
    b. cold, windy
*   c. warm, colder
    d. warm, windy

58. When you see your breath on a cold morning the air temperature
    a. must be above freezing.
    b. must be below freezing.
*   c. can be above or below freezing.
    d. must be equal to the relative humidity.

59. On a cold, calm autumn morning the formation of fog above a relatively warm lake would most likely be
    a. radiation fog.
*   b. steam fog.
    c. frontal fog.
    d. advection fog.
    e. upslope fog.

60. Which fog does not necessarily form in air that is cooling?
    a. advection fog
    b. radiation fog
*   c. evaporation (mixing) fog
    d. upslope fog

61. On a cold winter morning the air near the surface is full of smoke particles. If fog should form in this air, it will probably be ___ fog that forms in cleaner air.
*   a. thicker than
    b. thinner than
    c. practically the same as
    d. a different color than

62. On a cold, winter morning the most likely place for radiation fog to form is
    a. at the top of a hill or mountain.
*   b. in a valley.
    c. along the side of a hill.
    d. over a body of water.

63. The term "cirro" tells you something about cloud ___
    a. composition.
    b. thickness.
*   c. altitude.
    d. motion.

64. When fog lifts above the ground it normally forms this gray sheetlike cloud.
*   a. stratus
    b. altostratus
    c. nimbostratus
    d. cirrostratus
    e. cumulonimbus

65. When naming clouds, the term "strato" means
    a. thick clouds.
    b. storm clouds.
    c. low altitude clouds.
*   d. layer clouds.

66. Which of the following tell you something about the altitude where a cloud has formed?
*   a. cirro
    b. nimbo
    c. strato
    d. cumulo

67. The term "cumulo" tells you something about cloud
    a. altitude.
    b. composition.
    c. temperature.
*   d. appearance.

68. Which association below is not correct?
    a. cirrocumulus - high cloud
    b. cumulus - cloud of vertical extent
*   c. altostratus - high cloud
    d. stratus - low cloud

69. The name given to ragged-looking clouds that rapidly drift with the wind beneath a rain-producing cloud is
    a. pileus.
    b lenticular clouds.
    c. castellanus.
*   d. scud.

70. At which city might you be able to observe cirrus clouds at an altitude of 3000 m (10,000 feet) above the surface?
*   a. Barrow, Alaska
    b. Honolulu, Hawaii
    c. Miami, Florida
    d. Chicago, Illinois

71. A "mackerel sky" describes what type of cloud?
*   a. cirrocumulus
    b. stratocumulus
    c. cumulonimbus
    d. nimbostratus
    e. cumulus

72. When viewed from the surface, the smallest individual cloud elements (puffs) are observed with which cloud?
    a. stratocumulus
    b. cumulus
*   c. cirrocumulus
    d. altocumulus
    e. cumulonimbus

73. At middle latitudes, the base of an altostratus or altocumulus cloud would generally be found between
    a. 200 and 6500 feet.
*   b. 6500 and 23,000 feet.
    c. 23,000 and 43,000 feet.
    d. above 43,000 feet.

74. The name given to a towering cloud that has <u>not</u> fully developed into a thunderstorm is
    a. cumulus humilis.
*   b. cumulus congestus.
    c. cumulonimbus.
    d. altocumulus.

75. Which association below is <u>not</u> correct?
*   a. cirrocumulus - layer cloud
    b. cumulonimbus - thunderstorm
    c. stratocumulus - low cloud
    d. cirrostratus - ice cloud

76. A middle cloud that sometimes forms in parallel waves or bands is
    a. cirrocumulus.
    b. cumulonimbus.
*   c. altocumulus.
    d. stratocumulus.
    e. altostratus.

77. A low, lumpy cloud layer that appears in rows, patches or rounded masses would be classified
    a. nimbostratus.
    b. stratus.
    c. cumulus.
    d. altocumulus.
*   e. stratocumulus.

78. Which association below is <u>not</u> correct?
*   a. cumulus congestus - anvil top
    b. cumulus - fair weather cumulus
    c. altocumulus castellanus - resemble "little castles"
    d. stratus fractus - scud
    e. cumulonimbus - thunderstorm clouds

79. A dim, watery sun visible through a gray sheet-like cloud layer is often a good indication
    of ___ clouds.
    a. stratocumulus
    b. cirrostratus
    c. cumulonimbus
*   d. altostratus
    e. nimbostratus

80. An anvil-shaped top is most often associated with
*   a. cumulonimbus.
    b. cumulus congestus.
    c. altocumulus.
    d. cumulus humilis.

81. Which cloud is <u>least</u> likely to produce precipitation that reaches the ground?
   a. stratus
   b. nimbostratus
   c. cumulonimbus
* d. cirrocumulus

82. In middle latitudes, which cloud will have the highest base?
* a. cirrostratus
   b. cumulonimbus
   c. altostratus
   d. cumulus

83. Cirrus clouds are composed primarily of
   a. water droplets.
   b. water vapor.
* c. ice particles.
   d. meteoritic dust.
   e. salt aerosols.

84. Detached clouds of delicate and fibrous appearance, without shading, usually white in color and sometimes of a silky appearance are
   a. stratus.
   b. cirrocumulus.
   c. altostratus.
* d. cirrus.
   e. cumulonimbus.

85. Hail is usually associated with what cloud?
   a. stratus
   b. cumulus
   c. stratocumulus
   d. altocumulus
* e. cumulonimbus

86. The cloud with the greatest vertical growth is
   a. cumulus congestus.
   b. cumulus humilis.
* c. cumulonimbus.
   d. cirrocumulus.
   e. altocumulus.

87. Which of the following clouds would form in the stratosphere?
   a. cirrostratus
* b. nacreous
   c. lenticular
   d. mammatus

88. A halo around the moon means that
* a. cirrostratus clouds are present.
   b. the clouds overhead are low clouds.
   c. rain is falling from the clouds overhead.
   d. the clouds are composed of water droplets.

89. Which cloud type is composed of ice crystals and can cause a halo to form around the sun or moon?
     a. altostratus
     b. stratus
     c. nimbostratus
   * d. cirrostratus
     e. angelitus

90. Which of the following associations is <u>not</u> correct?
     a. altostratus - middle cloud
     b. cirrus - high cloud
   * c. stratocumulus - cloud of vertical development
     d. cirrocumulus - high cloud
     e. cumulonimbus - cloud of vertical development

91. Suppose the sky is completely covered with a thin, white layered-type cloud. You look at the ground and see that objects cast a distinct shadow. From this you conclude that the cloud type must be
     a. stratus.
     b. nimbostratus.
   * c. cirrostratus.
     d. stratocumulus.

92. Light or moderate-but-steady precipitation is most often associated with ____ clouds.
   * a. nimbostratus
     b. cirrostratus
     c. cirrocumulus
     d. cumulonimbus

93. As Apollo 12 ascended into the atmosphere, the height of the surrounding clouds was noted to be 42,000 feet. A lightning stroke was seen within these clouds, indicating that they must have been
     a. cumulus congestus.
   * b. cumulonimbus.
     c. cirrus.
     d. cirrocumulus.
     e. lenticular.

94. In middle latitudes, which cloud will have the lowest base?
     a. cirrostratus
   * b. stratocumulus
     c. altocumulus
     d. cirrus

95. If you hold your hand at arm's length and cloud elements appear to be about the size of your fist, the cloud type is probably
     a. cumulus humilis.
     b. altocumulus.
     c. cirrocumulus.
   * d. stratocumulus.

96. Which cloud forms in descending air?
     a. cumulus fractus
     b. cumulonimbus
   * c. mammatus
     d. pileus

97.   Which of the following clouds would be found at the highest elevation above the earth's surface?
        a. cumulonimbus
        b. cirrocumulus
*   c. noctilucent
        d. cumulus congestus

98.   Which below is <u>not</u> a way in which a contrail may form?
        a. from water vapor in the engine exhaust mixing with air
        b. by air cooling as it passes over the aircraft's wings
*   c. due to heating of the air by the engine exhaust
        d. all of the above

99.   The small smooth cloud that may form just above the top of a towering cumulus cloud is called
        a. mammatus.
*   b. a pileus cloud.
        c. a contrail.
        d. a banner cloud.
        e. scud.

100.   The cloud-like streamer often seen forming behind an aircraft flying at high altitude is called
*   a. a contrail.
        b. a pileus cloud.
        c. mammatus.
        d. a banner cloud.
        e. scud.

101.   Clouds that have a characteristic lens-shaped appearance are referred to as
*   a. lenticular clouds.
        b. mammatus.
        c. a contrail.
        d. banner clouds.

102.   Clouds that appear as bag-like sacks hanging from beneath a cloud are
        a. pileus clouds.
        b. lenticular clouds.
*   c. mammatus.
        d. castellanus clouds.
        e. scud.

103.   Which of the following pairs of cloud types could be very similar in appearance?
        a. cumulus and cirrus
        b. cirrostratus and stratus
*   c. altocumulus and cirrocumulus
        d. cirrocumulus and cumulonimbus

True False Exam Questions

1.   Transpiration from plants and evaporation from continental areas account for the majority of the water vapor added to the atmosphere each year.
        (ans: FALSE)

2.   The total pressure inside a parcel of air is equal to the sum of the pressures of the individual gases.
        (ans: TRUE)

3.   It is possible to change the relative humidity even if moisture is not added to or removed from the air.
        (ans: TRUE)

4.   Hot air with a low relative humidity may actually contain more water vapor than cool air with a high relative humidity.
        (ans: TRUE)

5.   Dry air will always have a low dew point temperature and a low relative humidity.
        (ans: FALSE)

6.   Dry air is less dense than humid air with the same temperature.
        (ans: FALSE)

7.   One common instrument uses human hair to measure relative humidity.
        (ans: TRUE)

8.   Dew is more likely to form on a clear night than on a cloudy night.
        (ans: TRUE)

9.   The relative humidity must reach 100% before water vapor can begin to condense onto condensation nuclei.
        (ans: FALSE)

10.   Nacreous and noctilucent clouds are unusual because they form above 30 km (100,000 ft.) in the stratosphere and mesosphere.
        (ans: TRUE)

Word Choice Exam Questions

1   When air is saturated, the rate of evaporation is GREATER than, EQUAL to, LESS than the rate of condensation. (circle one answer)
        (ans: EQUAL)

2.   Water departments in many cities in the desert southwest encourage their customers to water lawns early in the day. This is because the relative humidity is at its HIGHEST LOWEST value in the morning and the rate of evaporation from wet soil will be relatively HIGH LOW. (choose one word from each pair)
        (ans: HIGHEST, LOW)

3.   If you warm moist air the saturation vapor pressure will INCREASE DECREASE and the relative humidity will INCREASE DECREASE. (choose one word from each pair)
        (ans: INCREASE, DECREASE)

4.   An air temperature of 100° F and a dew point temperature of 75° F would result in COMFORTABLE OPPRESSIVE conditions. The heat index in this case would be GREATER than, LESS than, EQUAL to the 100° F air temperature. (choose one word from each group)
        (ans: OPPRESSIVE, GREATER)

5.   Humid air is slightly MORE LESS dense than dry air with the same temperature. (circle one answer)
        (ans: LESS)

6.   If frozen dew forms on Monday and frost is observed on Tuesday, you could conclude that the air on Tuesday was DRIER MOISTER than on Monday. (circle one answer)
        (ans: DRIER)

7. A large wet-bulb depression measured with a sling psychrometer means that water is evaporating RAPIDLY SLOWLY from the wet-bulb thermometer and that the relative humidity is HIGH LOW. (choose one word from each pair)
(ans: RAPIDLY, LOW)

8. If frost is observed in Dallas on a night when dew forms in Kansas City, you could conclude that the dew point temperature in Dallas was HIGHER LOWER than the dew point in Kansas City and that the nighttime minimum temperature in Dallas was WARMER COLDER than the minimum in Kansas City. (choose one word from each pair)
(ans: LOWER, COLDER)

9. Visibility will generally IMPROVE WORSEN when the relative humidity increases and dry haze becomes wet haze. (circle one answer)
(ans: WORSEN)

10. The term "alto" tells you something about cloud SHAPE ALTITUDE. (circle one answer)
(ans: ALTITUDE)

11. At polar latitudes, high and middle altitude clouds are generally CLOSER FURTHER to(from) the ground than at tropical latitudes. (circle one answer)
(ans: CLOSER)

12. The thickest layer clouds are those found at HIGH MIDDLE LOW altitude. (circle one answer)
(ans: LOW)

13. Haloes are sometimes observedin THICK THIN layer clouds composed of WATER ICE particles. (choose one word from each pair)
(ans: THIN, ICE)

14. A LOW MIDDLE HIGH altitude cumuliform cloud will have cloud elements that are about the size of your thumbnail. (circle one answer)
(ans: MIDDLE)

Short Answer Exam Questions

1. A water vapor pressure of 10 mb in an air parcel at sea level would indicate a water vapor concentration of about _____ percent.
(ans: 1%)

2. When you warm moist air _____ will decrease, _____ will increase, and _____ will remain constant. (fill in each blank with water vapor pressure (e), saturation water vapor pressure (e_s), or relative humidity (RH)).
(ans: RH, e_s, e)

3. _____ fog will sometimes form over a heated outdoor swimming pool in the winter.
(ans: EVAPORATION or STEAM)

4. Towering cumulus (cumulus congestus) would refer to which of the clouds sketched at right?
(ans: b)

5. _____ is one of the two names given to an instrument that is used to measure humidity.
(ans: HYGROMETER or PSYCHROMETER)

6. What three basic cloud types are missing from the list at right? (ans: STRATUS, ALTOCUMULUS, CIRRUS)

     altostratus   cirrostratus   cumulonimbus
     nimbostratus   cirrocumulus   cumulus
                   stratocumulus

7. Name the three cloud features indicated at right choosing from the terms below.
stratus fractus (scud)   anvil
lenticular   mammatus
(ans: a. ANVIL, b. MAMMATUS, c. LENTICULAR)

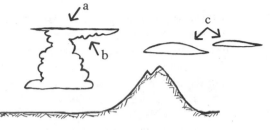

8. Fair weather _____ clouds resemble white balls of cotton.
(ans: CUMULUS)

9. The flat top of a thunderstorm is referred to as a(n) _____ cloud.
(ans: ANVIL)

10. Moist air crossing a mountain range may form several lens shaped clouds stacked above each that are called _____ clouds.
(ans: LENTICULAR)

Essay Exam Questions

1. What is meant by the terms water vapor saturation and saturation vapor pressure? Why does the saturation vapor pressure increase with increasing air temperature?

2. In terms of the air temperature and water vapor content, explain how the relative humidity normally changes during the course of a 24-hour day.

3. In order to reduce evaporation and conserve water, do you think it would be better to water a lawn in the early morning or early evening?

4. Would lowering the temperature in your home during the winter cause the relative humidity to increase or decrease? Why? What physiological effects might you experience during humid and dry conditions?

5. Explain why the dew point temperature provides a better indication of the actual amount of water vapor in the air than the relative humidity.

6. Describe how a sling psychrometer can be used to determine the relative humidity or dew point.

7. Small particles of ordinary table salt are hygroscopic. What does hydroscopic mean? Suggest a likely natural source for salt particles.

8. Water vapor is an invisible gas. How can an increase in rleative humidity affect visibility?

9. It is a cold winter night and a fog cloud forms. If it continues to cool during the night would you expect to find that the dew point has changed overnight? If so, would you expect to find that dew point has increased or decreased?

10. Would you expect your sunglasses to "fog up" when you move cold to warm surroundings or when you move from warm to cold surroundings? Explain.

11.   List the main types of fog, then briefly explain how each one forms.

12.   List one or more key identifying features for each of the ten basic cloud types. Which cloud types might have fairly similar appearances and thus be difficult to identify?

13.   With which cloud type would each of the following phenomena be associated?
        lightning   hail   tornadoes   mackerel sky
        brief heavy rain   steady rain   milky sun   halo

14.   List the major height categories of clouds. What differences might you expect to find in the clouds that form at these different levels?

15.   Fog is often described as a cloud that forms at ground level. In what ways are the formation of fog and clouds similar and different?

16.   Explain why clouds form in rising air. Would it be possible for rising air to remain cloud-free?

Chapter 5
Cloud Development and Precipitation

Summary

This chapter examines atmospheric stability and factors that affect the development of clouds. The treatment continues with a discussion of precipitation processes and the different types of precipitation that can be produced by clouds.

The concept of stable and unstable equilibria is introduced using an instructive analogy. Stability in the atmosphere depends on the change of temperature in a moving parcel relative to its surroundings. In a stable atmosphere, a parcel which is given an upward push will become colder and denser than its surroundings and will resist further upward motion. Clouds which form in a stable atmosphere tend to develop horizontally and have a layered structure. In an unstable atmosphere, a rising air parcel will become warmer and less dense than its surroundings and will continue to move upward on its own, often forming cumuliform clouds. The rising air motions that are needed to form clouds can be produced in a variety of ways including convection, topographic uplifting, convergence, and lifting at frontal boundaries. A variety of factors can affect atmospheric stability such as warming or cooling at the ground and the influx of warm or cold air at upper levels.

In the second part of the chapter, the student learns that the water droplets or ice crystals found in clouds are themselves too small and not heavy enough to be able to reach the ground as precipitation. Larger raindrops can form rapidly in warm clouds when water droplets collide and coalesce. Formation of rain by this process works best in thick clouds with strong updrafts. The formation and growth of ice crystals, which is important for precipitation formation in cold clouds, is discussed. An understanding of the processes that produce precipitation has led to attempts to enhance precipitation by cloud seeding.

Precipitation can reach the ground in a variety of forms depending on the type of cloud producing it and also on the atmospheric conditions between the cloud base and the ground. Rain and snowfall amounts can be measured using simple instruments or estimated remotely using weather radar.

Key Terms

(Listed in approximately the same order they appear in the text. Terms in boldface are emphasized and appear at the end of the chapter in the text.)

stable equilibrium

unstable equilibrium

air parcel

adiabatic process

dry adiabatic rate

moist adiabatic rate

irreversible pseudoadiabatic
   process

lapse rate

**absolutely stable
   atmosphere**

**supercooled (water
   droplet)**

environmental lapse rate

subsidence inversion

**absolutely unstable
   atmosphere**

superadiabatic

condensation level

level of free convection

**conditionally unstable
   atmosphere**

thermal

orographic uplift

acid rain

snow

orographic clouds

rain shadow

lenticular clouds

mountain wave clouds

rotor clouds

condensation nuclei

terminal velocity

coalescence

surface tension

warm clouds

cold clouds

snow pellets

soft hail

ice nuclei	fall streaks	hailstones
ice crystal (Bergeron)	dendrite	hailstone embryo
process	aggregate	hail streak
accretion	flurries (of snow)	standard rain gauge
riming	snow squall	trace (of precipitation)
graupel	blizzard	tipping-bucket rain
snowflake	ice pellet	gauge
cloud seeding	sleet	weighing-type rain
dry ice	freezing rain	gauge
glaciated (cloud)	glaze	water equivalent
seed drops	freezing drizzle	radar
rain	rime	target
drizzle	aircraft icing	radar echo
virga	clear ice	Doppler radar
shower (rain)	rime ice	algorithm
cloudburst	snow grains	Doppler shift

Teaching Suggestions, Demonstrations, and Visual Aids

1.   Free convection can be demonstrated by filling a dark-colored balloon with hydrogen or helium gas. Tape a small piece of paper to the balloon to add weight. Trim the paper until the balloon is just heavy enough that it will sink very slowly when released. Heat the balloon using an infrared heat lamp or a high-wattage flood light. As the balloon warms, it will expand slightly and begin to rise. The balloon will float out of range of the heat lamp, cool and sink back toward the floor. The demonstration can be repeated several times.

Or, alternatively, plunge a helium-filled balloon in liquid nitrogen. Remove the balloon and quickly place it on a table top. The balloon will expand as it warms. Eventually, the density of the gas in the balloon will be less than that of the surrounding air and the balloon will float upward off the table.

Convection currents can also be demonstrated by mixing a small amount of aluminum powder in a test tube of water. Shake the test tube to get a good homogeneous distribution of the particles. Currents will be established when the bottom of the test tube is warmed (ref: E.J. Carlone, "Convection Demonstration," *The Phys. Teacher,* p. 464, October, 1983).

2.   An interesting class discussion can sometimes be generated by writing two statements, "rising air cools" and "warm air rises," on the board and asking the students whether the statements are contradictory.

3.   This chapter might be an appropriate place to introduce Archimedes' Law. Students should be able to understand that the vertical pressure gradient force and the downward pull of gravity are generally very nearly balanced in the atmosphere. A slight change in an air parcel's density (with respect to its surroundings) will upset the balance and cause the parcel to rise or sink. For a surprising demonstration of density differences, place a can of diet and sugar-sweetened softdrink in an aquarium filled with water. The can of diet drink will generally float, while the sweetened beverage will sink. A large amount of corn syrup is added to soft drinks and the resulting mixture has a density greater than water (refs: Toepker, T.P., "Floaters and Sinkers," *The Phys. Teacher,* p. 164, March, 1986 and Heckathorn, D., "A Density Demonstration", *The Phys. Teacher,* p. 39, Jan., 1987).

4.   Temperature inversions and atmospheric stability are discussed in "Temperature Inversions Have Cold Bottoms" in <u>What Light Through Yonder Window Breaks</u> by C.F. Bohren (see reference on p. 44 of this manual).

5.   Satellite cloud photographs often illustrate stable and unstable atmospheric conditions. A spotty cumulus cloud pattern is often visible when cold air moves out over warm ocean water, for example.

6.   Fill a glass tube (18 to 24 inches tall and 2 to 3 inches in diameter) with glycerin (or corn syrup). Glycerin is sufficiently viscous that steel ball bearings dropped into glycerin will accelerate and quickly attain their terminal

velocity. The terminal velocity can readily be measured and the dependence of fall velocity on bearing diameter can be investigated (the terminal velocity should be proportional to the square of the ball bearing radius). Typical fall speeds for 3/32″ and 3/8″ diameter bearings are 1 to 2 cm/sec and 20 cm/sec, respectively.

Student Projects

1.   Strong radiation inversions frequently develop overnight in many locations. Have students plot an early morning sounding and identify the top of the inversion layer. In larger cities, an associated hazy layer may be visible over the city in the early morning. Plot the afternoon sounding for the same day and determine whether the inversion layer has disappeared. Are any other inversion layers visible? Have the students investigate what meteorological conditions favor strong inversions and pollution episodes for their location. (Tabulated sounding data will generally use pressure as the vertical coordinate; in this case it is probably sufficient to assume a 1 mb decrease per 10 meters)

2.   A variety of experiments dealing with cloud droplet and ice crystal formation have appeared in *Weatherwise* magazine (see for example, articles by I.W. Geer and V.J. Schaeffer in the April, June, August, October, and December 1979 and the April, June, August, and December 1980 issues).

3.   Supercooling of water can be readily demonstrated and studied using the apparatus at right. Two aluminum plates (3/8″ or 1/2″ thick and 3 to 4 inches in diameter) are connected to the ends of an aluminum rod (about 12″ long). Clean and coat the upper plate with a thin layer of petroleum jelly and use a medicine dropper to place 25 to 50 drops of distilled water on the plate (the petroleum jelly will cause the drops to bead up). Cover the drops with a clear cover (a plastic petri dish cover works well) and tape the cover in place. Insert a dial thermometer into a hole drilled into the side of the upper plate. Place the stand in a styrofoam ice chest and pour about 1 L of liquid nitrogen into the chest.

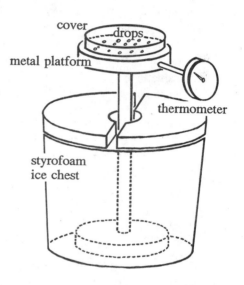

One student can record the time and temperature at 30 second intervals. A second student can carefully watch the drops and indicate when they freeze. Drops generally won't begin to freeze until the plate temperature is several degrees below 0° C. Each 30 second interval can be indentified with a letter from the alphabet. As each drop freezes, the student can write the corresponding letter above the drop. Have the students plot a freezing temperature distribution and calculate the mean freezing temperature for the drops.

A simpler and more readily performed demonstration of supercooling of water can be found in <u>Clouds in a Glass of Beer</u> by C.F. Bohren (see reference on p. 59 of this manual).

4.   Rainfall measurement, the construction of simple and inexpensive raingauges, and student projects have been discussed by J.T. Snow and S.B. Harley (ref: "Basic Meteorological Observations for Schools: Rainfall," *Bull. Am. Meteorol. Soc., 69*, 498-507, 1988).

Multiple Choice Exam Questions

1.   A rising parcel of air that does not exchange heat with its surroundings is referred to as
         a. isothermal ascent.
*   b. an adiabatic process.
         c. forced lifting.
         d. advection.

2.   If the environmental lapse rate is 5° C per 1000 m and the temperature at the earth's surface is 25° C, then the air temperature at 2000 m above the ground is
      a. 25° C.
      b. 30° C.
      c. 20° C.
*   d. 15° C.

3.   If a parcel of unsaturated air with a temperature of 30° C rises from the surface to an altitude of 1000 m, the unsaturated parcel temperature at this altitude would be about
      a. 10° C warmer than at the surface.
*   b. 10° C colder than at the surface.
      c. 6° C colder than at the surface.
      d. impossible to tell from the data given

4.   The rate at which the actual air temperature changes with increasing height above the surface is referred to as the
*   a. environmental lapse rate.
      b. dry adiabatic rate.
      c. moist adiabatic rate.
      d. thermocline.

5.   If an air parcel is given a small push upward and it falls back to its original position, the atmosphere is said to be
*   a. stable.
      b. unstable.
      c. isothermal.
      d. neutral.
      e. adiabatic.

6.   If an air parcel is given a small push upward and it continues to move upward on its own accord, the atmosphere is said to be
      a. stable.
*   b. unstable.
      c. bouyant.
      d. dynamic.

7.   The rate at which the temperature changes inside a rising (or descending) parcel of saturated air is called
      a. the environmental lapse rate.
      b. the dry adiabatic lapse rate.
*   c. the moist adiabatic lapse rate.
      d. the latent heat release rate.

8.   The dry adiabatic rate is the rate at which
      a. an air parcel rises.
*   b. temperature changes in a rising or descending parcel of unsaturated air.
      c. volume changes when a parcel expands or is compressed.
      d. latent heat energy is released in a rising air parcel.

9.   The most latent heat would be released in a ____ parcel of ____ saturated air.
*   a. rising, warm
      b. rising, cold
      c. sinking, warm
      d. sinking, cold

10. Which of the following environmental lapse rates would represent the most <u>unstable</u> conditions in a layer of unsaturated air?
    a. 1° C per 1000 m
    b. 3° C per 1000 m
    c. 6° C per 1000 m
    d. 9° C per 1000 m
    * e. 11° C per 1000 m

11. In a conditionally unstable atmosphere, the environmental lapse rate will be ___ than the moist adiabatic rate and ___ than the dry adiabatic rate.
    * a. greater, less
    b. greater, greater
    c. less, greater
    d. less, less

12. A conditionally unstable atmosphere is ___ with respect to unsaturated air and ___ with respect to saturated air.
    a. unstable, stable
    b. unstable, unstable
    * c. stable, unstable
    d. stable, stable

13. If the environmental air temperature decreases at a rate of 8° C/km, the atmosphere would be considered
    a. absolutely stable.
    * b. conditionally unstable.
    c. absolutely unstable.
    d. neutrally stable.

14. The reason that rising saturated air cools at a lesser rate than rising unsaturated air is
    a. rising saturated air is heavier.
    b. rising saturated air is lighter.
    c. unsaturated air expands more rapidly.
    d. saturated air has a higher heat capacity.
    * e. latent heat is released by rising saturated air.

15. If the environmental lapse rate is less than the moist adiabatic rate, the atmosphere is
    a. conditionally unstable.
    * b. absolutely stable.
    c. absolutely unstable.
    d. neutrally stable.

16. The difference between the "moist" and "dry" adiabatic rates is due to the fact that
    a. saturated air is always unstable.
    b. an unsaturated air parcel expands more rapidly than a saturated air parcel.
    c. moist air weighs less than dry air.
    * d. latent heat is released by a rising parcel of saturated air.

17. A knowledge of air stability is important because
    a. it determines the direction of movement of storms.
    * b. it determines the vertical motion of air.
    c. it determines the movement of high pressure areas.
    d. it determines seasonal weather patterns.

18.   Which condition below would make a layer of air more unstable?
a. an increase in wind speed
b. lifting the entire air layer
*   c. cooling the upper part of the layer
d. all of the above

19.   When the environmental lapse rate decreases more rapidly with height than the dry adiabatic rate, the atmosphere is
a. absolutely stable.
*   b. absolutely unstable.
c. convectively unstable.
d. conditionaly unstable.

20.   Most thunderstorms do not extend very far into the stratosphere because the air in the stratosphere is
a. unstable.
*   b. stable.
c. too cold.
d. too thin.
e. too dry.

21.   An inversion represents an extrememly stable atmosphere because air that rises into the inversion will eventually become ___ and ___ dense than the surrounding air.
a. warmer, less
b. warmer, more
c. colder, less
*   d. colder, more

22.   Which set of conditions, working together, will make the atmosphere the most stable?
*   a. cool the surface and warm the air aloft
b. cool the surface and cool the air aloft
c. warm the surface and cool the air aloft
d. warm the surface and warm the air aloft

23.   What two sets of conditions, working together, will make the atmosphere the most unstable?
a. cool the surface and warm the air aloft
b. cool the surface and cool the air aloft
*   c. warm the surface and cool the air aloft
d. warm the surface and warm the air aloft

24.   Which cloud type would most likely form in absolutely stable air?
a. cumulus congestus
b. cumulonimbus
*   c. stratus
d. altocumulus

25.   Which cloud type below would most likely form in an unstable atmosphere?
*   a. cumulonimbus
b. stratus
c. cirrostratus
d. nimbostratus
e. cumulus humilis

26.   Just above cumulus humilis clouds you would expect to find
*   a. a stable layer.
      b. an unstable layer.
      c. a conditionally unstable layer.
      d. unusually strong horizontal winds.

27.   Subsidence inversions are best developed with high pressure areas because of
      the ___ air motions associated with them causes the air to ___.
      a. rising, cool
      b. sinking, cool
      c. rising, warm
*   d. sinking, warm

28.   Which of the following sets of conditions would produce a cumulus cloud with the <u>lowest</u> base?
      a. air temperature 90° F, dew point temperature 50° F
      b. air temperature 90° F, dew point temperature 40° F
*   c. air temperature 90° F, dew point temperature 60° F
      d. air temperature 90° F, dew point temperature 20° F

29.   Which of the following statements is correct?
      a. convection can occur over the ocean
      b. air motions are usually downward around a cumulus cloud
      c. the temperature of the rising air at a given level inside a cumulus cloud is
         normally warmer that the air around the cloud
*   d. all of the above

30.   The vertical motion of air caused by sun heating the ground is called
*   a. convection.
      b. orographic lifting.
      c. subsidence.
      d. convergence.

31.   Which of the following is <u>not</u> a way of producing clouds?
      a. lifting air along a topographic barrier
      b. lifting air along a front
      c. warming the surface of the earth
      d. convergence of surface air
*   e. air motions caused by subsidence

32.   An example of orographic clouds would be
      a. clouds forming over a warm ocean current.
*   b. clouds forming on the windward slope of a mountain.
      c. clouds forming behind a jet airplane.
      d. clouds formed by surface heating.

33.   Which of the following is <u>not</u> an important factor in the production of rain by the collision-coalescence
      process?
      a. the updrafts in the cloud
      b. relative size of the droplets
*   c. the number of ice crystals in the cloud
      d. cloud thickness
      e. the electric charge of the droplets

34. The name commonly used to describe the drier region observed on the downwind (leeward) side of a mountain range is
    a. orographic.
    b. inversion region.
*   c. rain shadow.
    d. compression region.

35. Which of the following cloud types would commonly be found downwind of a mountain?
*   a. lenticular clouds
    b. anvil clouds
    c. mammatus clouds
    d. contrails

36. The merging of liquid cloud droplets by collision is called
*   a. coalescence.
    b. riming.
    c. accretion.
    d. deposition.
    e. condensation.

37. If you observe large raindrops hitting the ground, you could probably say that the cloud overhead was ___ and had ___ updrafts.
    a. thick, weak
*   b. thick, strong
    c. thin, weak
    d. thin, strong

38. Which cloud type below will only produce precipitation by the collision-coalescence process?
    a. a thick, cold nimbostratus cloud
*   b. a thick, warm cumulus cloud
    c. a thick, cold cumulus cloud
    d. a thick, supercooled cumulonimbus cloud with abundant nuclei
    e. a supercooled cumulus congestus cloud

39. During the ice crystal process of rain formation
    a. only ice crystals need be present in a cloud.
*   b. ice crystals grow larger at the expense of the surrounding liquid cloud droplets.
    c. the temperature in the cloud must be -40° C (-40° F) or below.
    d. the cloud must be a cumuliform cloud.

40. Most rain at middle latitudes is produced by the ice crystal process. This is because
    a. ice crystal nuclei are more plentiful than condensation nuclei.
*   b. most clouds form in cold regions of the atmosphere.
    c. ice crystals evaporate more slowly than water droplets.
    d. most rain occurs during the winter.

41. Which of the following is found in the greatest concentration in the mixed ice and water phase region of a cold cloud?
    a. ice crystal nuclei
    b. ice crystals
*   c. supercooled water droplets
    d. graupel particles

42.   Particles in the atmosphere on which ice crystals grow are called
        a. virga.
*   b. ice nuclei.
        c. condensation nuclei.
        d. graupel.

43.   The ice crystal process of precipitation formation operates in the mixed ice and water phase region of a cold
        cloud where there are ice crystals and
*   a. supercooled drops.
        b. updrafts and downdrafts.
        c. cloud condensation nuclei.
        d. positive and negative electrical charges.

44.   The growth of a precipitation particle by the collision of an ice crystal (or snowflake) with a supercooled
        liquid droplet is called
*   a. accretion.
        b. spontaneous nucleation.
        c. condensation.
        d. deposition.

45.   The falling ice crystal at right is colliding
        with supercooled water droplets which stick
        and freeze. This process is called
        a. nucleation.
        b. agglomeration.
*   c. riming.
        d. deposition.

46.   The most common ice crystal shape is
        a. graupel.
*   b. a dendrite.
        c. rime.
        d. virga.

47.   Cloud seeding using silver iodide only works in
        a. cold clouds composed entirely of ice crystals.
        b. warm clouds composed entirely of water droplets.
*   c. cold clouds composed of ice crystals and supercooled droplets.
        d. cumuliform clouds.

48.   If rain falls on one side of a street and not on the other side, the rain most likely fell from a
        a. nimbostratus cloud.
        b. stratus cloud.
*   c. cumulonimbus cloud.
        d. altostratus cloud.
        e. altocumulus cloud.

49.   Another name for an intense snow shower is
        a. sleet.
        b. blizzard.
*   c. snow squall.
        d. snow grains.
        e. hailstorm.

50. Which of the following would you not expect to fall from a nimbostratus cloud?
    a. snow
    b. drizzle
    c. sleet
  * d. graupel

51. Aircraft icing would be heaviest and most severe
    a. in the cloud at warmer than freezing temperatures.
  * b. in the cloud at just below freezing temperatures.
    c. in the cloud at well below freezing temperatures.
    d. outside the cloud at below freezing temperatures.

52. A raindrop which freezes before reaching the ground is called
    a. snow.
    b. graupel.
  * c. sleet.
    d. glaze.

53. Fall streaks most often form with
    a. nimbostratus clouds.
    b. cumulonimbus clouds.
    c. stratus clouds.
    d. altostratus clouds.
  * e. cirrus clouds.

54. Which of the following might be mistaken for hail?
    a. virga
  * b. graupel
    c. dendrite
    d. supercooled droplet

55. Rain which falls from a cloud but evaporates before reaching the ground is referred to as
    a. sleet.
  * b. virga.
    c. graupel.
    d. dry rain.

56. A true blizzard is characterized by
    a. low temperatures.
    b. strong winds.
    c. reduced visibility.
    d. blowing snow.
  * e. all of the above.

57. In the winter you read in the newpaper that a large section of the Midwest is without power due to downed power lines. Which form of precipitation would most likely produce this situation?
    a. snow
    b. hail
  * c. freezing rain
    d. sleet
    e. rain

58. The largest snowflakes would probably be observed in ___ air whose temperature is ___ freezing.
 *   a. moist, near
  b. dry, near
  c. moist, well below
  d. dry, well below

59. An aggregate of ice crystals is
 *   a. a snowflake.
  b. freezing rain.
  c. sleet.
  d. glaze.
  e. hail.

60. You would use a wooden stick to measure rainfall in the
  a. tipping bucket rain gauge.
 *   b. standard rain gauge.
  c. weighing rain gauge.
  d. Ozarks.

61. Radar gathers information about precipitation in clouds by measuring the
  a. energy emitted by the precipitation particles.
  b. absorption characteristics of falling precipitation.
 *   c. amount of energy reflected back to a transmitter.
  d. amount of sunlight scattered off the precipitation.
  e. amount of solar energy passing through the cloud.

62. If a city were to receive 1/2 inch of rain in the morning and then 5 inches of snow that afternoon, about how much precipitation would the weather service report for that day?
  a. 5 1/2 inches
  b. 1/2 inch
 *   c. 1 inch
  d. 10 inches

True False Exam Questions

1. Rising parcels of dry and moist air cool at the same rate as long as the moist air doesn't become saturated.
(ans: TRUE)

2. The temperature of the air in a rising parcel of air will always be the same as that of the surrounding air.
(ans: FALSE)

3. A rising air parcel will always cool. Environmental temperatures can increase or decrease with increasing altitude.
(ans: TRUE)

4. Relatively small precipitation particles fall from thunderstorms because the strong updrafts tend to break apart growing raindrops.
(ans: FALSE)

5. In the summer at middle latitudes, the collision-coalescence process is the dominant precipitation-producing process.
(ans: FALSE)

88

6. Supercooled water droplets may be more plentiful than ice crystals in certain sub-freezing regions of cold clouds.
(ans: TRUE)

7. Supercooled water droplets and ice crystals form readily in cold clouds because of the abundance of cloud droplet and ice crystal nuclei.
(ans: FALSE)

8. Falling raindrops have a nearly spherical shape because that is the profile that minimizes air resistance.
(ans: FALSE)

9. Visibility generally improves after a rain storm.
(ans: TRUE)

10. Hail can fall from both cumulonimbus and nimbostratus clouds.
(ans: FALSE)

Word Choice Exam Questions

1. In a stable atmosphere, a rising parcel of air will become WARMER COLDER than and MORE LESS dense than the surrounding atmosphere. (choose one word from each pair)
(ans: COLDER, MORE)

2. Stratiform clouds form in a STABLE UNSTABLE atmosphere and grow mainly in a HORIZONTAL VERTICAL direction. (choose one word from each pair)
(ans: STABLE, HORIZONTAL)

3. The air at point A in the figure at right will be WARMER COLDER than at B and will have a HIGHER LOWER dewpoint. (choose one word from each pair)
(ans: COLDER, HIGHER)

4. Would you expect a region in a "rain shadow" to have ABUNDANT or INFREQUENT precipitation? (circle one answer)
(ans: INFREQUENT)

5. Would you expect the largest raindrops to form in a cloud with STRONG or WEAK updrafts? (circle one answer)
(ans: STRONG)

6. Does the collision and coalescence process work best when all the drops are the SAME or DIFFERENT sizes? (circle one answer)
(ans: DIFFERENT)

7. For precipitation to develop via the ice crystal process, it is important to have many MORE FEWER ice crystals than supercooled droplets in the mixed ice and water phase region of a cold cloud. (circle one answer)
(ans: FEWER)

8. A mixed ice and water phase region is found in clouds at temperatures just ABOVE BELOW freezing. (circle one answer)
(ans: BELOW)

9. Does accretion (riming) occur during the ICE CRYSTAL process or the COLLISION COALESCENCE process? Does accretion make a precipitation particle LARGER or SMALLER? (choose one word from each pair)
(ans: ICE CRYSTAL, LARGER)

10. The water droplet and the ice crystal in the figure at right have the same temperature. Will the saturation vapor pressure surrounding the water droplet be HIGHER than, LOWER than, or the SAME as that surrounding the ice crystal? (circle one answer)
(ans: HIGHER)

Short Answer Exam Questions

1. Temperatures in a rising parcel of air are shown at various altitudes at right. The data indicate that a cloud must have formed at _____ kilometer(s). At what altitude will the parcel start to become warmer than the surroundings if the environmental lapse rate is 8° C/km?
(ans: 1 km, 2 km)

2. In an adiabatic process, there is no exchange of _____ between a parcel and the surrounding environment.
(ans: HEAT)

3. Which of the environmental temperature profiles at right indicates the most stable atmosphere?
(ans: d)

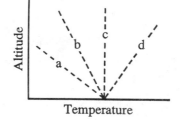

4. The stability of the air is determined by comparing the _____ in a rising air parcel to that of the surrounding environment.
(ans: TEMPERATURE or DENSITY)

5. In a(n) _____ environmental temperatures increase with increasing altitude.
(ans: INVERSION)

6. A(n) _____ is a hot "bubble" of air that breaks away from the ground and starts to rise.
(ans: THERMAL)

7. Convection and convergence are two ways of causing rising air motions. What two additional processes are there?
(ans: FRONTAL LIFTING and OROGRAPHIC LIFTING)

8. A drop will fall at a constant "terminal" velocity when _____ balances the pull of gravity.
(ans: AIR RESISTANCE, DRAG, or FRICTION)

9. Falling drops of water greater than 0.5 mm in diameter are called rain. What would drops with diameters less than 0.5 mm be called?
(ans: DRIZZLE)

10. The amount of air resistance acting on a falling drop depends on the drop's size and on _____.
(ans: FALL SPEED)

11. Water vapor moves from supercooled water droplets towards ice crystals in cold clouds because the _____ just above the drop is greater than above the ice crystal surface.
(ans: SATURATION VAPOR PRESSURE)

12. The common name for an aggregate of ice crystals is a(n) _____.
(ans: SNOWFLAKE)

13. The largest precipitation particle is _____.
(ans: HAIL)

14. Fill in the blanks at left using terms from the list at right.
a. "soft hail" _____   virga
b. rain which evaporates before   graupel
   reaching the ground _____   dendrite
c. most common ice crystal shape _____ sleet
(ans: a. GRAUEL, b. VIRGA, c. DENDRITE)

15. _____ or _____ can cause a noticeable change in the appearance of precipitation falling below a cloud.
(ans: EVAPORATION or MELTING)

16. On average about _____ inches of snow is equivalent to one inch of rain.
(ans: TEN)

17. Following its discovery and development during World War II, _____ began to be used by atmospheric scientists to examine the inside of a cloud.
(ans: RADAR)

18. By measuring the change in the _____ of reflected radio waves, scientists can use Doppler radar to measure the speed at which precipitation is moving toward or away from the radar antenna.
(ans: FREQUENCY)

Essay Exam Questions

1. Explain how the stability of the atmosphere can affect the types of clouds that form.

2. Would you expect to find a subsidence inversion to be associated with high or low pressure? What effects might a subsidence inversion have on weather conditions at the ground?

3. Does radiational cooling at the ground at night act to increase or decrease atmospheric stability? How does daytime heating at the ground during the day affect atmospheric stability?

4. Based on atmospheric stability considerations, do you think it would be best to burn agricultural debris in the early morning or the afternoon?

5. Explain why the surface air on the downwind side of a mountain can be drier than the surface air on the upwind side. What is this effect called? Can you think of a location in the United States where this might actually occur?

6. Is silver iodide used as a cloud seeding agent in warm or cold clouds? Explain why.

7.   What types of clouds might you expect to see form when a cold mass of air moves over warmer water?

8.   Would you expect the largest forms of precipitation particles to occur during the warmest or the coldest time of year? Explain.

9.   What is the main difference between a raindrop and a cloud droplet?

10. The first raindrops to reach the ground at the beginning of a rain shower are often very large. Why do you think this is so?

11. Thunderstorm cloud bases are generally higher above the ground in Arizona than in Florida. Why do you think this is true?

12. How large can raindrops get? Why can't they get any larger?

13. Would you expect the heaviest snowfall to occur on an unusually cold night or a night when the temperature was just a little below freezing?

14. Cumulonimbus clouds indicate unstable atmospheric conditions. What causes the tops of cumulonimbus clouds to flatten out into an anvil?

15. How would you explain the changing appearance of the falling precipitation in the sketch at right?

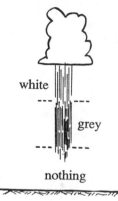

Chapter 6
Air Pressure and Winds

Summary

This chapter basically explains how and why the wind blows. To provide some needed background, the chapter begins by reviewing and extending a few of the basic concepts introduced earlier in the text. The ideal gas law is discussed and used to explain how temperature differences between regions can produce a horizontal force that will cause the air to begin to move from high to low pressure. Because of its importance in determining wind motions, a variety of instruments have been developed to accurately measure atmospheric pressure, and pressure patterns at the ground and at upper levels are routinely drawn on meteorological charts.

Once the forces that can cause air to move have been identified, Newton's laws of motion can be used to understand the wind motions that develop. The relatively simple case of air motions above the ground is studied first. Winds aloft are affected by just the pressure gradient force and the Coriolis force. Horizontal pressure gradients initially set the air in motion; the Coriolis force then exerts a force to the right or left of the wind's direction of motion. Winds at upper levels blow parallel to the height contour lines on an isobaric chart. When the contour lines are straight, the Coriolis and pressure gradient forces are equal and opposite and the wind blows in a straight line at constant speed.

Near the ground, the frictional force acts to slow the wind speed, with the result that winds blow across the isobars slightly toward lower pressure. This accounts for the rising and sinking air motions found in high and low pressure centers. Converging or diverging air motions above the ground can cause surface features to strengthen or weaken.

The chapter ends with descriptions of some of the common methods used to measure wind direction and speed at the ground and aloft. Examples of a few of the practical uses for wind data are given.

Key Terms
(Listed in approximately the same order they appear in the text. Terms in boldface are emphasized and appear at the end of the chapter in the text.)

air pressure
gas law (equation
  of state)
bar
newton
millibar (mb)
hectopascal (hPa)
inches or mercury (Hg)
**standard atmospheric
  pressure**
barometer
barometric pressure
mercury barometer

aneroid barometer
altimeter
barograph
instrument error
station pressure
altitude correction
sea level pressure
isobar
sea level pressure
  chart
surface map
anticyclone
depression

mid-latitude cyclone
extratropical cyclone
isobaric map
500-mb map
contour line (height)
isotherm
ridge
trough
Newton's laws of motion
acceleration
pressure gradient
**pressure gradient
  force (PGF)**

94

Coriolis force	planetary boundary layer	wind sock
geostrophic wind	convergence	**anemometer**
cyclonic flow	divergence	cup anemometer
anticyclonic flow	**hydrostatic equilibrium**	**aerovane**
gradient wind	**onshore wind**	skyvane
centripetal force	**offshore wind**	radiosonde
centrifugal force	upslope wind	rawinsonde observation
meridional flow	downslope wind	wind sounding
zonal flow	**prevailing wind**	**wind profiler**
Buys-Ballot's law	"flag" trees	wind turbine
friction	**wind rose**	wind farm
friction layer	**wind vane**	

Teaching Suggestions, Demonstrations, and Visual Aids

1.   A one-inch-square iron bar cut approximately 53 inches long weighs 14.7 pounds. When placed on end, the pressure at its base will be 14.7 pounds/sq.in., the same as that of the atmosphere at sea level. The bar can be passed around class and the students are generally surprised at how heavy it is. The bar can be used to motivate a discussion of the concept of density and the workings of the mercury barometer. If the bar were constructed of mercury, it would only need to be 30 inches long. If the bar were made of water, it would need to be close to 34 feet tall. Students should understand also why they are not crushed by the weight of many "iron bars" pressing in on every square inch of their bodies. One misconception that the bar might create is that pressure exerts only a downward force. The next demonstration might help clear that up. (ref: C.E. Meloan, *J. Chem. Educ.*, *65*, 69, 1988)

2.   There are a variety of "crushed-can" demonstrations. For example, put a small amount of water into a clean, metal can. Heat the can until the water boils and then tightly seal the spout. The can will be crushed by the weight of the atmosphere as it cools. The water is not necessary, but it enhances the effect. A proper explanation of this demonstration requires a discussion of the ideal gas law.

3.   This is a good place to illustrate and discuss current local, regional and national weather events using actual examples of surface and upper level charts. With some experience students will begin to be able to locate and follow large scale troughs and ridges on the 500 mb chart and to find the associated surface features. If possible, show the associated satellite photographs of cloud cover and radar depiction. This might be an appropriate place, also, to introduce the station model notation used to plot weather observations on surface charts.

4.   Show students a surface weather map without any isobars drawn on it. The students will appreciate how difficult it is to assimilate the large quantity of data plotted on the map. It will not be apparent at all what large scale weather features are present nor what is causing the observed weather conditions. Then, show the students the same map with a completed isobaric analysis. The positions of important high and low pressure centers will become clear immediately and their effect on the weather conditions in their vicinity will be apparent.

5.   The diagram at right shows how a fairly sensitive instrument can be constructed to measure the variation of pressure with height. One end of a U-shaped tube is inserted through a stopper into a flask. A second, shorter tube with a valve passes through a second hole in the stopper. Insert the stopper tightly and open the valve to equalize the pressure inside and outside the flask.

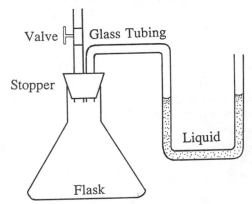

With the levels of the liquid in the manometer tube equal, close the valve and ask the students what they would expect to see if the "instrument" were carried from the bottom to the top of a multi-story building. Have someone conduct the experiment. The instrument is most sensitive with a low-density liquid (light weight oil) in the manometer. Take care to avoid heating or cooling the air in the flask or this will become a sensitive thermometer.

6. Pass around two small, but identical bottles (clear unbreakable plastic). Fill one bottle with 30 to 50 mL of water. Fill the second bottle with the same volume of mercury. Ask the students why mercury is used in a barometer instead of water or some other liquid.

7. Students are often surprised to find that a net inward force is needed to keep an object moving in a circular path at constant speed. To illustrate this fact, attach weights to opposite ends of a 3 or 4 foot long piece of nylon cord or rope. Pass the rope through a short piece of plastic pipe. Holding the pipe, swing one of the weights in a circle with just enough speed to begin to lift and suspend the weight hanging from the other end of the cord. The pull of gravity on the bottom weight supplies the centripetal force needed by the other weight moving in a circle. Ask the students what force is needed to keep a satellite in orbit around the earth?

8. A discussion of the Coriolis force will sometimes lead to a question about whether the direction water spins when draining out of a sink or toilet bowl is different in the Southern Hemisphere than it is in the Northern Hemisphere. The instructor can demonstrate that water can be made to rotate in either direction when draining from a plastic soft drink bottle (ref: J. Walker, The Flying Circus of Physics, p. 95, John Wiley and Sons, New York, 1977).

Student Projects

1. Give the students a simplified surface weather chart and have them perform an isobaric analysis. Initially, to keep the map as simple as possible, it might be best to plot only the wind and pressure data. Once students have located centers of high and low pressure, have them transfer the positions to a second map with additional data (temperature, cloud cover, weather, dew point). Have students circle regions with overcast skies or stations that are reporting precipitation. Are the stormy regions associated with high or low pressure?

2. Have students plot daily average pressure and observed weather condition for several weeks. Are stormy periods well correlated with lower-than-average pressures?

3. Determine the direction of upper-level winds by observing mid-level cloud motions. Have students draw the orientation of contour lines that would produce the observed motion and then compare their sketch with an actual upper-air chart.

4. Have students find examples of weather reports and weather maps from other countries in the foreign newspaper collection at the university or local library. Students should attempt to find at least one example from a city in the Southern Hemisphere.

5. Atmospheric pressure and surface wind measurements are discussed in two articles by J.T. Snow, M.E. Akridge, and S.B. Harley (refs: "Basic Meteorological Observations for Schools: Atmospheric Pressure," *Bull. Am. Meteorol. Soc.*, 73, 781-794, 1992; "Basic Meteorological Measurements for Schools: Surface Winds," *ibid.*, 7, 493-508, 1989). The articles give examples of high-quality instrumentation available commercially and contain plans for simpler instruments that students could construct and operate. A few suggestions for related student and class projects are also included.

Multiple Choice Exam Questions

1. If the earth's gravitational force were to increase, atmospheric pressure at the ground would
*   a. increase.
    b. decrease.
    c. remain the same.
    d. cause the atmosphere to expand vertically.

2. Which of the following correctly expresses the gas law relationship between pressure, P, density, ρ, and temperature, T, in a parcel of air (R is a constant)?
*   a. $P = ρ \times R \times T$
    b. $P = (ρ \times R) / T$
    c. $P = (R \times T) / ρ$
    d. $P = R / (ρ \times T)$

3. An increase in the ____ in(of) a parcel of air will <u>not</u> cause the pressure to rise.
    a. number of air molecules
*   b. volume
    c. temperature
    d. density of air

4. Two air columns extend from sea level up to an altitude of 10 km. If one column is cold and the other is warm, the air pressure in the <u>cold</u> column will ____ the air pressure in the warm column.
*   a. decrease more rapidly with increasing height than
    b. decrease less rapidly with increasing height than
    c. increase more rapidly with increasing height than
    d. increase at the same rate as

5. The surface pressures at the bases of warm and cold columns of air are equal. Which of the following statements is <u>not</u> correct?
*   a. pressure will decrease with increasing height at the same rate in both columns
    b. the cold air is more dense than the warm air
    c. both columns of air contain the same total number of air molecules
    d. the weight of each column of air is the same

6. The surface pressures at the bases of warm and cold columns of air are equal. Air pressure in the warm column of air will ____ with increasing height ____ than in the cold column.
    a. decrease, more rapidly
*   b. decrease, more slowly
    c. increase, more rapidly
    d. increase, more slowly

7. The mercury barometer was invented by
    a. Newton.
    b. Coriolis.
*   c. Torricelli.
    d. Aristotle.

8. Mercury is used in barometers primarily because of which one of the following properties?
    a. mercury is a good conductor of electricity
    b. mercury doesn't freeze
    c. mercury is a good conductor of heat
*   d. mercury has a high density

9.   Sea-level pressure values generally fall in the range
        a. 750 to 950 mb.
        b. 500 to 1500 mb.
        c. 100 to 1000 mb.
*   d. 950 to 1050 mb.

10.   Which of the following instruments measures pressure?
*   a. barometer
        b. thermometer
        c. radiometer
        d. hygrometer
        e. densitometer

11.   The pressures are equal, in the barometer
        at right, at points
        a. A and D.
        b. B and D.
*   c. A and C.
        d. C and D.

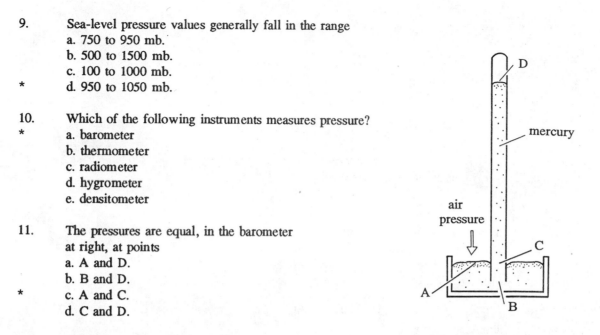

12.   If a liquid with a lower density than mercury were used in a barometer the height of the column in the barometer would
*   a. increase.
        b. decrease.
        c. remain the same.
        d. not provide an accurate measure of atmospheric pressure.

13.   A station at an altitude of 900 m (about 3000 feet) above sea level measures an air pressure of 930 mb. Under normal conditions, which of the values below do you think would be the most realistic sea level pressure for this station?
        a. 840 mb
        b. 930 mb
*   c. 1020 mb
        d. 1830 mb

14.   The scale on an altimeter indicates altitude, but an altimeter actually measures
        a. temperature.
        b. density.
*   c. pressure.
        d. humidity.

15.   To correctly monitor horizontal changes in air pressure, the most important correction for a mercury barometer measurement is the correction for
        a. temperature.
*   b. altitude.
        c. density.
        d. gravity.

16.   On a 500 millibar chart, ____ are drawn to represent horizontal changes in altitude which correspond to horizontal changes in pressure.
*   a. contour lines
        b. isobars
        c. isotherms
        d. isotachs

98

17. The unit of pressure most commonly found on a surface weather map is
    a. inches of mercury.
*   b. millibars.
    c. pounds per square inch.
    d. atmospheres.

18. To obtain the station pressure you must normally make corrections for
*   a. temperature and gravity.
    b. temperature and altitude.
    c. operator error and temperature.
    d. temperature and time.

19. Pressure changes
    a. more rapidly in the horizontal direction than in the vertical.
*   b. more rapidly in the vertical direction than in the horizontal.
    c. at the same rate in the horizontal and vertical directions.
    d. more rapidly in the vertical over land than over the ocean.

20. A ___ usually indicates clearing weather or fair weather.
    a. constant pressure
*   b. steadily rising pressure
    c. steadily falling pressure
    d. fluctuating pressure

21. The surface weather map is a sea level chart. Thus, a surface weather map is also called
    a. a constant pressure chart.
*   b. a constant height chart.
    c. an isobaric chart.
    d. a constant latitude chart.

22. Lines connecting points of equal pressure are called
*   a. isobars.
    b. millibars.
    c. contours.
    d. isotherms.

23. Low ___ on a constant height chart corresponds to low ___ on a constant pressure chart.
    a. pressures, pressures
*   b. pressures, heights
    c. heights, pressures
    d. heights, heights

24. The contour lines drawn on a 500 mb chart are lines of constant
    a. pressure.
*   b. altitude.
    c. density.
    d. wind direction.

25. Warm air aloft is associated with constant pressure surfaces that are found at ___ altitude than normal and ___ than normal atmospheric pressure aloft.
*   a. higher, higher
    b. higher, lower
    c. lower, higher
    d. lower, lower

26. On an upper-level chart, normally we find warm air associated with ___ pressure, and cold air associated with ___ pressure.
    a. high, high
  * b. high, low
    c. low, low
    d. low, high

27. A surface low pressure center is generally associated with ___ on an upper level isobaric chart.
  * a. a trough
    b. a ridge
    c. zonal flow
    d. convergence

28. A ridge on an upper-level isobaric chart indicates
  * a. higher-than-average heights.
    b. lower-than-average heights.
    c. average heights.
    d. a region with calm winds.

29. The fundamental laws of motion were formulated by
    a. Galileo.
  * b. Newton.
    c. Coriolis.
    d. Aristotle.
    e. Plato.

30. Newton would have been alive in
    a. 1492.
  * b. 1647.
    c. 1835.
    d. 1934.
    e. 1066.

31. An object is falling at constant speed. The net force is
    a. upward.
    b. downward.
    c. horizontally directed.
  * d. zero.

32. The "force exerted on an object equals its mass times the acceleration produced" is a description of
  * a. Newton's second law of motion.
    b. Buys-Ballot's law.
    c. geostrophic balance.
    d. hydrostatic equilibrium.

33. Newton's ___ law of motion says that the acceleration that results when a force is applied to an object is ___ proportional to mass.
    a. first, directly
    b. first, inversely
    c. second, directly
  * d. second, inversely

34. The net force on air moving in a circle at constant speed is
* a. inward toward the center of rotation.
b. zero.
c. in the direction of wind motion.
d. outward from the center of rotation.

35. The net force acting on air which is blowing parallel to straight contours at constant speed is
a. in the direction of wind motion.
b. to the right of the wind's motion in the Northern Hemisphere.
* c. zero.
d. in a direction opposite the wind's motion.

36. The amount of pressure change that occurs over a given horizontal distance is called the
a. pressure tendency.
b. coriolis parameter.
* c. pressure gradient.
d. potential gradient.
e. slope.

37. What is the direction of the pressure gradient force at point A in the figure at right?
a. up
b. down
c. toward the right
* d. toward the left

38. Which of the following forces does not have a direct effect on horizontal wind motions?
a. pressure gradient force
b. frictional force
* c. gravitational force
d. Coriolis force

39. The ___ is an apparent force created by the earth's rotation.
a. pressure gradient force
* b. Coriolis force
c. centripetal force
d. gravitational force

40. The pressure gradient force is directed from higher pressure toward lower pressure
a. only at the equator.
b. at all places on earth except for the equator.
c. only in the Northern Hemisphere.
d. only in the Southern Hemisphere.
* e. at all places on earth.

41. Which statement below is not correct concerning the Coriolis force?
a. It causes the winds to deflect to the right in the Northern Hemisphere
* b. It is strongest at the equator
c. It can cause winds to change direction, but not to increase or decrease in speed
d. It deflects winds in opposite directions in the Northern and Southern Hemispheres

42.   Which of the statements below is <u>not</u> correct concerning the pressure gradient force?
        a. the PGF points from high to low pressure in the Northern Hemisphere
*   b. it is non-existent at the equator
        c. it can cause the wind to speed up or slow down
        d. the PGF points from high to low pressure in the Southern Hemisphere

43.   The force that would cause a stationary parcel of air to begin to move horizontally is called the
        a. Coriolis force.
*   b. pressure gradient force.
        c. centripetal force.
        d. frictional force.

44.   The rate of the earth's rotation determines the strength of the
        a. pressure gradient force.
*   b. Coriolis force.
        c. frictional force.
        d. gravitational force.

45.   The Coriolis force is caused by
        a. wind motions.
        b. day/night temperature differences.
*   c. the rotation of the earth.
        d. gravitational attraction from the moon.
        e. the fact that the poles are colder than the equator.

46.   Which of the following combinations produces the strongest Coriolis force?
        a. fast winds and low latitude
*   b. fast winds and high latitude
        c. slow winds and low latitude
        d. slow winds and high latitude

47.   A wind blowing at a constant speed parallel to straight line isobars with the pressure gradient force
        (PGF) and the Coriolis force in balance is called a
        a. gradient wind.
        b. meridional wind.
*   c. geostrophic wind.
        d. cyclostrophic wind.
        e. zonal wind.

48.   Which of the following is <u>not</u> true of a geostrophic wind?
        a. blows parallel to straight contour lines
        b. blows at constant speed
        c. the net force is zero
*   d. found at the surface and upper levels

49.   A wind flow pattern that takes on a more or less north-south trajectory is called
        a. gradient flow.
        b. zonal flow.
        c. cyclostrophic flow.
*   d. meridional flow.
        e. geostrophic flow.

50.   On an upper-level chart the wind tends to blow
          a. at right angles to the isobars or contour lines.
*   b. parallel to the isobars or contours.
          c. at an angle between 10 and 30 to the contours and towards lower pressure.
          d. at constant speed.

51.   When the wind blows in a more or less west to east direction, the wind flow pattern is called
          a. gradient.
          b. meridional.
          c. centripetal.
*   d. zonal.

52.   A wind that blows at a constant speed parallel to curved isobars or contour lines is called a
          a. geostrophic wind.
          b. cyclonic wind.
          c. convergent wind.
*   d. gradient wind.

53.   Upper-level winds can turn to the right or the left. The turning is caused by
          a. the pressure gradient force only.
          b. the Coriolis force only.
          c. friction.
*   d. either the pressure gradient or the Coriolis force.

54.   The winds aloft in the middle latitudes would not blow from the west if
          a. the earth's rotation slowed or increased slightly.
          b. the tilt of the earth changed slightly.
*   c. the air over high latitudes became warmer than over the equator.
          d. the direction of the moon's orbit around the earth were reversed.

55.   The wind around a surface low pressure center in the Southern Hemisphere blows
          a. counterclockwise and outward from the center.
          b. counterclockwise and inward toward the center.
          c. clockwise and outward from the center.
*   d. clockwise and inward toward the center.

56.   The winds aloft in the middle latitudes of the Southern Hemisphere generally blow
*   a. from west to east.
          b. from east to west.
          c. from north to south.
          d. from south to north.

57.   Surface winds blow across the isobars at an angle due to
          a. the Coriolis force.
          b. the pressure gradient force.
*   c. the frictional force.
          d. the centripetal force.

58.   Winds blow slightly inward
          a. around surface low pressure centers in the Northern Hemisphere only.
          b. around surface low pressure centers in the Southern Hemsisphere only.
*   c. around surface low pressure centers in the Northern and Southern Hemispheres.
          d. at the poles in both hemispheres.

59.   Suppose that the winds aloft in the Northern Hemisphere are
        geostropic and blowing from the north. Low pressure is located to the
        a. north.
        b. south.
*   c. east.
        d. west.

60.   Cyclonic flow means ___ in either the Northern or Southern Hemisphere.
        a. clockwise wind flow
        b. counterclockwise flow
*   c. circulation around a low pressure center
        d. circulation around a high pressure center

61.   Suppose that the winds aloft are geostrophic and blowing from the north. With the same orientation of
        isobars at the surface, the winds would blow from the
        a. southwest.
*   b. northwest.
        c. northeast.
        d. southeast.

62.   If, at your home in the Northern Hemisphere, the surface wind is blowing from the northwest, then the
        region of lowest pressure will be to the ___ of your home.
        a. north
        b. south
*   c. east
        d. west

63.   Buys-Ballot's law states that, "In the Northern Hemisphere if you stand with your back to the surface
        wind, then turn clockwise about 30°, lower pressure will be ___ ."
        a. to your right
*   b. to your left
        c. behind you
        d. in front of you

64.   We can generally expect the air to be ___ above areas of surface low pressure and ___ above areas of
        surface high pressure.
        a. rising, rising
*   b. rising, sinking
        c. sinking, sinking
        d. sinking, rising

65.   The surface air around a strengthening low pressure area normally ___ , while, above the system, the
        air normally ___ .
        a. diverges, diverges
        b. diverges, converges
        c. converges, converges
*   d. converges, diverges

66.   Winds blow parallel to the contour lines
*   a. on upper-level charts, but not on surface charts.
        b. on surface maps, but not on upper-level charts.
        c. on both surface and upper-level charts.
        d. on neither surface nor upper-level charts.

67. The wind around a surface high pressure center in the Northern Hemisphere blows
   a. counterclockwise and outward from the center.
   b. counterclockwise and inward toward the center.
* c. clockwise and outward from the center.
   d. clockwise and inward toward the center.

68. The atmosphere around the earth would rush off into space if the vertical pressure gradient force were not balanced by
   a. the Coriolis force.
   b. the horizontal pressure gradient force.
* c. gravity.
   d. the centripetal force.
   e. friction.

69. In the vertical, the pressure gradient force points ___ and gravity points ___ .
   a. toward the earth, away from the earth
   b. toward the earth, toward the earth
   c. away from the earth, away from the earth
* d. away from the earth, toward the earth

70. When the upward-directed pressure gradient force is in balance with the downward pull of gravity, the atmosphere is in
* a. hydrostatic equilibrium.
   b. unstable equilibrium.
   c. geostrophic balance.
   d. isobaric balance.

71. An offshore wind
* a. blows from land to water.
   b. blows from water to land.
   c. only blows at night.
   d. only blows during the day.

72. A wind rose indicates
   a. the wind speed at a location at a particular time.
* b. the percentage of time that the wind blows from different directions.
   c. observed wind speed and direction on a surface map.
   d. spinning wind patterns caused by buildings or other obstructions.

73. The most practical location for building a wind turbine would be
   a. in a region of strong, gusty winds.
   b. on the downwind side of a mountain.
   c. in a narrow valley.
* d. in a region of moderate, steady winds.

74. What instrument would you use for a rawinsonde observation?
   a. cup anemometer
* b. radiosonde
   c. aerovane
   d. wind profiler
   e. laser

75.   An instrument used to measure wind speed is called a(an)
*   a. anemometer.
       b. ceilometer.
       c. psychrometer.
       d. tachometer.

76.   A wind reported as 225° would be a wind blowing from the
       a. NE.
       b. NW.
       c. SE.
*   d. SW.

77.   A wind profiler obtains wind information using
       a. an aerovane.
       b. a theodolite.
       c. an infrared radiometer.
*   d. a Doppler radar.

True/False Exam Questions

1.   If the earth's gravity were to increase in strength, the atmospheric pressure at sea level would increase
       but the reading on a mercury barometer would remain the same.
       (ans: TRUE)

2.   A sea level pressure reading of 30 inches of mercury would be about average.
       (ans: TRUE)

3.   Two parcels of air with the same volume and temperature will also always have the same pressure.
       (ans: FALSE)

4.   The idea that cold air is more dense that warm air assumes that the two volumes of air have the same
       pressure.
       (ans: TRUE)

5.   An altimeter is often just an aneroid barometer that has been calibrated to indicate altitude.
       (ans: TRUE)

6.   A "high" on an upper-level isobaric chart indicates a region where pressure decreases rapidly with
       increasing altitude.
       (ans: FALSE)

7.   The net force exerted on an object moving in a circle at constant speed is zero.
       (ans: FALSE)

8.   Contrary to popular belief, the Coriolis force does not cause water to turn clockwise or counterclockwise
       when draining from a sink.
       (ans: TRUE)

9.   The Coriolis force will only change the wind's direction and not its speed.
       (ans: TRUE)

10.   The net force points inward for air blowing around an upper level center of low pressure and outward
       for air blowing around and upper level high.
       (ans: FALSE)

11. Upper-level winds blow from west to east in both the northern and southern hemispheres.
(ans: TRUE)

12. Because pressure decreases with increasing altitude, there is always a strong downward pointing pressure gradient force.
(ans: FALSE)

Word Choice Exam Questions

1. Pressure decreases most rapidly with increasing altitude in WARM COLD air because the air has HIGH LOW density. (choose one word from each pair)
(ans: COLD, HIGH)

2. If the air pressure were to increase, the height of the column in a mercury barometer would INCREASE, DECREASE, remain CONSTANT. (circle one answer)
(ans: INCREASE)

3. When pressure is constant, the density of an air parcel is DIRECTLY INVERSELY proportional to temperature. (circle one answer)
(ans: INVERSELY)

4. Points A and B in the figure at right are at the same altitude. The solid line indicates the 850 mb pressure level. Does point A lie in an upper-level RIDGE or TROUGH? Is the air at A WARMER or COLDER than at B? Is the pressure at A HIGHER or LOWER than at B? (choose one word from each pair)
(ans: RIDGE, WARMER, HIGHER)

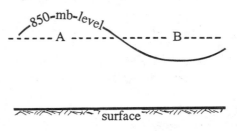

5. Generally speaking, you will find PRESSURE HEIGHT contours on a surface weather chart and PRESSURE HEIGHT contours on an upper-level chart. (choose one word from each pair)
(ans: PRESSURE, HEIGHT)

6. Pressure is decreasing most rapidly with increasing altitude on the RIGHT LEFT side of the figure at right. The warmest air would be found on the RIGHT LEFT side of the picture. There is more air found between 0 and 1.5 km altitude on the RIGHT LEFT side of the figure. (choose one word from each pair)
(ans: RIGHT, LEFT, RIGHT)

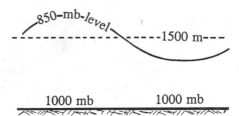

7. Would you expect to hear MILLIBAR or INCHES OF MERCURY pressure units used on a television weather report? (circle one answer)
(ans: INCHES OF MERCURY)

8. Three forces are acting on the straight line wind on the chart at right. Is this an UPPER LEVEL or a SURFACE map? Is the wind blowing across the contour lines toward HIGH or LOW pressure? Is this a NORTHERN or a SOUTHERN Hemisphere map? (choose one word from each pair)
(ans: SURFACE, LOW, SOUTHERN)

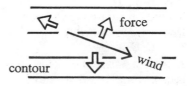

9. If you look in the direction the upper-level wind is blowing in the northern hemisphere, low pressure will be to your RIGHT LEFT. (circle one answer)
    (ans: LEFT)

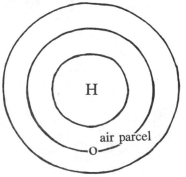

10. The pressure gradient force would cause the stationary parcel of air to begin to move INWARD OUTWARD on the upper level chart shown at right. In the Northern Hemisphere the Coriolis force would then bend the wind to the RIGHT LEFT. Eventually the wind will end up blowing in a CLOCKWISE COUNTERCLOCKWISE direction around the high. (choose one word from each pair)
    (ans: OUTWARD, RIGHT, CLOCKWISE)

11. Rising air motions are associated with surface centers of HIGH LOW pressure in the Northern Hemisphere and HIGH LOW pressure in the Southern Hemisphere. (choose one word from each pair)
    (ans: LOW, LOW)

12. Upper-level divergence by itself would cause surface pressure to INCREASE DECREASE. (circle one answer)
    (ans: DECREASE)

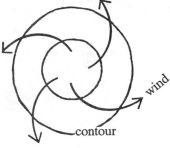

13. The figure at right depicts SURFACE UPPER-LEVEL winds blowing around HIGH LOW pressure in the NORTHERN SOUTHERN hemisphere. (choose one word from each pair)
    (ans: SURFACE, HIGH, SOUTHERN)

Short Answer Exam Questions

1. The 850 mb level is usually found at about 1.5 km altitude. If pressure continues to decrease at the same rate with increasing altitude above 850 mb, about how high would the 700 mb level be?
    (ans: 3 km)

2. To detect small horizontal pressure differences, station pressure measurements must be corrected for _____.
    (ans: ALTITUDE)

3. Evangelista Torricelli, a student of Galileo, invented the _____ in 1643.
    (ans: BAROMETER)

4. The mercury barometer sketched at right is currently reading _____ inches of mercury.
    (ans: 30)

5. Record low sea-level pressure values have all occurred in _____.
    (ans: HURRICANES)

6. A newton is a unit of force. Pascals are units of _____ and are equal to newtons per square meter.
    (ans: PRESSURE)

108

7. What type of instrument would likely have
a dial like the one shown at right?
(ans: ANEROID BAROMETER)

8. Acceleration can be a change in speed or a change in _____.
(ans: DIRECTION of MOTION)

9. According to Newton's second law of motion,
the acceleration of the object at right
depends on what two factors?
(ans: FORCE and MASS)

10. The rate of change of some quantity with distance is known as the _____.
(ans: GRADIENT)

11. A stationary parcel of air would begin to move toward the
_____ on the upper level chart shown at right. In the
Northern Hemisphere, the wind would end up blowing in a
straight line toward the _____. (fill in each blank
with NORTH, SOUTH, EAST, or WEST)
(ans: WEST, NORTH)

12. In addition to the rate of rotation of the earth on its axis, the strength of the Coriolis force depends on
_____ and _____.
(ans: LATITUDE and WIND SPEED)

13. The strength of the _____ force determines the speed of the upper-level wind.
(ans: PRESSURE GRADIENT FORCE)

14. The _____ force is zero at the equator.
(ans: CORIOLIS)

15. Which of the types of upper level air
motions shown at right would be possible
if the Coriolis force were equal to zero?
(ans: a)

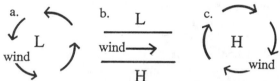

16. In a(n) _____ flow pattern, upper-level winds blow from west to east without any large
excursions to the north or south.
(ans: ZONAL)

17. Because of the effect of _____ wind speeds generally increase with height above the ground.
(ans: FRICTION)

18. Ordinarily, the downward force of _____ acting on a parcel of air is balanced by an upward
_____ force, producing a condition known as hydrostatic equilibrium.
(ans: GRAVITY, PRESSURE GRADIENT)

19. Rawinsonde observations provide vertical profiles of temperature, pressure, humidity,
and _____.
(ans: WINDS)

Essay Exam Questions

1. Under what conditions (if any) might you record a station pressure of 750 mb?

2. What differences might you expect to see between the weather conditions depicted on the surface in your city and at the 500 mb level above your city?

3. If the pressure gradient force remained the same but the earth's rate of rotation decreased slightly, would you expect the speed of the geostrophic wind to increase, decrease or remain about the same?

4. Briefly explain the principle of the mercury barometer. Mercury is relatively expensive and toxic. Why do you think mercury is used in barometers instead of another fluid such as water?

5. Name some things that you might observe in a location unfamiliar to you that might provide some clue as to the direction of the prevailing wind.

6. How might a knowledge of the direction of the prevailing wind at a given location be used in the design and construction of an energy-efficient home?

7. If the earth were to begin rotating in the other direction, would air still rise in the center of surface low pressure?

8. Is a force needed to keep a satellite orbiting at constant speed around the earth?

9. Sketch the wind flow patterns around surface high and low pressure centers in the Northern and Southern Hemispheres.

10. The pressure announced on last night's television weather broadcast was 29.92. Explain how this was measured and give the units. Would this be considered an unusually large or low pressure value?

11. Explain briefly why upper-level winds at middle latitudes in the Northern Hemisphere blow from West to East. In what direction do upper level winds at middle latitudes in the Southern Hemisphere blow?

12. If the earth did not rotate, how would you expect winds to blow with respect to high and low pressure centers?

13. Explain why closely-spaced contour lines on an upper-level isobaric chart are associated with fast winds.

14. Draw a simple Northern Hemisphere upper-air pressure pattern consisting of several straight, uniformly-spaced contour lines running from left to right across your paper. Assume that lower heights are found at the top of your chart. Use arrows to indicate the direction that the wind would blow and the direction of the pressure gradient force and Coriolis force acting on a moving parcel of air.

15. Explain why strong upper-level divergence will cause the pressure in the center of a surface low to decrease.

Chapter 7
Atmospheric Circulations

Summary

A wide variety of types of air motion are examined in this chapter, ranging from short-lived microscale phenomena to the semi-permanent circulation patterns found in the earth's global circulation.

The chapter can be divided roughly in half. The first portion begins with a quick classification of the scales of atmospheric motion and looks at the formation of eddies. Wind shear and the turbulent eddies that can form in clear air are of practical importance because they can present a hazard to aviation. The formation of thermal circulations is then covered in some detail. Sea, lake, and land breezes are common examples of thermal circulations and students may have lived in or visited a region where these occur. The role that seasonal changes play in the development of the Asian monsoon, which resembles a large thermal circulation, will also be better appreciated. Several additional local scale winds including mountain and valley breezes, katabatic winds, chinook, and the Santa Ana winds are described.

The earth's global scale wind and surface pressure patterns are treated in the second half of the chapter. Single-cell and three-cell models have been developed in an effort to understand the underlying cause of the general circulation pattern. Despite some unrealistic assumptions, the three-cell model contains many of the surface features found in the real world. These features and their seasonal movement can have an important effect on regional climate. Approximately 70% of the earth's surface is covered with oceans; weather and climate are strongly affected by interactions between the atmosphere and oceans. The major ocean currents are identified and the chapter ends with a discussion of the El Niño/Southern Oscillation phenomenon and some of the possible climatological effects associated with it.

Key Terms

(Listed in the approximately the same order they appear in the text. Terms in boldface are emphasized and appear at the end of the chapter in the text.)

scales of motion	thermal (warm core) low	**Santa Ana wind**
microscale	**sea breeze**	sandstorm
mesoscale	lake breeze	**haboob**
synoptic scale	**land breeze**	**dust devil (whirlwind)**
planetary (global) scale	sea breeze front	willy-willy
macroscale	smoke (smog) front	**general circulation**
eddy	**monsoon wind system**	**of the atmosphere**
rotor	**valley breeze**	single-cell model
mountain wave eddy	**mountain breeze**	**Hadley cell**
wind shear	gravity (drainage) wind	three-cell model
clear air turbulence	**katabatic (fall) wind**	**doldrums**
(CAT)	bora	**subtropical highs**
air pocket	mistral	horse latitudes
thermal circulation	Columbia Gorge wind	**trade winds**
thermal (cold core) high	**chinook wind**	northeast trades

southeast trades	Pacific high	stratospheric polar jet
intertropical convergence zone (ITCZ)	Icelandic low	Gulf Stream
	Aleutian low	North Atlantic Drift
prevailing westerlies	Siberian high	Canary Current
westerlies	Canadian high	California Current
polar front	jet stream	**upwelling**
subpolar low	subtropical jet stream	El Niño
Ferrel cell	polar front jet stream	major El Niño event
polar easterlies	isotach	countercurrent
polar cell	jet maximum or	Southern Oscillation
semipermanent highs and lows	jet streak	ENSO
Bermuda high	low-level jet stream	La Niña
	tropical easterly jet	

Teaching Suggestions, Demonstrations, and Visual Aids

1.   Clouds produced by some of the mesoscale and global scale wind circulation patterns discussed in this chapter can be seen on satellite photographs. The ITCZ is often very clearly defined on a full or half disk photograph from a geostationary satellite. Sea breeze convergence zones may be visible along the eastern or western coastline of Florida. Ask students why a strong convergence zone will form along the west coast one day and then along the east coast another day. A recent book by T.S. Loebl has good examples of waveclouds produced by winds blowing over mountain ranges (ref: T.S. Loebl, View From Low Orbit, Imaging Publications, Hubbardston, Mass., 1991).

2.   A simple demonstration of a thermal circulation has been described by H. Neuberger and G. Nicholas (ref: Manual of Lecture Demonstrations, Laboratory Experiments, and Observational Equipment for Teaching Elementary Meteorology in Schools and Colleges, Pennsyvania State University, 1962). Construct a box approximately 12″ wide x 12″ high x 4″ deep. The front side of the box should be constructed out of clear plastic. Place two "catfood" cans at opposite ends of the bottom of the box. Fill one can with dark soil, the other with water. Place a 150 or 200 Watt bulb so that light shines equally onto the two cans in the box. After a few minutes, carefully introduce some smoke into the chamber from a hole near the middle of the bottom edge of the plastic. With some care, a closed circulation cell will be visible.

3.   During the winter, bring a surface weather map to class and compare temperatures to the north and the south of the polar front. There is often a very sharp temperature gradient. Locate the polar jet stream on an upper-level chart and determine the region where the maximum winds are found.

Student Projects

1.   Have students research and plot the path of some of the early voyages of discovery made aboard sailing ships (Columbus or Magellan, for example). Do the routes appear reasonable in light of what the students know about the earth's general circulation pattern?

2.   Have students collect climatological data for their location (or another region) during one or two strong El Niño events. Select two or three periods when there was not a strong El Niño to act as a control. What effects might the El Niño have on local weather or climate. Do the students see any evidence of this in their climate data?

3.   Have students summarize the weather conditions prevailing during a period when strong Santa Ana winds are being observed in southern California.

4.   Have students research and summarize the weather conditions that produce any local scale winds that are unique to their area. Do these local winds have any important effects on the local climate?

Multiple Choice Exam Questions

1.   The smallest scale of atmospheric motion is the
     a. mesoscale.
     b. synoptic scale.
*   c. microscale.
     d. macroscale.
     e. global scale.

2.   An example of mesoscale motion is
     a. winds on a surface weather map of North America.
     b. winds on a 500 mb chart.
*   c. winds blowing through a city.
     d. winds blowing past a chimney.
     e. the average wind patterns around the world.

3.   An example of microscale motion is
     a. winds on a surface weather map of North America.
     b. winds on a 500 mb chart.
     c. winds blowing through a city.
*   d. winds blowing past a chimney.
     e. the average wind pattern around the world.

4.   Which of the following associations is most accurate?
     a. microscale - chinook wind
     b. synoptic scale - sea breeze
*   c. mesoscale - land breeze
     d. planetary scale - lake breeze

5.   An abrupt change in wind speed or wind direction is called
*   a. wind shear.
     b. an air pocket.
     c. flurry.
     d. squall.

6.   Violent, rotating eddies that create hazardous flying conditions beneath the crest of a mountain wave are called
     a. montainadoes.
     b. dust devils.
     c. rollers.
     d. seiches.
*   e. rotors.

7.   Which below is not true concerning an "air pocket?"
     a. can form in a downdraft of an eddy
*   b. often form in the atmosphere where the air is too thin to support the wings of an airplane
     c. often form in regions that exhibit strong vertical wind shear
     d. can develop in clear air

8.   Clear Air Turbulence (CAT) can occur
     a. near a jet stream.
     b. in areas of mountain waves.
     c. where strong wind shear exists.
*   d. all of the above.

114

9.   Which is <u>not</u> a characteristic of a thermal low?
        a. forms in a region of warm air
        b. forms in response to variations in surface air temperature
*   c. becomes stronger with increasing height
        d. lowest pressure is at the center

10.   Which below is usually <u>not</u> true concerning a sea breeze circulation?
*   a. they mainly occur at night
        b. they usually occur when the water is cooler than the land
        c. they occur when the surface wind blows from the water toward the land
        d. can cause clouds to form over the land

11.   A sea breeze circulation will reverse direction and become a land breeze
        a. once every few days.
        b. at the beginning and the end of the summer.
        c. several times per day.
*   d. once per day .

12.   A sea breeze circulation is caused by ___ differences.
        a. humidity
*   b. temperature
        c. altitude
        d. surface roughness

13.   The nighttime counterpart of the sea breeze circulation is called a
        a. chinook.
        b. Santa Ana.
*   c. land breeze.
        d. night breeze.
        e. foehn.

14.   A smog front is most often associated with which wind system?
        a. monsoon
        b. chinook
        c. Santa Ana
        d. mountain breeze
*   e. sea breeze

15.   When a sea breeze moving north meets a sea breeze moving south they form a
        a. land breeze.
*   b. sea breeze convergence zone.
        c. monsoon depression.
        d. katabatic wind.
        e. valley breeze.

16.   A cool, summertime wind that blows from sea to land is called a
        a. Santa Ana wind.
        b. land breeze.
        c. chinook wind.
        d. valley breeze.
*   e. sea breeze.

17. In summer, during the passage of a sea breeze, which of the following is not usually observed?
    a. a drop in temperature
    * b. a drop in relative humidity
    c. a wind shift
    d. an increase in relative humidity

18. In south Florida the prevailing winds are northeasterly. Because of this, the strongest sea breeze is usually observed on Florida's ___ coast, and the strongest land breeze on Florida's ___ coast.
    * a. east, west
    b. west, east
    c. west, west
    d. east, east

19. Clouds and precipitation are frequently found on the downwind side of a large lake. This would indicate that the air on the downwind side is
    * a. converging and rising.
    b. converging and sinking.
    c. diverging and sining.
    d. diverging and rising.

20. During the summer along the coast, a sea breeze is usually strongest and best developed
    * a. in the afternoon.
    b. just after sunrise.
    c. just before sunset.
    d. just before noon.
    e. around midnight.

21. Monsoon depressions are
    a. large shallow lakes that are filled during the heavy summer monsoon rains.
    * b. low pressure areas that enhance rainfall during the summer monsoon.
    c. short periods of time when monsoon rainfall is suppressed.
    e. a mental affliction brought on by the nearly continuous heavy monsoon rainfall.

22. The summer monsoon in eastern and southern Asia is characterized by
    a. wet weather and winds blowing from land to sea.
    b. dry weather and winds blowing from land to sea.
    * c. wet weather and winds blowing from sea to land.
    d. dry weather and winds blowing from sea to land.

23. The winter monsoon in eastern and southern Asia is characterized by
    a. wet weather and winds blowing from land to sea.
    b. wet weather and winds blowing from sea to land.
    c. dry weather and winds blowing from sea to land.
    * d. dry weather and winds blowing from land to sea.

24. While fly fishing in a mountain stream, you notice that the wind is blowing upstream. From this you might deduce that the wind is a
    a. chinook wind.
    * b. valley breeze.
    c. Santa Ana wind.
    d. mountain breeze.
    e. katabatic wind.

116

25. The name given to a wind system that seasonally changes direction is
    a. katabatic.
    b. chinook.
    c. mountain breeze.
 * d. monsoon.
    e. diurnal breeze.

26. Surface low pressure becomes best developed over the Asian continent in the
 * a. summer.
    b. winter.
    c. fall.
    d. spring.

27. Cumulus clouds that appear above isolated mountain peaks are often the result of
    a. katabatic winds.
    b. mountain winds.
    c. fall winds.
    d. Santa Ana winds.
 * e. valley breezes.

28. A valley breeze would develop its maximum strength
    a. at sunrise.
 * b. in early afternoon.
    c. about an hour after sunset.
    d. about midnight.

29. A strong, usually cold, downslope wind is called a
    a. valley wind.
 * b. katabatic wind.
    c. monsoon wind.
    d. haboob wind.
    e. chinook wind.

30. Which of the following is not considered to be a katabatic wind?
    a. bora
    b. mistral
 * c. haboob
    d. mountain breeze
    e. fall wind

31. A katabatic wind on the Oregon coast would most likely blow from the
    a. north.
    b. south.
 * c. east.
    d. west.

32. A chinook wind in the Alps is called a
    a. haboob.
    b. monsoon.
 * c. foehn.
    d. bora.
    e. Santa Ana.

33.   A katabatic wind is a ___, ___ wind.
        a. cold, upslope
        b. warm, upslope
*   c. cold, downslope
        d. warm, downslope

34.   The heat from a chinook wind is generated mainly by
*   a. compressional heating.
        b. sunlight.
        c. warm ocean water.
        d. friction with the ground.
        e. forest fires.

35.   A chinook wall cloud is a
        a. sand storm that marks the leading edge of the chinook.
        b. row of intense thunderstorms that bring heavy rain to eastern Colorado.
        c. cloud of smoke the marks the advancing edge of the chinook.
*   d. bank of clouds that form over the mountains and signal the possible onset of a chinook.
        e. line of fog that moves over the plains as a chinook advances.

36.   On the eastern side of the Rocky Mountains, chinook winds are driest when
*   a. clouds form and precipitation falls on the upwind side of the montains.
        b. the air aloft is cold.
        c. the sun is shining.
        d. the winds are blowing from the east.
        e. surface friction is greatest on the downwind side of the mountain.

37.   Chinook winds are
*   a. warm, dry, downslope winds.
        b. warm, moist, downslope winds.
        c. cold, dry, downslope winds.
        d. cold, moist, downslope winds.
        e. warm, dry, upslope winds.

38.   The main reason Santa Ana winds are warm is because
        a. latent heat is released in rising air.
*   b. sinking air warms by compression.
        c. condensation occurs.
        d. solar heating warms the air.
        e. they are heated by forest fires in canyons.

39.   The Santa Ana wind is a ___, ___ wind that blows into
        southern California.
        a. cold, damp
        b. cold, dry
        c. warm, moist
*   d. warm, dry

40.   The surface pressure pattern shown at right could lead
        to which of the following?
        a. land breeze
        b. Chinook wind
        c. Nor'easter
*   d. Santa Ana wind

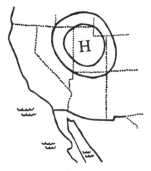

41. Strong Santa Ana winds develop in Los Angeles during the fall when
    a ___ pressure center forms to the ___ of Los Angeles over the Great Basin.
    *   a. high, northeast
        b. high, southwest
        c. low, northeast
        d. low, southwest

42. Devastating fires that occur in southern California during the fall are often spread by
        a. monsoon winds.
    *   b. Santa Ana winds.
        c. trade winds.
        d. sea breezes.

43. Which of the following conditions favor the development of dust devils?
        a. hot, moist days
    *   b. hot, dry days
        c. cold, moist days
        d. cold, dry days

44. Another name for a small, rotating whirlwind observed at the surface is
        a. seiche.
        b. haboob.
        c. rotor.
    *   d. dust devil.
        e. foehn.

45. A dust- or sandstorm that forms along the leading edge of a thunderstorm is a
        a. foehn.
    *   b. haboob.
        c. chinook.
        d. bora.
        e. Santa Ana.

46. The intertropical convergence zone (ITCZ) is a region where
        a. the polar front meets the subtropical high.
    *   b. northeast trades meet the southeast trades.
        c. northeast trades converge with the subtropical high.
        d. the Ferrel cell converges with the Hadley cell.
        e. polar easterlies converge with the air at the doldrums.

47. Chicago, Illinois (latitude 42° N) is located in the
        a. northeast trades.
        b. southeast trades.
    *   c. westerlies.
        d. doldrums.

48. In the three-cell model of the general circulation, areas of surface low pressure should be found at
        a. the equator and the poles.
        b. the equator and 30° latitude.
    *   c. the equator and 60° latitude.
        d. 30° latitude and 60° latitude.
        e. 30° latitude and the poles.

49. In Honolulu, Hawaii (latitude 21° N), you would most likely experience winds blowing from the
*   a. northeast.
     b. south.
     c. southwest.
     d. northwest.

50. At Barrow, Alaska (latitude 70° N), you would expect the prevailing wind to be
     a. northerly.
*   b. easterly.
     c. southerly.
     d. westerly.

51. Which of the following is not considered a semi-permanent high or low pressure area?
     a. Bermuda high
     b. Aleutian low
*   c. Siberian high
     d. Pacific high
     e. Icelandic high

52. The position of the Pacific high over the north Pacific Ocean shifts ____ in winter and ____ in summer.
     a. northward, southward
*   b. southward, northward
     c. eastward, westward
     d. westward, eastward

53. Generally, along the polar front one would not expect to observe
     a. temperatures on one side lower than on the other side.
     b. an elongated region of lower pressure.
     c. clouds and precipitation.
     d. converging surface air.
*   e. sinking air aloft.

54. According to the three-cell general circulation model, at the equator we would not expect to find
     a. the ITCZ.
*   b. a ridge of high pressure.
     c. cumuliform clouds.
     d. light winds.
     e. heavy showers.

55. The large semi-permanent surface anticyclone that is normally positioned over the ocean, west of
     California, is called the
     a. Hawaiian high.
     b. Aleutian high.
     c. California high.
     d. Baja high.
*   e. Pacific high.

56. The wind belt observed on the poleward side of the polar front is called the
     a. polar easterlies.
     b. prevailing westerlies.
     c. northeast trades.
     d. doldrums.

57.   On a weather map of the Northern Hemisphere, one would observe the westerlies
       a. north of the subpolar lows.
       b. south of the tropical highs.
       c. between the doldrums and the horse latitudes.
*   d. between the subpolar lows and the subtropical highs.

58.   The large convection cell that is driven by convective "hot" towers along the equator is the
       a. Ferrel cell.
*   b. Hadley cell.
       c. Ekman spiral.
       d. El Niño cell.

59.   The majority of the United States lies within a ___ wind belt.
*   a. westerly
       b. easterly
       c. northerly
       d. southerly

60.   On a weather map of the Northern Hemisphere, the trade winds would be observed
       a. north of the polar front.
       b. between the polar front and the subtropical highs.
*   c. south of the subtropical highs.
       d. between the subpolar lows and the subtropical highs.

61.   The semi-permanent pressure systems associated with the polar front are called
*   a. subpolar lows.
       b. equatorial lows.
       c. polar highs.
       d. subtropical highs.

62.   In the general circulation of the atmosphere, one would find the region called the doldrums
       a. near 30° latitude.
*   b. at the equator.
       c. at the poles.
       d. near 60° latitude.

63.   Warm southwesterly and cold northeasterly surface winds meet at the
       a. horse latitudes.
*   b. subpolar low.
       c. equatorial low.
       d. continental divide.

64.   In terms of the three-cell general circulation model, the driest regions of the earth should be near
       a. the equator and the polar regions.
       b. the equator and 30° latitude.
       c. the equator and 60° latitude.
       d. 30° latitude and 60° latitude.
*   e. 30° latitude and the polar regions.

65.   In the 3-cell model, converging surface winds and rising air motions are found at
       a. the equator and 30° latitude.
*   b. the equator and 60° latitude.
       c. 30° latitude and 60° latitude.
       d. 30° latitude and the poles.

66. The world's deserts are found at 30° latitude because
   a. the intertropical convergence zone is located there.
   b. of sinking air found near the polar front.
   c. of the convergence of the prevailing westerlies and the Northeast Trades.
   * d. of the sinking air of the subtropical highs.

67. Which of the following is the primary cause of the jet stream?
   a. the Coriolis force is stronger at higher latitude
   b. there is not frictional force at upper level
   * c. a large pressure gradient is found above the polar front
   d. land/ocean temperature differe

68. Which of the following does not describe the subtropical jet stream?
   * a. forms along the polar front
   b. generally blows from west to east
   c. is found at the tropospause
   d. is normally equatorward of the polar front jet stream

69. Which below does not describe the polar front jet stream?
   a. is strongest in winter
   b. moves farther south in winter
   c. forms near the boundary called the polar front
   * d. is normally found at a higher elevation than the subtropical jet

70. In the Northern Hemisphere, the polar jet stream is strongest when
   * a. air north of the polar front is much colder than air south of the polar front.
   b. air north of the polar front is much warmer than air south of the polar front.
   c. air temperatures on opposite sides of the polar front are about equal.
   d. air temperatures on the East Coast of the US are much colder than on the West Coast of the US.

71. The polar jet stream is strongest and moves furthest south in the
   * a. winter.
   b. spring.
   c. summer.
   d. fall.

72. The jet stream blows
   a. directly from west to east.
   b. directly from east to west.
   c. from the equator towards the poles.
   * d. in a wavy pattern from west to east.

73. The average winds aloft are strongest in
   a. summer.
   * b. winter.
   c. fall.
   d. spring.

74. In the Northern Hemisphere, air found to the north of the polar front
   is ___ , while air further south is ___ .
   * a. cold, warm
   b. cold, cold
   c. warm, cold
   d. warm, warm

75. Average winter temperatures in Great Britain and Norway would probably be much colder if it were not for the
   a. Labrador current.
   * b. North Atlantic Drift.
   c. Canary current.
   d. North Equatorial current.
   e. Greenland current.

76. Upwelling is
   a. the lifting of air along the polar front.
   * b. the rising of cold ocean water from below.
   c. increasing heights in an upper-level ridge.
   d. the rising air motion found in a low pressure center.

77. Along a north-south oriented coastline in the Southern Hemisphere, upwelling would occur when winds blow from the
   a. north.
   * b. south.
   c. east.
   d. west.

78. The ocean current that brings cold water southward along the coast of Maine and New Jersey is the
   a. Canary current.
   b. North Atlantic Drift.
   c. Gulf Stream.
   * d. Labrador current.

79. Upwelling occurs along the northern California coast because
   * a. winds cause surface waters to move away from the coast.
   b. of seismic activity on the ocean bottom.
   c. of gravitational attraction between the earth and the moon.
   d. water flows from the Atlantic ocean into the Pacific because they are at different levels.

80. The ocean current that flows southward parallel to the west coast of North America is the
   a. Aleutian current.
   * b. California current.
   c. Gulf Stream.
   d. Baja Drift.

81. The cold water observed along the northern California coast in summer is due mainly to
   a. the California current.
   b. oceanic fronts.
   * c. upwelling.
   d. cold air moving over the water.
   e. evaporation.

82. In the Northern Hemisphere, ocean currents in the Atlantic and the Pacific move in a generally circular pattern. The direction of this motion is ____ in the Atlantic and ____ in the Pacific.
   a. clockwise, counterclockwise
   b. counterclockwise, counterclockwise
   * c. clockwise, clockwise
   d. counterclockwise, clockwise

83.   Major ocean currents that flow parallel to the coast of North America are the _____ currents.
        a. Labrador, Canary, and California
*   b. California, Gulf Stream, and Labrador
        c. Kuroshio, California, and Labrador
        d. Labrador, Canary, and Gulf Stream

84.   The name given to the current of warm water that replaces cold surface water along the coast of Peru and Equador during December is
        a. Brazil current.
        b. Humbolt current.
        c. Benguela current.
*   d. El Niño.

85.   The two ocean currents, warm and cold, that produce fog off the coast of Newfoundland are the
        a. Gulf stream and Canary current.
        b. Labrador current and Canary current.
*   c. Gulf stream and Labrador current.
        d. North Atlantic Drift and Canary current.
        e. North Atlantic Drift and Gulf stream.

86.   Which of the following would <u>not</u> be associated with a major El Niño event?
        a. drought in Australia
        b. westerly winds at the equator
*   c. record fish catch in the ocean off the coasts of Peru and Ecuador
        d. warmer than normal ocean water in the eastern tropical Pacific

87.   During a major El Niño event
        a. Peruvian fishermen harvest a record amount of fish near Christmas time.
*   b. extensive ocean warming occurs over the eastern tropical Pacific.
        c. the Northeast trade winds increase in strength.
        d. California experiences severe drought conditions.

88.   The reversal of positions of surface high and low pressure at opposite ends of the Pacific Ocean is called
        a. the El Niño.
*   b. the Southern Oscillation.
        c. upwelling.
        d. the La Niña.

True/False Exam Questions

1.   Generally speaking larger scale air motions last longer than smaller scale air motions.
        (ans: TRUE)

2.   The El Niño is an example of a mesoscale wind circulation system.
        (ans: FALSE)

3.   Strong winds blowing over a mountain may produce surface
        winds that blow in the opposite direction.
        (ans: TRUE)

4.   Average rainfall amounts of over 400 inches per year occur in portions of northeastern India.
        (ans: TRUE)

5.   Surface winds and upper-level winds blow in the same direction in a thermal circulation.
     (ans: FALSE)

6.   The circulation of a dust devel usually begins at the surface while a tornado begins and descends from the base of a cloud.
     (ans: TRUE)

7.   Small cumulus clouds forming above a mountain in the early afternoon could indicate a well developed valley breeze.
     (ans: TRUE)

8.   A chinook is a warm, dry, upslope wind.
     (ans: FALSE)

9.   Compressional heating can warm and lower the humidity in a downslope wind.
     (ans: TRUE)

10. The surface pressure pattern in the 3-cell model largely determines the direction of global surface winds but has very little effect on the global distribution of precipitation.
     (ans: FALSE)

11. The trade winds blow from the east and away from the equator.
     (ans: FALSE)

12. The polar jet stream is strongest in the winter when surface temperature contrasts are greatest.
     (ans: TRUE)

13. A warm northward flowing ocean current is found along the east coast of the United States and a cold southward moving current is found along the west coast.
     (ans: TRUE)

14. Winter temperatures in Great Britain and Norway are warmer than one might expect to find at high latitudes because westerly winds steer the warm Gulf Stream current eastward away from the east coast of North America and toward Europe.
     (ans: TRUE)

15. Surface winds are much too weak and variable to have any appreciable effect on the major ocean currents of the world.
     (ans: FALSE)

Word Choice Exam Questions

1.   The figure at right shows a layer of relatively fast moving air overlying a layer of more slowly moving air. Would you expect to find eddies and turbulent air motions forming in the TOP layer, the BOTTOM layer, or near the BOUNDARY between the two layers? (circle one answer)
     (ans: BOUNDARY)

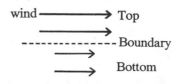

2.   In a thermal circulation, the pressure gradient force is STRONGER than, WEAKER than, the SAME strength as the Coriolis force. (circle one answer)
     (ans: STRONGER)

3.   Would you expect a thermal LOW or HIGH to develop over the desert southwest region of the US during the summer? (circle one answer)
(ans: LOW)

4.   The clouds shown in the figure at right most likely form during the DAY NIGHT when the land is WARMER COLDER than the water. (choose one word from each pair)
(ans: DAY, WARMER)

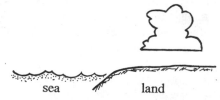

sea   land

5.   A cold, dry, downslope wind would probably be called a KATABATIC CHINOOK wind. (circle one answer)
(ans: KATABATIC)

6.   The wind pattern shown at right is a MOUNTAIN VALLEY breeze. It would form during the DAY NIGHT when the mountain side is relatively WARM COLD. (choose one word from each pair)
(ans: VALLEY, DAY, WARM)

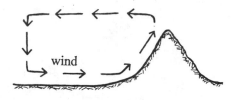

wind

7.   In the one-cell model of the earth's global circulation we find a large thermal circulation cell in the northern and southern hemispheres. Do the surface winds in this case blow TOWARD or AWAY from the equator? (circle one answer)
(ans: TOWARD)

8.   The clouds and precipitation that have formed on the windward side of the mountains in the figure at right would make the resulting chinook wind WARMER COLDER and MOISTER DRIER than would otherwise be the case. (choose one word from each pair)
(ans: WARMER, DRIER)

west   east

9.   The "roaring 40s" are strong surface winds found near 40°S latitude. Would these be EASTERLY or WESTERLY winds? (circle one answer)
(ans: WESTERLY)

10. Are the TRADE WINDS or the PREVAILING WESTERLIES found just north and south of the equator? Do these winds CONVERGE or DIVERGE at the equator? (choose one word from each pair)
(ans: TRADE WINDS, CONVERGE)

11. The doldrums are a region of HIGH LOW surface pressure and STRONG WEAK surface winds. (choose one word from each pair)
(ans: LOW, WEAK)

12. The term "horse latitudes" refers to a belt of HIGH LOW pressure where winds are STRONG WEAK and precipitation is ABUNDANT SCARCE. (choose one word from each group)
(ans: HIGH, WEAK, SCARCE)

13. The Pacific high moves NORTH SOUTH in the summer. Because of RISING SINKING air along its eastern side, relatively DRY WET conditions prevail along the California coast. (choose one word from each pair)
(ans: NORTH, SINKING, DRY)

126

14. The Bermuda HIGH LOW is shown just off the east coast of the US in the figure at right. The southerly winds along the east coast are generally MOISTER DRIER than the northerly winds along the west coast. (choose one word from each pair)
(ans: EAST, MOISTER)

15. The Aleutian Islands are found off the EAST WEST coast of North America. (circle one answer)
(ans: WEST)

Short Answer Exam Questions

1. Wind _____ is an abrupt change in wind direction or wind speed.
(ans: SHEAR)

2. Based on the isobaric surfaces drawn in the figure at right you would expect to find the warmest air on the _____ side of the figure. The highest surface pressure would be found on the _____ side of the figure. The upper level winds would blow from the _____. (fill in each blank with RIGHT or LEFT)
(ans: RIGHT, LEFT, RIGHT)

isobaric surfaces
– 1 km
0 km

3. Differences in _____ create pressure gradients that cause sea and land breezes to blow.
(ans: TEMPERATURE)

4. _____ winds are dry, warm winds that have been referred to as "snow eaters."
(ans: CHINOOK)

5. A _____ is a wind system with a seasonal change in direction.
(ans: MONSOON)

6. A mountain breeze is also called a(n) _____ wind because of the force that drives the wind downhill.
(ans: GRAVITY)

7. The serious brush fires that occur in southern California in autumn are often driven by _____ winds.
(ans: SANTA ANA)

8. The steady surface winds that blow between the equator and 30° S latitude are called the _____ and blow from the _____.
(ans: TRADE WINDS, SOUTHEAST)

9. Most of the world's deserts are found near what feature in the 3-cell model of the earth's global circulation?
(ans: SUBTROPICAL HIGHS)

10. The polar jet stream is found above what feature in the 3-cell model of the earth's general circulation?
(ans: POLAR FRONT or SUBPOLAR LOW)

Essay Exam Questions

1. What changes might you expect to see in the earth's general circulation if the earth's rotation were in the opposite direction?

2. You are hiking on a mountain trail at sunrise when you smell the smoke from cooking bacon. You can't see where the smoke is coming from. Would you expect the camp to be above you or below you on the mountain?

3. List the scales of atmospheric motion from largest to smallest and give an example of each. From what you know about the various types of wind systems, are the size and duration related?

4. Draw a sketch to show where eddies can form when air blows rapidly over a mountain range. Show on your sketch where you might expect clouds to form. How would these clouds appear when viewed from the ground?

5. What is clear air turbulence (CAT)? Why does clear air turbulence represent a hazard to aviation?

6. Would you expect a well-developed sea breeze circulation to cause clouds to form over the land or over the ocean?

7. Briefly sketch or describe the formation of a chinook wind. Would you expect chinook winds to form more often on the eastern or the western slopes of the Cascade mountains in Oregon?

8. Briefly sketch or describe the conditions that lead to the formation of a Santa Ana wind. Is the Santa Ana wind dry or moist, warm or cold?

9. What is meant by the term monsoon wind system? Briefly describe or sketch the wind and pressure pattern during the summer and winter monsoon in Asia.

10. Will a valley breeze or a mountain breeze produce clouds?

11. Briefly describe where each of the following features is found in the earth's general circulation. What meteorological conditions might you find associated with each feature?
    horse latitudes   trade winds   ITCZ
    polar front   doldrums

12. Sketch and name the major ocean currents adjacent to the coastlines of the United States. Indicate the direction of motion of each current and indicate whether it is a warm or cold current.

13. What occurs during a major El Niño event? How might this affect global wind and precipitation patterns?

14. What is the polar jet stream and where is it found? Does the position of the polar jet stream change during the year?

15. What features in the earth's general circulation help determine where the driest and wettest places on earth are found?

Chapter 8
Air Masses, Fronts, and Middle Latitude Cyclones

Summary

This chapter examines the typical weather conditions associated with air masses and the weather produced at frontal boundaries between air masses. The chapter also reviews our modern understanding of the formation and development of middle latitude storms.

Students will first see how and where air masses form and how they are classified according to their temperature and moisture content. Once upper level winds cause an air mass to move, it will carry characteristics of its source with it and may have a strong influence on conditions in the region it invades. Continental polar air moving down from Canada, for example, may bring clear skies but bitterly cold temperatures to the United States in winter.

The converging air motions associated with areas of low pressure will often bring air masses with very different properties into contact. The fronts that form at the boundaries between air masses are often the site of changeable, sometimes violent, weather. When warm and cold air masses collide, the warm low density air is forced upward. The rising motion is relatively gradual in the case of a warm front, and a variety of types of precipitation can fall over a large area ahead of the front. Air is generally forced upward more abruptly at cold fronts with the result that precipitation may be quite heavy in a narrower zone near the front. With a basic understanding of the structures of fronts, students will be in a position to appreciate and even forecast the weather associated with their approach and passage.

A relatively recent contribution to the science of meteorology, the polar front theory of middle latitude storm development, is reviewed in the final portion of the chapter. The influence that upper-level wind patterns have on storm development is also covered. Students will see, for example, that diverging air motions at upper levels are needed in order for a surface low pressure area to intensify. Divergence will often occur when a shortwave passes through a longwave trough. The jet stream can also play a role in storm development. Strong divergence can be found near the jet stream maximum where wind speeds change rapidly.

Key Terms
(Listed in approximately the same order they appear in the text. Terms in boldface are emphasized and appear at the end of the chapter in the text.)

air mass	**continental polar (cP)**	upslope snow
source region	**(air mass)**	Pacific air
(for air masses)	**continental arctic (cA)**	**maritime tropical (mT)**
polar	**(air mass)**	**(air mass)**
tropical	**lake effect snows**	subtropical air
continental	fetch	"the pineapple connection"
maritime	Siberian express	**continental tropical (cT)**
arctic	**maritime polar (mP)**	**(air mass)**
equatorial	**(air mass)**	**air mass weather**

130

front	**polar front theory**	**divergence**
frontal surface	**frontal wave**	confluence
stationary front	**wave cyclone**	difluence
cold front	**open wave**	speed convergence
pressure tendency	warm sector	speed divergence
trough	"family" of cyclones	deepening
squall line	**cyclogenesis**	filling
back door cold front	**lee-side low**	building
warm front	**northeaster (nor'easter)**	longwave
overrunning	Hatteras low	Rossby wave
occluded front	Alberta clipper	shortwave
(occlusion)	Colorado low	jet maximum
cold-type occluded front	**convergence**	**jet streak**
warm-type occluded front		

Teaching Suggestions, Demonstrations, and Visual Aids

1.   Have the students read the section on air masses and air mass weather. Then, instead of repeating the text material in class, answer question number 11 from the text during the lecture. Add additional weather condition examples that might pertain to your region. Ask the students whether the air mass producing the described conditions would need to be warm or cold, moist or dry. Where would air like this originate? What upper level wind flow pattern would produce the required motion? This is a good point also to insure that students are familiar with the geography of the United States and North America.

2.   A satellite photograph of the spotty pattern of cumuliform clouds or rows of clouds that are produced when continental polar air moves out over warm ocean water (such as in Figure 8.4) can be used to complement a discussion of the lake effect. Ask the students what type of weather conditions they would expect if the winds in Figure 8.4 changed direction and began to blow from the ocean toward the land.

3.   Show the students a good example of the "comma-shaped" cloud pattern associated with a mature middle latitude storm. Ask the students where they would expect the center of low pressure and the fronts to be found.

4.   A line of thunderstorms forming along a strong cold front can often be seen clearly on satellite photographs.

5.   After covering the material in this chapter, students should be able to understand and enjoy discussions of the current weather conditions depicted on surface weather charts. Show the positions and movement of air masses and fronts. Show the upper air chart and relate this to the surface features.

6.   The Pacific and Atlantic surface analysis maps will generally show several middle latitude storm storms approaching and leaving the US. Examples of storms in various stages of development can often be seen.

7.   Students will sometimes be confused to find precipitation associated with a stationary front. It is worth explaining that warm air may still override the cold air even though the cold air mass and the frontal boundary remain stationary.

8.   Students will often have difficulty, initially, trying to locate shortwaves on an upper-level chart. Instead of a single chart, show the students a sequence of charts covering a period of 2 or 3 days. Shortwaves will be more apparent as they move and distort different portions of the longwave pattern.

9.   Fronts, and the polar front theory are discussed in Chapter 8 (Motion) in Hands-On Meteorology (see reference on p. 2 of this manual).

Student Projects

1.   Provide the students with surface weather observations plotted on a map. Have the students first locate centers of high and low pressure. Then using the weather changes summarized in Tables 8.2 and 8.3 have them attempt to locate warm and cold fronts on the map. The instructor can supply students with simple examples at first and then move to more complex situations. Having students forecast the future movement of a middle latitude storm would fit in well with material covered in the next chapter.

Have students draw isotherms on the surface weather chart. A southward bulge of cold air will often be visible to the west of a strong surface low pressure center. The cold front should correspond to the front edge of this cold air mass. Similarly, the warm front will be found at the advancing edge of a warm air mass east of the low.

2.   Have students record and plot daily average weather data (maximum and minimum temperature, average dew point and pressure, precipitation amounts) and weather observations (cloud cover, cloud types, winds) for a few days before and following the passage of a strong front. The change in weather conditions can sometimes be quite dramatic. Also, students will often be surprised to see how closely the sequence of events described in the text corresponds to events in the real world.

Students could repeat this same exercise for another location using data that appears in the daily newspaper.

3.   Have students describe and document an unusual weather event that occurs during the semester, such as an outbreak of polar air, a squall line with severe thunderstorms in the southeastern US, a strong storm with gale force winds reaching the northwestern US, or a strong storm along the East Coast of the US. The study should be confined to air mass weather or a middle latitude storm system. The student's report should include a surface weather map and an upper level map. In each case students should attempt to find one or more reasons for these extreme weather conditions. Was the central pressure in a surface low, for example, lower than normal? Was the temperature gradient across a cold front unusually large? Was the upper level wind flow pattern atypical?

Students might also document an unusual weather event that they or someone from their family remembers.

Multiple Choice Exam Questions

1.   A good source region for an air mass would be
   a. mountains with deep valleys and strong surface winds.
*   b. generally flat areas of uniform composition with light surface winds.
   c. hilly with deep valleys and light winds.
   d. generally flat area of uniform composition with strong surface winds.

2.   The origin of cP and cA air masses that enter the United States is
   a. Northern Siberia.
   b. The northern Atlantic Ocean.
   c. Antarctica.
*   d. Northern Canada and Alaska.

3.   A warm, moist air mass that forms over water is called
   a. cP.
   b. mP.
*   c. mT.
   d. wT.

4. Compared to an mP air mass, mT air is
    a. warmer and drier.
    * b. warmer and moister.
    c. colder and drier.
    d. colder and moister.

5. One would expect a cP air mass to be
    * a. cold and dry.
    b. cold and moist.
    c. warm and dry.
    d. warm and moist.

6. Which air mass forms over North America only in summer?
    a. mT
    b. mP
    * c. cT
    d. cP

7. During the winter, an air mass that moves into coastal sections of Oregon and Washington from the northwest would most likely be
    * a. mP.
    b. mT.
    c. cP.
    d. cT.

8. The upper air flow on the adjacent map would bring ___ air masses into the Pacific Northwest and ___ air masses into the eastern United States.
    a. mT, mP
    b. mP, cP
    * c. mT, cP
    d. mP, cT

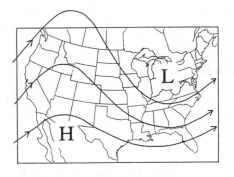

9. The greatest contrast in both temperature and moisture will occur along the boundary separating which air masses?
    a. cP and cT
    b. mP and mT
    c. mP and cT
    * d. mT and cP
    e. cT and mT

10. Wintertime mP air masses are less common along the Atlantic coast of North America than along the Pacific coast mainly because
    a. the water is colder along the Pacific coast.
    * b. the prevailing winds aloft are westerly.
    c. the source region for mP air on the Atlantic coast is western Europe.
    d. the water is warmer along the Atlantic coast.
    e. the land is colder along the Atlantic coast.

11. Which air mass would show the most dramatic change in both temperature and moisture content as it moves over a large body of very warm water?
    a. cT in summer
  * b. cP in winter
    c. mP in winter
    d. mT in summer

12. An air mass is characterized by similar properties of ___ and ___ in any horizontal direction.
    a. temperature, pressure
    b. pressure, winds
    c. pressure, moisture
    d. winds, moisture
  * e. temperature, moisture

13. The designation for a cool, moist air mass is
    a. mT.
  * b. mP.
    c. cT.
    d. cP.

14. The air mass with the highest actual water vapor content is
  * a. mT.
    b. cT.
    c. mP.
    d. cP.

15. The upper air flow on the adjacent map would bring ___ air masses into western Canada and the United States, and ___ air masses into the eastern United States.
    a. mP, mT
    b. cA, mP
    c. mP, cP
  * d. cA, mT
    e. cT, mT

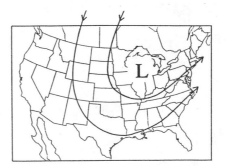

16. The coldest of all air masses is
    a. mT.
    b. mP.
    c. cT.
    d. cF.
  * e. cA.

17. What type of air mass would be responsible for hot, muggy summer weather in the eastern half of the United States?
    a. mP
  * b. mT
    c. cP
    d. cT
    e. cA

18. In Southern California, which air mass is mainly responsible for heavy rains, flooding in low-lying valleys, and melting of snow at high elevations?
*   a. mT
     b. mP
     c. cP
     d. cA

19. Record breaking low temperatures are associated with which air mass?
     a. mT
     b. mP
*   c. cP
     d. cT

20. During the spring, which air mass would most likely bring record-breaking high temperatures to the eastern half of the United States?
*   a. mT
     b. mP
     c. cP
     d. cT

21. What type of air mass would be responsible for refreshing cool, dry breezes after a long summer hot spell in the Central Plains?
     a. mP
     b. mT
*   c. cP
     d. cT

22. What type of air mass would be responsible for hot, dry summer weather in southern Arizona?
     a. mP
     b. mT
     c. cP
*   d. cT

23. What type of air mass would be responsible for snow showers on the western slopes of the Rockies?
     a. mT
     b. cP
*   c. mP
     d. cA

24. What type of air mass would be responsible for daily afternoon thunderstorms along the Gulf Coast?
     a. mP
*   b. mT
     c. cP
     d. cT

25. What type of air mass would be responsible for summer afternoon thunderstorms along the eastern slopes of the Sierra Nevada mountains in California?
     a. mP
*   b. mT
     c. cT
     d. cP
     e. cA

26.　　What type of air mass would be responsible for heavy summer rainshowers in southern Arizona?
　　　　a. cP
　　　　b. cT
　　　　c. mP
*　　　d. mT

27.　　Clear sunny days with very cold nights would be associated with what type of air mass?
　　　　a. mP
　　　　b. mT
*　　　c. cP
　　　　d. cT

28.　　An mT air mass lying above a cold ground surface represents a(an) ___ situation.
*　　　a. stable
　　　　b. unstable
　　　　c. occluded
　　　　d. stationary

29.　　Cumuliform cloud development would be most likely in which of the following?
　　　　a. cT air mass moving over a mountain range
*　　　b. cP air mass moving over warm water
　　　　c. mT air mass moving over cold land surface
　　　　d. cT air mass moving over cold water

30.　　What type of air mass would be responsible for persistent cold, damp weather with drizzle along the east coast of North America?
*　　　a. mP
　　　　b. mT
　　　　c. cP
　　　　d. cT

31.　　Lake-effect snows are best developed around the Great Lakes during
　　　　a. early spring when moist, tropical air moves over the frozen lakes.
*　　　b. late fall and early winter when cold, dry polar air moves over the relatively warm water.
　　　　c. late fall and early winter when moist, polar air sweeps in from the east.
　　　　d. middle winter when the unseasonably warm air mass moves over the cold water.

32.　　The lake effect occurs when ___ air mass moves over a ___ body of water.
　　　　a. a mT, cold
　　　　b. a mT, warm
　　　　c. a cP, cold
*　　　d. a cP, warm

33.　　Generally, the greatest lake effect snow fall will be on the ___ shore of the Great Lakes.
　　　　a. northern
　　　　b. southern
*　　　c. eastern
　　　　d. western

34.　　When two air masses collide at a front, one air mass is pushed upward by the other. This is because
　　　　a. one air mass is moving faster than the other.
*　　　b. one air mass is denser than the other.
　　　　c. pressure is falling in one air mass and rising in the other.
　　　　d. one of the air masses encounters topographical features on the ground.

Questions number 35-37
refer to the adjacent diagram

North
Surface Map

35.   A cold front is positioned
       between points
       a. 1 and 2.
*   b. 2 and 3.
       c. 2 and 5.
       d. 3 and 4.

36.   An occluded front is positioned
       between points
*   a. 1 and 2.
       b. 2 and 3.
       c. 2 and 5.
       d. 3 and 4.

37.   A warm front is positioned between points
       a. 1 and 2.
       b. 2 and 3.
*   c. 2 and 5.
       d. 3 and 4.

38.   When two air masses collide at a front, one air mass rises because it has lower
       a. pressure.
       b. temperature.
*   c. density.
       d. humidity.

39.   A true cold front on a weather map is always
       a. associated with precipitation.
       b. associated with a wind shift.
       c. followed by drier air.
*   d. followed by cooler air.

40.   Occluded fronts may form as
*   a. a cold front overtakes a warm front.
       b. a warm front overtakes a cold front.
       c. a cold front overtakes a squall line.
       d. overrunning occurs along a warm front.

41.   On a weather map, the transition zone between two air masses with sharply contrasting properties is
       marked by
       a. the letter "H".
       b. the words "air mass weather".
*   c. a front.
       d. the letter "L".

42.   Which of the following is not correct concerning a cold front?
       a. it marks the position of a trough of low pressure
       b. it marks a zone of shifting winds
*   c. it is colored purple on a weather map
       d. it has cold air behind it

43. The adjacent diagram represents a side view of a ____ occluded front with the coldest air located at position ____.
    a. cold type, B
    b. warm type, B
    * c. cold type, A
    d. warm type, A

44. Which of the following is not correct concerning a warm front?
    a. it is colored red on a weather map
    * b. it has warm air ahead (in advance) of it
    c. in winter it is usually associated with stratiform clouds
    d. it normally moves more slowly than a cold front

45. The front shown in the figure at right is ____ front. The coldest air is at point ____.
    a. an occluded, 1
    b. an occluded, 2
    * c. a stationary, 1
    d. a stationary, 2

46. Alternating lines of blue and red on a surface weather chart indicate
    a. a cold front.
    b. a warm front.
    * c. a stationary front.
    d. an occluded front.

47. The adjacent diagram represents a side view of
    * a. a cold front.
    b. a warm front.
    c. an occluded front.
    d. a stationary front.

48. The rising of warm air up and over cold air is called
    * a. overrunning.
    b. frontolysis.
    c. frontogenesis.
    d. occlusion.

49. At a warm front, the warm air
    * a. rises and cools.
    b. rises and warms.
    c. sinks and cools.
    d. sinks and warms.

50. Before the passage of a cold front the pressure normally ____, and after the passage of a cold front the pressure normally ____.
    a. drops, drops
    * b. drops, rises
    c. rises, rises
    d. rises, drops

51. In winter, which sequence of clouds would you most likely expect to observe as a warm front with precipitation approaches your location?
    a. cirrus, nimbostratus, altostratus, cumulonimbus
 * b. cirrus, cirrostratus, altostratus, nimbostratus
    c. altostratus, cirrostratus, cumulonimbus, nimbostratus
    d. cirrostratus, nimbostratus, altostratus, fog
    e. cirrus, cirrostratus, altostratus, cumulonimbus

52. On a weather map this front, drawn in blue, represents a region where colder air is replacing warmer air
    a. warm front.
 * b. cold front.
    c. cold-type occluded front.
    d. warm-type occluded front.

53. When comparing an "average" cold front to an "average" warm front, which of the following is not correct?
    a. generally, cold fronts move faster than warm fronts
    b. generally, cold fronts have steeper slopes
 * c. generally, precipitation covers a much broader area with a cold front
    d. especially in winter, cumuliform clouds are more often associated with cold fronts

Questions 54 through 58 refer to
the adjacent surface weather map.

54. Heavy snow would most likely be falling at position
    a. 1.
 * b. 2.
    c. 3.
    d. 4.

55. Clearing skies are most likely at position
    a. 1.
    b. 2.
    c. 3.
 * d. 4.

56. Falling pressure would probably be observed at
    a. 1.
    b. 1 and 2.
 * c. 1, 2, and 3.
    d. 1, 2, 3, and 4.

57. Which position is located in the warm sector?
    a. 1
    b. 2
 * c. 3
    d. 4

58. The winds at point 3 would most likely be from the
 * a. southwest.
    b. northwest.
    c. northeast.
    d. southeast.

59. Squall lines most often form ahead of a
 * a. cold front.
 b. warm front.
 c. cold-type occluded front.
 d. warm-type occluded front.
 e. stationary front.

60. A stationary front does not move because
 a. winds on both sides of the front are calm.
 * b. the winds blow parallel to the front.
 c. the front is between high and low pressure.
 d. the winds blow against each other and are of equal strength.

61. In winter, thunderstorms are most likely to form along
 * a. cold fronts.
 b. warm fronts.
 c. stationary fronts.
 d. occluded fronts.

62. During the winter as you travel toward a warm front, the most likely sequence of weather you would experience is
 a. snow, freezing rain, hail, sleet.
 b. rain, snow, sleet, freezing rain.
 c. freezing rain, snow, sleet, rain.
 * d. snow, sleet, freezing rain, rain.

63. What type of weather front would be responsible for the following weather forecast: "Increasing cloudiness and warm today with the possibility of showers by this evening. Turning much colder tonight. Winds southwesterly becoming gusty and shifting to northwesterly by tonight."
 * a. cold front
 b. warm front
 c. cold-type occluded front
 d. stationary front

64. What type of weather front would be responsible for the following weather forecast: "Increasing high cloudiness and cold this morning. Clouds increasing and lowering this afternoon with a chance of snow or rain tonight. Precipitation ending tomorrow morning. Turning much warmer. Winds light easterly today becoming southeasterly tonight and southwesterly tomorrow."
 a. cold front
 * b. warm front
 c. stationary front
 d. warm-type occluded front

65. According to the model of the life cycle of a wave cyclone, the storm system is normally most intense
 a. as a frontal wave.
 b. as an open wave.
 c. as a stationary wave.
 * d. when the system first becomes occluded.

66. Which below is not a name given to a large cyclonic storm system that forms in the middle latitudes?
 a. middle latitude cyclone
 b. extratropical cyclone
 c. wave cyclone
 * d. anticyclone

67. In the polar front theory of a developing wave cyclone, energy for the storm is usually derived from all but one of the following.
    a. rising of warm air and the sinking of cold air
    b. latent heat of condensation
    c. an increase in surface winds
* d. heat energy stored in the ground

68. The development or strengthening of a middle latitude storm system is called
    a. convergence.
    b. divergence.
* c. cyclogenesis.
    d. frontolysis.

69. Which region is not considered to be a region where cyclogenesis often occurs
    a. eastern slopes of the Rocky Mountains.
    b. Atlantic Ocean near Cape Hatteras, North Carolina.
* c. California.
    d. the Great Basin of the United States.
    e. Gulf of Mexico.

70. For cyclogenesis to occur along a frontal wave, the winds aloft directly above the wave should be
* a. diverging.
    b. converging.
    c. blowing straight from west to east.
    d. increasing in speed uniformly over a broad area.

71. If the winds are all blowing at constant speed, confluence of air is occurring at point ___ in the diagram at right.
* a. 1
    b. 2
    c. 3
    d. 4

72. The piling up of air above a region is called
    a. thickening.
    b. divergence.
    c. cyclogenesis.
* d. convergence.

73. If the flow of air into a surface low pressure area is greater than the divergence of air aloft, the surface pressure in the center of the low will
* a. increase.
    b. decrease.
    c. remain the same.
    d. deepen.

74. Which of the following is not associated with rising air motions?
    a. overrunning
    b. convergence of air at the surface
* c. convergence of air aloft
    d. divergence of air aloft

75.   A surface low pressure area with a deep upper-level trough to the west will tend to move toward the
        a. northwest.
*   b. northeast.
        c. southwest.
        d. southeast.

76.   When a deep upper-level trough is located to the east of a surface anticyclone, the surface anticyclone
        will tend to move toward the
        a. northwest.
        b. northeast.
        c. southwest.
*   d. southeast.

77.   For a surface storm system to intensify, the upper-level low (or trough) should be located to the ___ of
        the surface low.
        a. north
        b. south
        c. east
*   d. west

78.   When upper-level divergence of air above a surface low pressure area is stronger than the convergence
        of surface air, the surface pressure will ___ and the storm itself will ___.
        a. increase, intensify
        b. increase, dissipate
*   c. decrease, intensify
        d. decrease, dissipate

Questions 79-81 refer to
the adjacent diagram

79.   A developing wave
        cyclone would most
        likely be found below
        a. 1.
        b. 2.
        c. 3.
*   d. 4.
        e. 5.

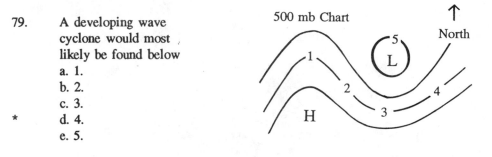

80.   A person at the earth's surface beneath position 2 in the previous diagram would observe clouds
        overhead (at the 500 mb level) moving from
        a. southwest to northeast.
*   b. northwest to southeast.
        c. west to east.
        d. southeast to northwest.
        e. east to west.

81.   A surface high pressure area moving toward the southeast would most likely be found beneath point
        a. 1.
*   b. 2.
        c. 3.
        d. 4.
        e. 5.

142

82. A building anticyclone means
*   a. the central pressure is increasing.
     b. the anticyclone is moving toward the east coast.
     c. separate anticyclones are merging.
     d. the anticyclone is causing a middle latitude storm to form.

83. Developing low pressure areas generally have ___ air near the surface and ___ air aloft.
*   a. converging, diverging
     b. diverging, converging
     c. converging, converging
     d. diverging, diverging

84. If the outflow of air around a surface high pressure area is greater than the convergence of air aloft, you would observe
     a. in increase in pressure in the center of the high.
     b. movement of the high toward the northeast.
*   c. a decrease in the central pressure.
     d. strengthening in the high.

85. Longwaves in the middle and upper troposphere usually have lengths on the order of
     a. tens of kilometers.
     b. hundreds of kilometers.
*   c. thousands of kilometers.
     d. millions of kilometers.

86. Rossby waves are also known as
     a. stable waves.
     b. shortwaves.
     c. tidal waves.
*   d. longwaves.

87. Atmospheric shortwaves usually move ___ at a speed that is ___ than longwaves.
     a. east to west, faster
*   b. west to east, faster
     c. east to west, slower
     d. west to east, slower

88. Atmospheric shortwaves usually move ___ than longwaves, and ___ when they move through a longwave ridge.
*   a. faster, weaken
     b. faster, strengthen
     c. slower, weaken
     d. slower, strengthen

89. A small, moving disturbance inbedded in a longwave is called
     a. a lee-side low.
     b. a wave cyclone.
*   c. a shortwave.
     d. a frontal wave.

True/False Exam Questions

1. Unstable atmospheric conditions result when an air mass is warmer than the surface below.
(ans: FALSE)

2. The middle latitudes, where there is a lot of surface terrain and moisture variability, make good air mass source regions.
    (ans: FALSE)

3. An extremely hot and humid air mass originating over a tropical ocean would be designated marine equatorial (mE).
    (ans: TRUE)

4. Stable atmospheric conditions usually result in good visiblity.
    (ans: FALSE)

5. Because it is located at middle latitudes, the United States is only rarely affected by polar and tropical air masses.
    (ans: FALSE)

6. Atlantic mP air masses are usually much colder than their Pacific counterparts.
    (ans: TRUE)

7. The Rockies, Sierra Nevada, and Cascades normally protect the Pacific Northwest from an invasion of cP air.
    (ans: TRUE)

8. A cP air mass that remains stagnant over an area for several days is often accompanied by unusually high surface pressure values.
    (ans: TRUE)

9. The pressure will generally fall as a warm or cold front approaches and then rise once the front has passed through.
    (ans: TRUE)

10. A "back door" cold front will move into a region from the east or northeast instead of from the west.
    (ans: TRUE)

Word Choice Exam Questions

1. Ideal air mass source regions are usually those dominated by a large HIGH LOW pressure system. (circle one answer)
    (ans: HIGH)

2. An air mass is a large volume of air with very little HORIZONTAL VERTICAL change in its moisture and temperature properties. (circle one answer)
    (ans: HORIZONTAL)

3. An unstable situation could result when an air mass is WARMER COLDER than the underlying surface. (circle one answer)
    (ans: COLDER)

4. Lake Effect snows result when an air mass moves across a large body of FROZEN UNFROZEN water. (circle one answer)
    (ans: UNFROZEN)

5. Occluded fronts form relatively EARLY LATE in a middle latitude storm's development. (circle one answer)
    (ans: LATE)

144

6. Are most of the clouds and precipitation associated with a warm front found AHEAD or BEHIND the surface front? (circle one answer)
    (ans: AHEAD)

7. Front A in the figure at right is a Southern Hemisphere COLD WARM front and is moving toward the NORTH SOUTH. (choose one word from each pair)
    (ans: COLD, NORTH)

8. The term "nor'easter" refers to the strong northeasterly winds that can develop around an intense center of HIGH LOW pressure positioned off the EAST WEST coast of the United States. (choose one word from each pair)
    (ans: LOW, EAST)

9. You would expect strong upper-level convergence to STRENGTHEN WEAKEN a middle latitude storm system. (circle one answer)
    (ans: WEAKEN)

10. Upper-level winds which slow as they move along produce speed CONVERGENCE DIVERGENCE. (circle one answer)
    (ans: CONVERGENCE)

11. You would use the term FILLING BUILDING DEEPENING to describe a storm system that is weakening because surface pressure is rising. (circle one answer)
    (ans: FILLING)

Short Answer Exam Questions

1. Air masses are classified according to their _____ and _____ characteristics.
    (ans: TEMPERATURE, MOISTURE)

2. The 'c' in cT air mass stands for _____ and means the air mass is _____.
    (ans: CONTINENTAL, DRY)

3. Fill in the blanks below to indicate whether the following weather changes would most often be associated with the approach and passage of a warm front, a cold front, or both types of front.
    a. Clouds may precede the arrival of the front by 1 or 2 days _____
    b. Falling pressure ahead of the front, rising pressure behind the front _____
    c. Southwest to northwest wind shift _____
    d. Showers followed by clear skies and cold nighttime temperatures _____
    (ans: a. WARM, b. BOTH, c. COLD, d. COLD)

4. Surface winds tend to blow parallel to a(n) _____ front.
    (ans: STATIONARY)

5. A line of showers or thunderstorms that develops parallel to an advancing front is called a(n) _____.
    (ans: SQUALL LINE)

6. The term _____ refers to winds blowing around a low pressure center.
    (ans: CYCLONE)

7. Development or strengthening of a middle latitude storm system is called _____.
    (ans: CYCLOGENESIS)

8. You might expect to find a lee-side low developing near a(n) _____.
(ans: MOUNTAIN)

9. Middle latitude cyclones will often form along the _____, a semicontinous global boundary separating cold polar air from warm subtropical air.
(ans: POLAR FRONT)

10. Frontal waves which grow into large middle latitude storms generally develop and dissipate over a period of several HOURS DAYS WEEKS. (circle one answer)
(ans: DAYS)

11. A strengthening or developing storm which forms on the eastern (downwind) slopes of the Rockies is called a _____.
(ans: LEE-SIDE LOW)

Essay Exam Questions

1. List the four basic types of air masses. Give an example of where each type could originate and describe how each air mass could affect local weather conditions if it moved into your region.

2. What type of clouds, if any, would you expect to see form when a cP air mass moves across warm water. Would conditions be any different when mT air moves across a cold land surface? Would types of clouds would form in this latter case?

3. When a warm and cold air mass collide, the warm air is forced upward. Why does this occur?

4. Describe some of the changes in weather conditions (winds, temperature, clouds, precipitation, pressure changes) you would expect to observe as a cold front approaches and passes through your location.

5. Draw side views of a typical warm and cold front. Clearly indicate the temperatures of the separate air masses and show their directions of motion. What types of clouds would you expect to find and where? Where would you expect precipitation to occur?

6. How would a warm front, a cold front, and a center of low pressure appear on a surface weather map in the Southern Hemisphere?

7. Explain why a halo around the moon or sun could forewarn of the arrival of a warm front.

8. Clouds in a middle latitude storm system are produced by rising air motions. Name the storm processes that could produce this upward motion.

9. Describe or illustrate the various phases in the life cycle of a middle latitude storm according to the polar front theory.

10. With the aid of a diagram, show why an intensifying surface low pressure center which is located just east of a deep upper-level trough will often move in a northeastly direction.

11. What does the term "shortwave" refer to? Why is it important locate and follow the movements of atmospheric shortwaves? How is this done? How is a shortwave different from a "longwave?"

12. Describe, in words or with a sketch, a wind flow pattern that will result in upper-level divergence.

13. Describe some of the ways in which the upper-level wind flow pattern can influence the development and movement of a middle latitude storm system.

Chapter 9
Weather Forecasting

Summary

Weather forecasts are an important part of many people's daily lives. This chapter looks at how weather observations are collected and analyzed, and at the wide variety of different types of weather forecasts that can be made using this data.

Forecasts are based on worldwide observations of weather conditions made several times a day. This large data set can be processed very quickly using modern computer technology, and meteorologists can provide early warning of developing hazardous weather conditions. The specific conditions that warrant issuance of various weather alerts and advisories are summarized.

Computers and weather satellites are used routinely in preparing a weather forecast. Computers perform the numerical calculations in complex mathematical models of the atmosphere. Some of factors which limit the accuracy of numerical weather predictions are listed and discussed. Satellite images from geosynchronous and polar orbiting satellites provide information about cloud height and thickness, and the circulation of water vapor in the atmosphere.

Different methods of predicting future weather including persistence and steady state forecasts, the analogue method, weather type, and climatological forecasts are examined. Often one method is appropriate in a short-range forecast, while another method would be employed when formulating a longer range seasonal outlook.

The chapter includes a practical guide to weather prediction that is based on observations of local conditions and basic weather principles. The chapter concludes with an example of how a fairly accurate short term forecast could be made using data from a surface chart and a knowledge of the upper level wind pattern. Students should find this example particularly instructive as it applies many of the concepts developed in previous chapters.

Key Terms

(Listed in approximately the same order they appear in the text. Terms in boldface are emphasized and appear at the end of the chapter in the text.)

World Meteorological
   Organization (WMO)
National Center
   for Environmental
   Prediction (NCEP)
soundings
weather watch
weather warning
advisories
wind advisory

high wind warning
wind-chill advisory
flash-flood watch
flash-flood warning
severe thunderstorm watch
severe thunderstorm
   warning
tornado watch
tornado warning
snow advisory

winter storm warning
blizzard warning
dense fog advisory
small craft advisory
gale warning
storm warning
hurricane watch
hurricane warning
analysis
atmospheric models

numerical weather prediction	polar-orbiting satellites	analogue forecasting method
grid points	TIROS I	weather type forecasting
prognostic chart (prog)	GOES (Geostationary Operational Environmental Satellite)	long-range weather forecasting
chaos		
AWIPS (Advanced Weather Interactive Processing System)	radiometer imager	ensemble forecasting
	radiometer sounder	climatological forecast
	infrared cloud pictures	probability forecast
ASOS (Automated Surface Observing System)	computer enhancement	forecast skill
	persistence forecast	teleconnections
algorithms	steady-state (trend) forecast	chroma key
meteorological indexes		Book of Signs
wind profilers	nowcasting	veering winds
geostationary satellites	pattern recognition	backing winds
geosynchronous satellites		

Teaching Suggestions, Demonstrations, and Visual Aids

1.   Show the students some of the weather forecasts issued by the National Meteorological Center such as the NGM 12, 24, 36 and 48 hour forecasts (sea-level pressure, 500 and 700 mb heights, precipitation), the SM126 0, 12, 24, 36, 48, 72 and 84 hour forecasts (500 mb heights), the 3 to 5 day and the 6 to 10 day temperature and precipitation outlooks. These charts contain a lot of information and will be confusing initially. Some maps may be redrawn and simplified. With time, students will begin to recognize features on the forecast maps that prompt the local television weather reporter to forecast a change in the weather by week's end.

It is worthwhile acquainting the students with other sources of weather forecast information if this has not been done already. Sources include the NOAA weather radio broadcast, the Weather Channel (see *Weatherwise, 45*, 9-15, 1992), the USA Today weather page (see *Weatherwise, 45*, 12-18, 1992). Students might also be interested in modern interactive computer displays of weather information such as the McIDAS, Gempak, and WXP packages.

2.   The person who presents the local television weather report may be willing to come and speak to the class. This would complement the focus section in the text. Or, in the case of a small class, it might be possible to arrange a visit to the studio to see a weather broadcast. A small class could also, in some cities, visit the local weather service office.

3.   Using the present surface and upper air charts, together with prognostic charts, make a 12, 24 and 36 hour forecast in class. Use a variety of forecast methods or let the students decide what type of forecast method they think would be most suitable. If the upper level forecast charts do not show a large change during the forecast period, a persistence forecast might be most appropriate. The steady state method could be used in the case of an approaching storm system or front. Some storms might resemble events from earlier in the semester in which case an analogue type forecast could be made. Define criteria that will allow verification of the various forecasts.

Student Projects

1.   Provide students with surface and upper level charts and have them predict the future motion of a middle latitude storm system using the methods listed in the text (past motion, upper-level winds, winds in the warm sector, and movement toward the region of maximum pressure decrease). Have the students compare their predicted location with the actual location at the end of the forecast period.

Using their predictions of storm positions, students could issue specific forecasts for cities that the storm is likely to affect. This exercise could be patterned after the example at the end of the chapter in the text.

2.   Have students compare the actual year-to-date average weather conditions (mean temperatures and precipitation amounts) with climatological averages for their region. Prepare a climatological forecast for the remainder of the semester or the year.

Students might try to forecast first or last frost dates, first snow fall, first day over 100 °F, or some other event using climatological data. They might modify their forecast by noting whether conditions thus far during the year have been above or below the climatological average. Can they account for any departure from average conditions?

Multiple Choice Exam Questions

1.   A weather warning indicates that
a. the atmospheric conditions are favorable for hazardous weather over a particular region.
* b. hazardous weather is either imminent or occurring within the forecast area.
c. hazardous weather is likely to occur within the forecast area during the next 24 hours.
d. hazardous weather is frequently observed in a particular region.

2.   A weather watch would probably be issued for which of the following conditions?
* a. there is a chance for tornadoes tomorrow
b. severe thunderstorms have been spotted in the forecast area
c. presently, extremely high winds are occurring at mountain summits
d. a tornado has been sighted at the outskirts of town
e. heavy snow has been falling over the forecast area

3.   An analysis is
a. a forecast chart that shows the atmosphere at some future time.
b. a forecast chart that compares past weather maps with those of the present.
* c. a surface or upper-level chart that depicts the present weather patterns.
d. a forecast method used in long range weather prediction.
e. a method used to determine skill in predicting the weather.

4.   A prog is
a. a chart that interprets the current state of the atmosphere.
b. an instrument that draws lines on an upper-level chart.
c. a new method of forecasting the weather.
* d. a forecast chart that shows the atmosphere at some future time.
e. another name for a probability forecast.

5.   The forecasting of weather by a computer is known as
a. weather type forecasting.
b. climatology forecasting.
c. extended weather forecasting.
d. analogue prediction.
* e. numerical weather prediction.

6.   Which of the following is presently a problem with modern-day weather predictions?
a. computer forecast models make assumptions about the atmosphere that are not always correct
b. there are regions of the world where only sparce observations are available
c. computer models do not always adequately interpret the surface's influence on the weather
d. the distance between grid points on some models is too large to pick up smaller-scale weather features such as thunderstorms
* e. all of the above

7.   Which of the following is true of geosynchronous satellites?
*   a. they orbit the earth once per day
     b. they are stationary in space and do not orbit around the earth
     c. they are in orbit around the sun, not the earth
     d. pass over the north and south poles of the earth several times each day

8.   Which of the following explain why it is possible to see clouds on satellite photographs taken at night?
     a. the clouds reflect visible light from the sun
     b. the clouds reflect light coming from the moon
     c. the clouds emit visible light
*   d. the clouds emit infrared light

9.   Bright white on an infrared cloud picture indicates
*   a. a cold, high altitude cloud.
     b. a cold, low altitude cloud.
     c. a warm, low altitude cloud.
     d. a warm, high altitude cloud.

10. Which of the following would probably be used to infer cloud altitude on a satellite photograph?
     a. high altitude wind speeds as indicated by cloud motions
*   b. intensity of infrared emissions
     c. cloud appearance
     d. cloud size

11. A tall cumulonimbus cloud would appear ___ on a visible satellite and ___ on an infrared cloud picture.
     a. white, grey
*   b. white, white
     c. grey, grey
     d. grey, white

12. A persistence forecast could be quite accurate when
     a. a frontal system approaches your location at constant speed.
*   b. you are positioned in the middle of a large, stationary air mass.
     c. the weather has been unusually cold for several days.
     d. upper level winds blow straight from west to east.

13. The least accurate forecast method of predicting the weather two days into the future during changeable weather conditions is usually the
     a. trend method.
*   b. persistence forecast.
     c. analogue method.
     d. prediction by weather types.
     e. numerical weather prediction.

14. Which forecasting method assumes that weather systems will move in the same direction and at the same speed as they have been moving?
     a. persistence forecast
     b. probability forecast
     c. weather type forecast
     d. climatological forecast
*   e. steady state (trend) forecast

15. Weather forecast that predicts that the future weather will be the same as the present weather is called
    a. a steady-state forecast.
    b. the trend method.
    * c. a persistence forecast.
    d. the analogue method.
    e. an extended weather forecast.

16. A weather forecast for the immediate future that employs the trend method is called
    * a. nowcasting.
    b. extrapolation.
    c. first order forecast.
    d. linear forecast.

17. Predicting the weather by weather types employs which forecasting method?
    a. probability
    b. steady-state
    * c. analogue
    d. persistence
    e. guess

18. A forecast method that compares past weather maps and weather patterns to those of the present is
    a. persistence forecasting.
    * b. the analogue method.
    c. the trend method.
    d. nowcasting.

19. A probability forecast that calls for a "40 percent chance of rain" means that
    a. there is a 40 percent chance that it will not rain within the forecast area.
    * b. there is a 40 percent chance that any random place in the forecast area will receive measurable rain.
    c. it will rain on 40 percent of the forecast area.
    d. it will rain during 40 percent of the time over the forecast area.

20. The greatest improvement in forecasting skill during the past decade has been
    a. predicting the strength and path of snowstorms along the eastern seaboard.
    * b. in the lead time for watches and warning of severe storms.
    d. predicting the movement of warm and cold fronts.
    e. estimating maximum and minimum temperature 6 to 10 days in the future.

21. The forecasting technique that produces several versions of a forecast model, each beginning with slightly different weather information to reflect errors in the measurements, is called
    a. climatology forecasting.
    b. redundancy analysis.
    c. peristence forecasting.
    * d. ensemble forecasting.
    e. probability forecasting.

22. Suppose that where you live the middle of January is typically several degrees warmer than the rest of the month. If you forecast this "January thaw" for the middle of next January, you would have made a
    a. forecast based on the analogue method.
    b. persistence forecast.
    c. forecast based on weather types.
    d. probability forecast.
    * e. climatological forecast.

23. Which of the following forecasts do you think would <u>not</u> be issued, based on the winter weather pattern on the adjacent 500 mb chart?

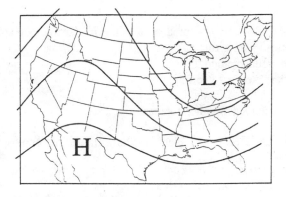

   a. warmer-than-average temperatures over the western half of North America

   b. lower-than-normal temperatures over the eastern half of North America

*   c. higher-than-normal precipitation over the southwestern section of North America

   d. dry weather over the NE United States

Questions 24-28 refer to the following illustration of a middle latitude cyclone. (the dashed lines show the positions of the fronts 6 hours ago)

Surface Weather Map

24. The storm system will apparently move toward the
*   a. northeast.
   b. east.
   c. southeast.
   d. northwest.

25. At which of the 4 positions would you expect to hear the following 12-hour forecast: "Cloudy and cold this morning with snow this afternoon and tonight?"
*   a. 1
   b. 2
   c. 3
   d. 4

26. At which of the 4 positions would you expect to hear the following 12-hour forecast: "Cloudy with possible showers today, turning colder by tonight?"
   a. 1
   b. 2
*   c. 3
   d. 4

27. At which of the 4 positions would you expect to hear the following 12-hour forecast: "Clearing and colder today with continued rising pressures?"
   a. 1
   b. 2
   c. 3
*   d. 4

28. At which of the 4 positions would you expect to hear the following 12-hour forecast: "Partly cloudy and continued warm through this afternoon and evening?"
   a. 1
*   b. 2
   c. 3
   d. 4

29. A forecast of an extended period of dry weather would be made for a region beneath
   a. an upper-level trough.
   b. the polar jet stream.
   c. a cold pool of air aloft.
 * d. an upper-level ridge.
   e. a shortwave trough.

30. By examining a surface map, the movement of a surface low pressure area can be predicted based upon the
   a. orientation of the isobars in the warm sector.
   b. region of greatest pressure decrease.
   c. movement during the previous 6 hours.
 * d. all of the above.

31. Suppose it is warm and raining, and a cold front is moving toward your location. Directly behind the cold front it is cold and snowing. Still further behind the front the weather is cold and clearing. If the front is scheduled to pass your area in 6 hours, a persistence forecast for your area for 12 hours from now would be
   a. cold and snowing.
   b. cold and clearing.
   c. cold and cloudy.
 * d. warm and raining.
   e. not enough information on which to base a forecast

True/False Exam Questions

1. While surface weather observations are made at over 10,000 locations around the world there is no international agency to insure that the same observational procedures are used by the different countries.
   (ans: FALSE)

2. Weather charts and maps are still plotted and analyzed entirely by hand.
   (ans: FALSE)

3. Commercial radio and television stations do not have the economic means and expertise to prepare weather forecasts on their own and station announcers simply read the National Weather Service forecast word for word.
   (ans: FALSE)

4. Geographical features on the earth such as mountain ranges do not have much effect on the weather because the features are small compared to the thickness of the atmosphere.
   (ans: FALSE)

5. A forecaster will use a prognostic chart for guidance in preparing a forecast, but will also rely on personal experience and a knowledge of local features that can affect the weather.
   (ans: TRUE)

6. A polar-orbiting satellite would provide a more detailed view of a severe thunderstorm than a geosynchronous satellite.
   (ans: TRUE)

7. A geostationary satellite must orbit the earth at the same rate and in the same direction as the earth spins on its axis.
   (ans: TRUE)

8. Satellites can observe the movement of the air in areas where there are no clouds by detecting IR radiation emitted by water vapor.
(ans: TRUE)

9. Forecasts made for 1 to 3 days are more accurate than the 12 to 24 hour and 7 day forecasts.
(ans: FALSE)

Word Choice Exam Questions

1. Small errors in weather observations generally AMPLIFY DIMINISH as computers predict weather farther and farther into the future (circle one answer)
(ans: AMPLIFY)

2. A visible satellite photograph is best used to distinquish cloud THICKNESS ALTITUDE. (circle one answer)
(ans: THICKNESS)

3. Polar-orbiting satellites circle the earth at HIGHER LOWER altitude than geosynchronous satellites. (circle one answer)
(ans: LOWER)

4. A tall cumulonimbus (Cb) cloud would appear WHITE GREY on a visible satellite and WHITE GREY on an infrared photograph. (choose one word from each group)
(ans: WHITE, WHITE)

5. Forecasting large scale weather events is MORE LESS accurate than smaller, shorter-lived events. (circle one answer)
(ans: MORE)

6. You would expect a relatively WARM COLD minimum temperature on a night with calm winds, clear skies, and low humidity. (circle one answer)
(ans: COLD)

Short Answer Exam Questions

1. What is needed first, before making a weather forecast?
(ans: WEATHER CONDITIONS must be known over a LARGE AREA)

2. A vertical profile of atmospheric conditions is known as a(n) _____.
(ans: SOUNDING)

3. The most widely separated surface weather observations come from what region on the earth?
(ans: OCEANS)

4. _____ are one of the means used to indicate weather advisories or warnings in maritime areas.
(ans: FLAGS)

5. A(n) _____ would be issued if snow and winds of at least 35 MPH reduce visibility to less than 1/4 mile for a period of several hours.
(ans: BLIZZARD WARNING)

6. A set of mathematical equations that approximate how atmospheric temperature, pressure, winds, and moisture vary with time is known as a(n) atmospheric _____.
(ans: MODEL)

7. A computer-derived forecast map is known as a(n) _____ or more simply as a(n) _____.
(ans: PROGNOSTIC CHART, PROG)

8. When weather conditions aren't expected to change, a(n) _____ forecast could be quite accurate.
(ans: PERSISTENCE)

9. A model is run several times with slight changes in the starting data to generate a(n) _____ forecast.
(ans: ENSEMBLE)

10. Surface winds from the east or southeast, cool or cold temperatures, high clouds thickening and lowering, and a halo around the sun or moon could warn of the approach of a(n) _____
(ans: WARM FRONT)

11. A satellite _____ image can show air motions in regions where there aren't any clouds.
(ans: WATER VAPOR)

12. Surface storm systems tend to move in the same direction and at about _____ the speed of the winds at the 500 mb level.
(ans: ONE HALF)

13. Temperature and precipitation in one part of the world can affect the weather in another widely separated region. These interactions are known as _____.
(ans: TELECONNECTIONS)

Essay Exam Questions

1. List some of the ways in which you can predict the future movement of surface middle latitude storms.

2. Describe four different types of weather forecasting methods and give an example of each.

3. List some of the factors that affect the accuracy of atmospheric models.

4. List some of the ways in which you use the daily weather forecast in your everyday life.

5. Describe the data and tools that a meteorologist assembles prior to making a weather forecast.

6. Which types of forecasts do you think would work best for the following time periods: short range (6 to 12 hours), medium range (24 to 48 hours), long range (5 to 10 days), and seasonal (3 month)?

7. Explain how and why the cloud brightness on an infrared satellite photograph can be related to cloud altitude.

8. About how far apart do you think weather observing stations should be in order to accurately depict a middle latitude storm and to be able to forecast the storm's movement?

9. What local signs would you look for to predict the approach of a low pressure center or a weather front?

10. Assuming you know last night's minimum temperature, what weather information would you use to predict tonight's minimum temperature?

Chapter 10
Thunderstorms and Tornadoes

Summary

Thunderstorms can be one of the most spectacular and destructive of weather phenomena. This chapter begins by describing the growth and development of common air mass thunderstorms and then examines the special atmospheric conditions that can lead to severe storm formation. Larger organized systems of thunderstorms, such as squall lines and mesoscale convective complexes, are covered here also. Many of the physical characteristics and some of the hazards associated with thunderstorms, such as gust fronts and roll clouds, microbursts, wind shear, and flash floods are explained and illustrated.

The chapter continues by reviewing our current understanding of thunderstorm electrification and summarizing the rapid sequence of events that occurs during a cloud-to-ground lightning discharge. A relatively simple device, the lightning rod, is still used to protect structures from lightning, and there are a few basic rules that one should observe, for personal safety, if caught in a lightning storm.

Tornadoes are discussed in the final portion of the chapter. Tornadoes occur more frequently in the United States than in any other country in the world. The chapter examines how, when, and where tornadoes form in the US, and explains why tornadoes can be so destructive. We look also at new technology, such as Doppler radar, that is beginning to be used to study tornado-producing thunderstorms and to remotely detect and warn of tornado occurrence. The chapter concludes with a brief discussion of waterspouts.

Key Terms

(Listed in approximately the order they appear in the text. Terms in boldface are emphasized and appear at the end of the chapter in the text.)

ordinary (air mass)
  thunderstorm
cumulus stage
entrainment
downdraft
mature thunderstorm
cell
overshooting
dissipating stage
multicell storms
severe thunderstorm
gust front
mesohigh
shelf cloud
arcus cloud
roll cloud
downburst
microburst

macroburst
wind shear
LLWSAS (Low-Level Wind
  Shear Alert System)
straight-line winds
derecho
bow echo
supercell storm
bounded weak echo
  region (BWER)
echo free vault
squall line
pre-frontal squall-
  line thunderstorms
gravity waves
ordinary squall lines
dry line
dew-point front

mesoscale convective
  complexes (MCCs)
flash flood
training
lightning
thunder
sonic boom
cloud-to-ground lightning
stepped leader
return stroke
dart leader
forked lightning
ribbon lightning
bead lightning
ball lightning
sheet lightning
heat lightning
red sprite

blue jet	tornado outbreak	**tornado watch**
corona discharge	super outbreak	**tornado warning**
St. Elmo's fire	tornado alley	hook echo
lightning direction finder	multi-vortex tornado	**Doppler radar**
tornadoes	**suction vortice**	Doppler shift
twisters	**Fujita scale**	tornado vortex
cyclones	**mesocylone**	signature (TVS)
funnel cloud	gustnado	Doppler lidar
dust-whirl stage	landspouts	**NEXRAD (Next Generation**
organizing stage	vortex tubes	**Weather Radar)**
mature stage	**wall cloud**	**waterspout**
shrinking stage	VORTEX (Verification of	tornadic waterspout
decay stage	the Origins of Rotation	"fair weather" waterspout
families (of tornadoes)	in Tornadoes Experiment)	

Teaching Suggestions, Demonstrations, and Visual Aids

1.   A table-top demonstration of a gust front produced at the ground by a cold thunderstorm downdraft can be performed relatively simply. Create a fog cloud by placing a piece of dry ice on a table (or in a shallow pan filled with warm water). Partially fill a styrofoam cup with dry ice or liquid nitrogen. Carefully tip the cup so that just the cold air spills out. When the cold downward sinking air hits the table top, it will "blow" the fog cloud outward from a point below the cup.

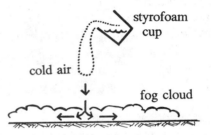

2.   The growth and decay of an air mass thunderstorm is illustrated well on time-lapse video photography. Unfortunately, home video equipment does not usually have a time-lapse filming capability. It may be possible to borrow suitable equipment from a university audio visual department or perhaps a local television station would be willing to record local thunderstorm activity. Clouds at different levels will often be observed to be moving in very different directions - a good visual demonstration of vertical wind shear.

3.   Spectacular video footage of tornadoes, often obtained by amateur photographers using home video equipment, is available for purchase from several sources. See a recent issue of *Weatherwise* magazine for advertisements. Interesting programs on thunderstorms, lightning, and tornadoes produced for the NOVA television series on the PBS network and for the Discovery Channel are also available for purchase.

     Weatherwise magazine is a good source of still photographs of tornadoes, thunderstorms and lightning. See, especially, the winning entries from the yearly weather photography contest (published in the August issue) and the yearly weather summary (published in the February issue).

Student Projects

1.   Depending on location and time of the year, students might use data from morning surface and upper-level data to prepare forecasts of thunderstorm activity for the coming afternoon or evening. Let the students decide which of the various weather elements or simple stability indices might be appropriate. Students should validate their forecast and attempt to improve forecast accuracy.

2.   Thunderstorms and lightning are good choices for student photography projects. Still photographs of a developing thunderstorm taken at intervals of 5 or 10 minutes will often illustrate how rapidly cumulonimbus clouds can develop. For a close storm, it will probably be difficult to fit the entire cloud into the camera's field of view unless a short focal length, wide-angle lens, is available.

If nighttime thunderstorm activity is frequent, students can attempt to photograph the cloud-to-ground lightning. Depending on the height of the cloud base and the focal length of the camera lens, the camera will probably need to be located several kilometers away from the thunderstorm and out of the rain. Students should operate from a protected location if the lightning activity is closer than this. The camera should be mounted on a tripod and exposures should be made using the B (bulb) setting and a shutter release cable. Keep the shutter open until a lightning flash is seen. Test exposures can be made to determine when background light will begin to overexpose the film. Close lightning discharges are sufficiently bright, that low speed film (ASA 25 or 64) gives satisfactory results.

By slowly panning the camera, it might be possible to resolve the separate strokes in a lightning flash (see, for example, J. Hendry Jr., "Panning for Lightning," *Weatherwise, 45*, 19, 1993.)

3.	As in the introduction to the chapter, many students may have themselves had or may know of a family member that has had a close encounter with a tornado. Have the student describe the experience.

4.	Have students report on a particularly destructive tornado or tornado outbreak. Significant tornado events include the 18 March 1925 Tri-State tornado (695 deaths, probably the greatest tornado disaster in the US), the 11 April 1965 Palm Sunday tornado outbreak (ref: T.T. Fujita, D.L. Bradbury and C.F. Van Thullenar, "Palm Sunday Tornadoes of April 11, 1965," *Monthly Weather Review, 98*, 29-69, 1970), and the 3-4 April 1974 super tornado outbreak (ref: T.T. Fujita, "Jumbo Tornado Outbreak of 3 April 1974, *Weatherwise, 27*, 116-126, 1974).

Multiple Choice Exam Questions

1.	An air-mass thunderstorm is a
	a. thunderstorm that does not produce lightning or thunder.
	b. thunderstorm that has a tilted updraft and downdraft.
*	c. scattered or isolated storm that is not severe.
	d. thunderstorm that does not produce hail.

2.	The initial stage of an air-mass thunderstorm is the
	a. mature stage.
	b. dissipating stage.
*	c. cumulus stage.
	d. multicell stage.

3.	Air mass thunderstorms only last about one hour and begin to dissipate when
	a. lightning neutralizes all the electrical charge in the cloud.
	b. when all the precipitation particles in the cloud turn to ice.
*	c. when the downdraft spreads throughout the cloud and cuts off the updraft.
	d. when solar heating at the ground begins to decrease.

4.	Downdrafts spread throughout a thunderstorm during the ___ stage.
	a. cumulus
*	b. dissipating
	c. precipitating
	d. developing

5.	An air-mass thunderstorm is most intense during the ___ stage.
*	a. mature
	b. multicell
	c. cumulus
	d. dissipating

6.   A group of thunderstorms which develop in a line one next to the other, each in a different stage of development, are called
     a. air-mass thunderstorms.
     b. a thunderstorm cluster.
*   c. a multicell thunderstorm.
     d. mature thunderstorms.

7.   The downdraft in an air-mass thunderstorm is created mainly by
     a. the melting of snow in the anvil.
     b. electrical attraction between the cloud and ground.
     c. the release of latent heat as water in the cloud freezes.
*   d. evaporating raindrops that make the air cold and heavy.
     e. upper level wind motions.

8.   The most turbulent part of a thunderstorm is
     a. above the top of the cloud.
     b. near the base of the cloud
     c. in the middle of the updraft
*   d. between the updraft and downdraft

9.   Severe thunderstorms are different from air-mass thunderstorms in that severe thunderstorms
     a. contain thunder and lightning.
     b. have an anvil.
     c. contain hail.
     d. have a strong updraft and downdraft.
*   e. have a tilted updraft in the mature stage.

10. A supercell storm is
     a. a thunderstorm that produces several tornadoes.
     b. a thunderstorm that produces a category F-5 tornado.
     c. a thunderstorm with an extremely large downburst.
*   d. an enormous thunderstorm that lasts for several hours.

11. The cloud that forms along the leading edge of a gust front is called
     a. an anvil cloud.
*   b. a roll cloud.
     c. a mammatus cloud.
     d. a wedge cloud.

12. The leading edge of a thunderstorm's cold downdraft is known as a
     a. downburst.
     b. squall line.
*   c. gust front.
     d. dry line.
     e. microburst.

13. The small area of high pressure created by the cold, heavy air of a thunderstorm downdraft is called
     a. an anticyclone.
     b. a microburst.
*   c. a mesohigh.
     d. a gust front.
     e. a mesocyclone.

14. Which of the following would you <u>not</u> expect to observe during the passage of a gust front?
   a. gusty winds
   b. rising surface pressures
   * c. increase in temperatures
   d. wind shift

15. A small thunderstorm cloud with virga falling out of its base and blowing dust at the ground could warn of a severe hazard to aircraft because
   a. this could be the first indication of a tornado.
   b. it is likely that hail will soon begin to fall.
   * c. this could indicate an intense downdraft or microburst.
   d. the airplane could be struck by lightning.

16. Blowing dust moving outward at the ground below a thunderstorm could indicate a
   a. wall cloud.
   b. dry line.
   c. squall line.
   * d. strong downdraft.

17. The main difference between a downburst and a microburst is
   a. duration.
   b. strength.
   * c. horizontal size.
   d. overall altitude.

18. The wind shear associated with several major airline crashes is believed to have been caused by
   * a. microbursts.
   b. dry lines.
   c. the jet stream.
   d. mesocyclones.

19. A relatively narrow downburst, less than 4 kilometers wide, is called
   * a. a microburst.
   b. a funnel cloud.
   c. a rain shaft.
   d. a narrow burst.
   e. a mesocyclone.

20. Many flash floods, including those that occurred in Rapid City, South Dakota, and in Colorado's Big Thompson Canyon, are the result of thunderstorms that
   a. contain no lightning.
   b. form in a dry air mass.
   * c. move slowly.
   d. have weak or non-existant downdrafts.

21. Squall lines generally do not form
   * a. behind a cold front.
   b. when the air aloft develops waves downwind from a cold front.
   c. along a dry line.
   d. in the warm sector where warm, dry air meets warm, humid air.
   e. ahead of an advancing cold front.

22. A line of thunderstorms that forms ahead of an advancing cold front is called a
     a. roll cloud.
*   b. squall line.
     c. wall cloud.
     d. gust front.
     e. dry line.

23. On a surface weather map, this marks the boundary where a warm, dry air mass encounters a warm, moist air mass.
     a. gust front
*   b. dry line
     c. storm front
     d. wall cloud

24. Most squall line thunderstorms form
*   a. in advance of a cold front.
     b. along a cold front.
     c. behind a cold front.
     d. in advance of a warm front.
     e. along an occluded front.

25. The greatest annual number of thunderstorms in the United States occurs in
     a. the Ohio valley.
     b. the Central Plains.
     c. the desert southwest.
*   d. Florida.
     e. Texas.

26. Nighttime thunderstorms tend to be more common
     a. in the Rocky Mountains.
     b. in the desert southwest.
*   c. in the Central Plains.
     d. in California.
     e. in Florida.

27. The most likely time for an air mass thunderstorm to form is
     a. just after sunrise.
     b. just before sunrise.
     c. around midnight.
*   d. late afternoon
     e. at noon.

28. A discharge of electricity from or within a thunderstorm is called
     a. static electricity.
*   b. lightning.
     c. a downburst.
     d. St. Elmo's fire.
     e. an atmospheric arc.

29. Lightning discharges within a cloud occur ____ cloud-to-ground lightning.
*   a. more frequently than
     b. less frequently than
     c. about as frequently as
     d. lightning cannot remain in the cloud, it must strike an object on the ground

30. In cloud-to-ground lightning, the stepped leader travels ___ and the return stroke travels ___ .
   a. upward, upward
   b. upward, downward
 * c. downward, upward
   d. downward, downward

31. The bluish halo that may appear above pointed objects underneath a thunderstorm is called
   a. heat lightning.
   b. fluorescence.
 * c. St. Elmo's fire.
   d. sheet lightning.

32. Distant lightning that is so far away you cannot hear the thunder is called
   a. sheet lightning.
 * b. heat lightning.
   c. false lightning.
   d. St. Elmo's fire.
   e. auroral lightning.

33. Electrons
 * a. are negatively charged.
   b. are positively charged.
   c. carry no charge.
   d. can carry either positive or negative charge.

34. The top of a thunderstorm is normally ___ charged, and the middle and lower parts are ___charged.
   a. negatively, negatively
   b. negatively, positively
   c. positively, positively
 * d. positively, negatively

35. A cloud-to-ground lightning discharge will sometimes appear to flicker. This is because
   a. you are able to see the separate steps of the stepped leader.
 * b. you are able to distinquish separate return strokes.
   c. the bright light causes you to blink.
   d. of refraction caused by turbulent thunderstorm winds.

36. What would be the proper sequence of events in a lightning flash?
   a. stepped leader, dart leader, return stroke, return stroke
   b. return stroke, stepped leader, return stroke, dart leader
   c. dart leader, return stroke, stepped leader, return stroke
 * d. stepped leader, return stroke, dart leader, return stroke

37. You a generally safe inside an automobile during a lighting storm because
   a. the car's radio antenna will act as a lightning rod.
   b. the rubber tires insulate you from the ground.
   c. metal cars do not become electrically charged.
 * d. the metal car body will carry the lightning current around the passengers inside.

38. Thunder is caused by
   a. the collision between two thunderstorms with opposite electrical charge.
 * b. the rapid heating of air surrounding a lightning channel.
   c. the explosion that occurs when + and - charge collide and neutralize each other.
   d. turbulent wind motions inside the thunderstorm.

39. If you see a lightning stroke and then, 15 seconds later, hear the thunder, the lightning is about ___ miles away.
    a. 45
    b. 15
    c. 5
*   d. 3

40. When caught in a thunderstorm in an open field, the best thing to do is to
    a. run for cover under the nearest tree.
    b. lie down flat on the ground.
*   c. crouch down as low as possible while minimizing contact with the ground.
    d. remove all metallic objects from your pockets.

41. Thunder will not occur
*   a. without lightning.
    b. in wintertime thunderstorms.
    c. in thunderstorms over the ocean.
    d. when a thunderstorm is producing precipitation.

42. Which of the following is the most accurate description of the principle of a lightning rod?
    a. the lightning rod acts to discharge the thunderstorm
*   b. the lightning rod intercepts the lightning and safely carries the lightning current around the object it protects
    c. lightning rods have been used since the 1700s, but the principle of their operation is not known
    d. positive charge induced in the lightning rod repels the negative charge in an approaching step leader

43. A tornado cloud that does not touch the ground is called
*   a. a funnel cloud.
    b. a wall cloud.
    c. a roll cloud.
    d. a mesocyclone.

44. A funnel cloud is composed primarily of
*   a. cloud droplets.
    b. dust and dirt from the ground.
    c. raindrops.
    d. hail.
    e. ice crystals.

45. Which of the following factors is most important in determining the strength of a tornado?
    a. diameter
    b. air temperature
    c. duration
*   d. central pressure

46. Which of the following statements about tornadoes is correct?
    a. all tornadoes rotate in a counterclockwise direction
    b. tornadoes never strike the same place twice
    c. all tornadoes make a distinction roar
*   d. the United States has more tornadoes that any other country in the world

47. The most frequent time of day for tornadoes to form is in the
    a. early morning at the time of sunrise.
    b. late morning just before noon.
*   c. afternoon.
    d. middle of the night.

48. Which of the following regions would you expect to have the most tornadoes in the winter?
    a. southern Great Plains
    b. Oklahoma
    c. northern Great Plains
*   d. southern Gulf States

49. A funnel cloud or tornado may develop from this rotating cloud that extends beneath a severe thunderstorm.
    a. mammatus cloud
    b. roll cloud
*   c. wall cloud
    d. suction vortice

50. The small, rapidly rotating whirls that sometimes occur within a large tornado are called
    a. microtornadoes.
    b. whirl winds.
*   c. suction vortices.
    d. mesocyclones.

51. The Fujita scale pertains to
    a. the size of a tornado producing thunderstorm.
    b. the amount of hail that falls from a mature thunderstorm.
    c. the size of the thunderstorm image on a radar screen.
*   d. the strength of a tornado.

52. Most tornadoes have winds that are
    a. greater than 300 MPH.
    b. greater than 200 MPH.
    c. between 100 and 200 MPH.
*   d. less than 100 MPH.

53. The rotating updraft inside a severe thunderstorm is called a
    a. mesohigh.
*   b. mesocyclone.
    c. funnel cloud.
    d. roll cloud.

54. Most tornadoes move from
    a. north to south.
    b. northwest to southwest.
*   c. southwest to northeast.
    d. southeast to northwest.

55. About two-thirds of all tornadoes fall into which of the following categories on the Fujita scale?
*   a. F0 or F1.
    b. F2 or F3.
    c. F0 or F5.
    d. F4 or F5.

166

56. If a tornado is rotating in a counterclockwise direction and moving toward the northeast, the strongest winds will be on its ___ side.
   a. southwestern
* b. southeastern
   c. northeastern
   d. northwestern

57. Thunderstorms which produce tornadoes
   a. have very little cloud-to-ground lightning.
   b. have updraft velocities that exceed 100 miles per hour.
* c. have rotating updrafts.
   d. will not produce hail.

58. Different tornadoes spawned by the same thunderstorm are said to occur
   a. in unison.
   b. in sequence.
   c. in repetition.
* d. in families.

59. In a region where severe thunderstorms with tornadoes are forming, one would not expect to observe
* a. a strong ridge of high pressure over the region.
   b. a dry tongue of cold air between the 700 and 500 mb levels.
   c. the polar jet stream above the region.
   d. moist warm air moving north at about the 850 mb level.

60. A hook-shaped echo on a radar screen often indicates
   a. a thunderstorm with very frequent lightning.
   b. a developing hurricane.
* c. the possible presence of a tornado-producing thunderstorm.
   d. a rotating anvil cloud at the top of a thunderstorm.

61. ___ measures the speed at which precipitation is moving toward or away from an observer is
   a. A radiosonde
   b. An anemometer
   c. A wind psychrometer
* d. Doppler radar

62. The signal detected by a Doppler radar is
   a. a radiowave emitted by lightning.
   b. a soundwave produced by thunder.
* c. a radiowave reflected by precipitation.
   d. a soundwave produced by wind shear.

63. Most waterspouts would fall into which category of the Fujita scale?
* a. F_0
   b. F_1
   c. F_2
   d. F_4 or F_5

64. On a Doppler radar screen, a tornado might appear as a
   a. a region of low pressure.
   b. a region of intense precipitation.
* c. a region of rapidly changing wind speeds.
   d. a region of intense lightning activity.

65. A Doppler radar determines precipitation ___ by measuring changes in
the ___ of the reflected radiowave.
   a. size, intensity
   b. velocity, intensity
 * c. velocity, frequency
   d. size, frequency

66. A tornado-like event that forms over water is a
   a. mesohigh.
   b. roll cloud.
   c. microburst.
 * d. waterspout.
   e. squall line.

True False Exam Questions

1. To be considered a mature thunderstorm, rain falling from the cloud must reach the ground.
   (ans: FALSE)

2. In some situations individual thunderstorms may organize into a convective weather system that may be 1000 times larger than an individual storm.
   (ans: TRUE)

3. Thunderstorm activity generally increases in frequency as you move from the east to the west coast of the United States.
   (ans: FALSE)

4. Electrical charge is produced in thunderstorms by collisions between different types of precipitation particles.
   (ans: TRUE)

5. Lightning is sometimes produced during snowstorms and dust storms, and by the clouds of erupting volcanoes.
   (ans: TRUE)

6. St. Elmo's Fire is a glowing electrical discharge that appears on ship's masts and power lines when a thunderstorm is nearby.
   (ans: TRUE)

7. Most cloud-to-ground lightning flashes consist of a single return stroke.
   (ans: FALSE)

8. Dim lightning discharges have been observed to shoot upward from the tops of thunderstorms into the upper atmosphere.
   (ans: TRUE)

9. Most tornadoes last only a few minutes; some tornadoes have existed for several hours.
   (ans: TRUE)

10. When the air is dry tornado winds can remain invisible until they reach the ground and pick up dust.
   (ans: TRUE)

11. Weak tornadoes sometimes form along a thunderstorm gust front.
   (ans: TRUE)

168

12. About equal numbers of clockwise- and counterclockwise-rotating tornadoes are observed in the United States every year.
(ans: FALSE)

13. An upper level inversion may actually favor severe thunderstorm development because the inversion will prevent many smaller weaker thunderstorms from forming.
(ans: TRUE)

14. Even if distinctive features that might indicate a tornado are observed on radar, a tornado must be observed visually before a tornado warning is issued.
(ans: FALSE)

Word Choice Exam Questions

1. In ordinary air mass thunderstorms, when the downdraft begins to expand laterally in the cloud, the thunderstorm will usually begin to STRENGTHEN WEAKEN. (circle one answer)
(ans: WEAKEN)

2. Surface winds are blowing from left to right in the figure at right. Once the thunderstorm downdraft reaches the ground and begins to spread out beneath the cloud would you expect to find convergence and new cell formation to occur on the RIGHT or LEFT side of the storm? (circle one answer)
(ans: LEFT)

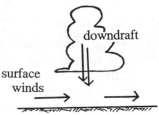

3. An anvil cloud forms near the TOP BOTTOM of a thunderstorm where the thunderstorm cloud reaches a STABLE UNSTABLE region of the atmosphere. (choose one word from each pair)
(ans: TOP, STABLE)

4. Evaporating precipitation beneath a thunderstorm will STRENGTHEN WEAKEN the downdraft. (circle one answer)
(ans: STRENGTHEN)

5. Potentially the strongest and longest-lived thunderstorm is one with a VERTICAL TILTED updraft. (circle one answer)
(ans: TILTED)

6. A gust front is caused by a thunderstorm UPDRAFT DOWNDRAFT. Do gust front winds blow INWARD toward or OUTWARD from the center of the storm? (choose one word from each pair)
(ans: DOWNDRAFT, OUTWARD)

7. The greatest potential for flooding is with thunderstorms that are FAST SLOW moving. (circle one answer)
(ans: SLOW)

8. Squall line thunderstorms will often form 100 to 300 km AHEAD of BEHIND a cold front. (circle one answer)
(ans: AHEAD)

9. Lightning flashes that stay within a cloud are MORE LESS frequent than discharges that strike the ground. (circle one answer)
(ans: MORE)

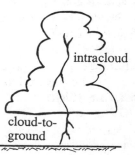

10. Florida has MORE FEWER thunderstorms in an average year than Oklahoma. (circle one answer)
(ans: MORE)

11. In an average year you would expect the highest incidence of severe thunderstorms in FLORIDA OKLAHOMA. (circle one answer)
(ans: OKLAHOMA)

12. Most lightning flashes that strike the ground begin with a(n) UPWARD DOWNWARD moving discharge that carries POSITIVE NEGATIVE charge. (choose one word from each pair)
(ans: DOWNWARD, NEGATIVE)

13. If you are caught outside during a lighting storm, an automobile would be a GOOD BAD place to seek shelter. (circle one answer)
(ans: GOOD)

14. Tornadoes form around intense cores of HIGH LOW pressure. (circle one answer)
(ans: LOW)

15. The strongest tornado is one with a THICK THIN funnel cloud and a VERTICAL TILTED orientation. (choose one word from each pair)
(ans: THICK, VERTICAL)

16. The most tornadoes occur in the United States in the SPRING FALL. The strongest tornadoes occur in the SPRING FALL. (choose one word from each group)
(ans: SPRING, SPRING)

Short Answer Exam Questions

1. A _____ thunderstorm produces wind gust of 50 knots or more and/or 3/4 inch or larger hail.
(ans: SEVERE)

2. Strong and gusty winds and a drop in temperature in the vicinity of a thunderstorm could indicate the passage of a(n) _____.
(ans: GUST FRONT)

3. Fill in each blank below with 1, 10, 100, or 1000.
An air mass thunderstorm will last about _____ hour(s).
The top of a moderate thunderstorm will grow to an altitude
of _____ km(s).
There are about _____ tornadoes in the United States every year.
About _____ people are killed by lightning every year in the United States.
(ans: 1, 10, 1000, 100)

4. Strong surface winds produced by a narrow intense thunderstorm downdraft called a(n) _____ are capable of producing the same degree of damage as a weak tornado.
(ans: MICROBURST)

5. A rapid change in wind speed or wind direction in a short distance is known as _____ and represents a serious hazard to aviation.
(ans: WIND SHEAR)

6. Thunderstorms are forming along the _____ at right which separates dry and moist air masses.
(ans: DRY LINE)

7. An intense thunderstorm that is moving slowly or is stalled present a risk of _____.
    (ans: FLASH FLOODING)

8. A(n) _____ is produced when aircraft travel faster than the speed of sound.
    (ans: SONIC BOOM)

9. A rotating thunderstorm updraft is called a(n) _____
    (ans: MESOCYCLONE)

Essay Exam Questions

1. List and discuss some of the atmospheric conditions that are needed for a thunderstorm to develop.

2. List and describe the stages of development of an air-mass thunderstorm. About how long does a single air-mass thunderstorm cell last?

3. Where does the energy contained in a mature thunderstorm come from?

4. In what ways are severe thunderstorms different from air mass thunderstorms? What are some of the meteorological or atmospheric conditions that favor the development of severe thunderstorms?

5. How does a thunderstorm gust front form? What might you expect to see and feel if a gust front were to approach and pass you on the ground?

6. What is wind shear? Why does wind shear represent a hazard to aviation?

7. Sketch a mature thunderstorm. On your sketch indicate approximately the altitude of the cloud's base and top and show where you might expect to see the anvil cloud, a pileus cloud, mammatus cloud, and a roll cloud. With arrows, indicate where the updraft and downdraft might be found in the cloud. Where would you expect to find strong vertical wind shear? Indicate where the largest concentrations of positive and negative charge would be found in the cloud.

8. What is a squall line? Where would you expect squall lines to form?

9. Where do thunderstorms form most frequently in the US? Why is this the case? Is this also where most tornadoes occur? Explain.

10. List and describe the sequence of events that occur during a cloud-to-ground lightning discharge.

11. Describe a tornado by giving average values for as many of the following characteristics as you can: diameter, duration, length of path on the ground, direction and speed of movement, when and where tornadoes occur, central pressure, tornado wind speeds.

12. Why do tornadoes have low pressure cores? Would it be possible for a tornado to form around a high pressure core?

13. What makes a tornado-producing thunderstorm different from other thunderstorms?

14. The region of greatest tornado activity shifts northward from early spring to summer. Why does this occur?

15. Most tornadoes move from the southwest toward the northeast. Why is this true?

Chapter 11
Hurricanes

Summary

Weather and storms in the tropics are discussed in this chapter. Several unusually strong and destructive hurricanes have affected the United States, Mexico, and countries of the Caribbean in recent years, so this subject should be especially relevant and interesting to students.

The chapter begins by comparing atmospheric conditions and storms in the tropics to those at middle latitudes. Horizontal temperature and pressure gradients are generally fairly weak at low latitudes, but moisture is abundant and thunderstorm formation is common. Zones of convergence, such as might be associated with an easterly wave or might be found near the ITCZ, will sometimes cause thunderstorm development in lines or clusters. On a few occasions each year special conditions will cause a mass of thunderstorms to become better organized and to develop into a tropical storm or hurricane. Hurricanes form above (and derive much of their energy from) a warm surface layer of ocean water. Hurricanes generally form between 5 and 20 degrees latitude, where steering winds will cause an overall east to west movement. Schematic diagrams illustrate the air motions in a mature hurricane and point out the characteristic eye, eye wall, and spiral rain band features.

Several of the unique hazards associated with hurricanes are discussed. In addition to powerful winds and flooding caused by heavy rainfall, extensive damage can be caused by the hurricane storm surge. Several recent examples of destructive and costly hurricanes are given, and we see that providing timely and accurate warning of a hurricane's approach and landfall is a particularly demanding task. A list of names proposed for future Northern Atlantic and Eastern Pacific hurricanes is included.

Key Terms
(Listed in approximately the same order they appear in the text. Terms in boldface are emphasized and appear at the end of the chapter in the text.)

non-squall cluster	eye wall	Ekman spiral
squall line	**trade wind inversion**	Ekman transport
streamlines	organized convection	**storm surge**
tropical wave	theory	**spin-up vortices**
(easterly wave)	heat engine theory	**(mini swirls)**
hurricane	feedback mechanism	**hurricane watch**
typhoon	**tropical disturbance**	**hurricane warning**
baguio	**tropical depression**	Project STORMFURY
cyclone	**tropical storm**	landfall
tropical cyclone	warm-core lows	**Saffir-Simpson scale**
eye (of hurricane)	polar lows	major hurricane
spiral rain bands	Arctic hurricanes	**super-typhoon**

Teaching Suggestions, Demonstrations, and Visual Aids

1.   Video footage of recent hurricanes is available for purchase from a variety of sources. See a recent issue of *Weatherwise* magazine for advertisements.

        A one-hour program about hurricanes has also been produced by the NOVA television series. This program includes dramatic aerial footage from inside the eye of hurricane Gilbert.

Student projects

1.   Depending on the time of the year students may be interested in plotting and following hurricane or tropical storm trajectories on a tracking chart. Students can investigate how large, synpotic scale weather features affect the storm's movement.

2.   Have students prepare a report on a strong recent hurricane or a hurricane of historical interest. A suitable choice could be made from the list in Table 11.1. Some additional possibilites can be found in the list of the ten deadliest hurricanes to have struck the United States in the 20th century (ref: J. Williams, The Weather Book, 2nd ed., p. 143, Vintage Books, New York, 1997).

Multiple Choice Exam Questions

1.   A weak trough of low pressure found in the tropics and along which hurricanes occasionally form is called
        a. an open wave.
*   b. an easterly wave.
        c. a baroclinic wave.
        d. a permanent wave.

2.   Streamlines on a weather map depict
        a. water temperature.
        b. pressure.
*   c. wind flow.
        d. dew point.
        e. ocean currents.

3.   Which of the following is not true concerning an easterly wave?
        a. moves from east to west
*   b. has converging winds on its western side
        c. showers and thunderstorms may be found on its eastern side
        d. indicates a region of lower-than-average pressure

4.   The center of a hurricane is called the
*   a. eye.
        b. eye wall.
        c. vortex.
        d. core.

5.   The skies in the center (eye) of a hurricane are often cloud free. This is because the air in the eye
*   a. is sinking.
        b. is very cold.
        c. is dry.
        d. is expanding.

6. An intense storm of tropical origin that forms over the Pacific Ocean adjacent to the west coast of Mexico would be called a
    *   a. hurricane.
        b. typhoon.
        c. cyclone.
        d. willy willy.
        e. baguio.

7. Hurricanes that move into India and Australia are usually called ____ in that part of the world.
        a. typhoons
        b. hurricanes
    *   c. cyclones
        d. extratropical cyclones

8. Pressure at the center of a hurricane is ____ than the surroundings at the surface and ____ than the surroundings aloft.
        a. higher, lower
    *   b. lower, higher
        c. lower, lower
        d. higher, higher

9. The vertical structure of the hurricane shows an upper-level ____ of air, and a surface ____ of air.
    *   a. outflow, inflow
        b. outflow, outflow
        c. inflow, outflow
        d. inflow, inflow

10. In the Northern Hemisphere, hurricanes and middle latitude cyclones are similar in that both
        a. have surface weather fronts.
        b. intensify with increasing height above the ground.
    *   c. have winds that blow counterclockwise around their centers.
        d. will generally move from west to east.

11. Which would you <u>not</u> expect to observe as the eye of a hurricane passes directly over your area?
        a. an increase in surface temperature
        b. a very low surface pressure reading
    *   c. high winds
        d. little or no precipitation

12. The ring of intense thunderstorms and strong winds located about 20 to 50 km from the center of a hurricane is referred to as the
    *   a. eye wall.
        b. vortex.
        c. spiral band.
        d. wall cloud.

13. In a hurricane, the eye wall represents
        a. the exact center of the storm.
        b. the area of broken cloudiness at the center.
        c. a region of light winds and low pressure.
    *   d. a zone of intense thunderstorms around the center.
        e. a layer of cirrus cloud in the center of the storm.

174

14.   The strongest winds in a hurricane are found
      a. at the center of the storm.
*   b. in the eye wall.
      c. in the rain bands.
      d. at upper levels, above the center of the hurricane.
      e. near the periphery of the hurricane.

15.   Hurricane winds rotate in a clockwise direction
      a. in the Northern Hemisphere only.
*   b. in the Southern Hemisphere only.
      c. in both the Northern and Southern Hemispheres.
      d. in neither hemisphere.

16.   At the periphery of a hurricane the air is ___, and several kilometers above the surface, in the eye, the air
      is ___.
*   a. sinking, sinking
      b. sinking, rising
      c. rising, sinking
      d. rising, rising

17.   The surface pressure at the center of hurricane Gilbert decreased to a value
      of ___, the record minimum value for Atlantic hurricanes.
      a. 953 mb
*   b. 888 mb
      c. 734 mb
      d. 238 mb

18.   The main reason hurricanes don't develop over the south Atlantic Ocean adjacent to South America is
      because
      a. the Coriolis force is too small there.
      b. the pressure gradient force is too weak in that area.
*   c. the surface water temperatures are too cold.
      d. the air at the surface is always diverging.

19.   Just before a storm becomes a fully developed hurricane, it is in the ___ stage.
      a. tropical depression
      b. tropical disturbance
*   c. tropical storm
      d. cyclone
      e. typhoon

20.   Hurricanes do not form
      a. along the ITCZ.
*   b. along the equator.
      c. with an easterly wave.
      d. when the trade wind inversion is weak.
      e. when the surface water temperature exceeds 25 °C.

21.   As surface air rushes in toward the eye of a hurricane, the air expands and should cool. The main reason
      the surface air is not cooler around the eye is because
      a. the sinking air near the eye warms the air.
      b. friction with the water adds heat to the air.
*   c. the warm water heats the air.
      d. sunlight heats the air.

22.   The main difference between a hurricane and a tropical storm is that
       a. hurricanes are larger.
       b. tropical storms are more than 500 miles from the US mainland.
 *   c. winds speeds are greater in a hurricane.
       d. hurricanes have a clearly defined eye on satellite photographs.

23.   The main source of energy for a hurricane is the
       a. upper-level jet stream.
       b. rising of warm air and sinking of cold air in the vicinity of weather fronts.
 *   c. warm ocean water and release of latent heat energy by condensation.
       d. ocean currents and tides.

24.   Which below is not an atmospheric condition conducive to the formation of hurricanes?
       a. a region of converging surface winds at the surface
       b. warm water
 *   c. strong upper-level winds
       d. cold air aloft
       e. moist, humid surface air

25.   Which below forms only over water?
       a. thunderstorms
       b. tornadoes
       c. mesocyclones
 *   d. hurricanes

26.   Hurricanes dissipate when
       a. they move over colder water.
       b. they move over land.
       c. surface inflow of air exceeds upper-level outflow of air.
 *   d. all of the above.

27.   The first three stages of a developing hurricane are (from first stage to third stage)
       a. tropical disturbance, tropical storm, typhoon.
       b. tropical depression, tropical disturbance, tropical storm.
 *   c. tropical disturbance, tropical depression, tropical storm.
       d. cyclone, typhoon, tropical storm.

28.   A tropical storm becomes a hurricane when
       a. a clear eye becomes visible on a satellite photograph.
       b. the central pressure drops below 950 mb.
 *   c. the winds exceed 64 knots (74 MPH).
       d. it reaches Category 3 on the Saffir-Simpson scale.

29.   As a northward-moving hurricane passes to the east of an area, surface winds should change from
       a. NW to N to NE.
       b. W to SW to S.
 *   c. NE to N to NW.
       d. S to SW to W.

30.   Which method below describes how scientists have tried to modify hurricanes?
       a. putting an oil slick over the ocean water and igniting it
 *   b. seeding the hurricanes with silver iodide
       c. igniting huge smoke bombs in the eye of the storm
       d. seeding the hurricanes with hair-thin pieces of aluminum called chaff

31.   Which of the following areas in the United States would most likely experience thunderstorms, hurricanes and tornadoes during the course of one year?
        a. Pacific Coast states
        b. New England states
*   c. Gulf Coast states
        d. Great Plains states

32.   Which statement below is <u>not</u> correct concerning hurricanes?
        a. they may contain tornadoes
        b. they may contain severe thunderstorms
*   c. a hurricane moving northward over the Pacific will normally survive for a longer time than one moving north over the Atlantic
        d. a weakening hurricane can move up to middle latitudes and turn into an extratropical cyclone

33.   On the Saffir-Simpson hurricane scale, a hurricane with winds in excess of 155 mi/hr (135 knots) and a central pressure of 910 mb (26.87 in.) would be classified as a category ____ hurricane.
        a. 1
        b. 2
        c. 3
        d. 4
*   e. 5

34.   Which below is the best indication that a hurricane will likely strike your area within 24 hours?
        a. a hurricane watch issued by the National Weather Service
        b. high cirrus clouds moving in from the east
*   c. a hurricane warning issued by the National Weather Service
        d. easterly or northeasterly winds with speeds in excess of 30 knots
        e. a rapid drop in pressure and heavy rains

35.   On the Saffir-Simpson scale a category 5 storm would indicate
        b. a weak hurricane.
        b. a moderately strong hurricane.
*   c. a very strong hurricane.
        d. none of the above, the Saffir-Simpson scale applies to tornadoes.

36.   The term storm surge refers to
        a. the leading edge of a hurricane.
        b. a higher-than-average incidence of tropical storm occurrence.
*   c. a rise in ocean level of several meters or more.
        d. the increasing speed of a hurricane as it moves in the middle latitudes.

37.   The strongest winds in a hurricane heading westward toward Florida would most likely be found on the ____ side.
*   a. northern
        b. southern
        c. eastern
        d. western

38.   Most of the destruction caused by a hurricane is due to
        a. high winds.
*   b. flooding.
        c. lightning.
        d. tornadoes.

39. A hurricane warning
    a. gives the exact location where a hurricane will make landfall.
    b. is usually issued several days ahead of a hurricane's arrival.
* c. gives the percent chance of a hurricane's center passing within 65 miles of a community.
    d. is issued when a hurricane approaches to within 500 miles of the US mainland.
    e. is issued whenever surface wind speeds exceed 74 mi/hr.

40. Along a coastline, most hurricane damage is caused by
    a. the pressure gradient force.
* b. the storm surge.
    c. wind shear.
    d. release of latent heat.

41. A rise in ocean levels along a coastline caused by an approaching hurricane.
    a. rip tide
    b. tsunami
* c. storm surge
    d. easterly wave

42. The ____ is a measure of hurricane strength based on hurricane winds and central pressure.
    a. Fujita scale
    b. Richter scale
* c. Saffir-Simpson scale
    d. Beaufort scale

43. Which of the following is true?
    a. hurricanes are given only male names
    b. hurricanes are given only female names
* c. hurricanes are alternately assigned male and female names
    d. Atlantic hurricanes are given male names and Pacific hurricanes are given female names

44. Storms that form in the tropics are given names when
* a. they reach tropical storm strength.
    b. they become fully developed hurricanes.
    c. they approach to within 250 miles of land.
    d. rotation becomes visible on a satellite photograph.

True False Exam Questions

1. Hurricane development is more likely when the trade wind inversion is well developed.
   (ans: FALSE)

2. There is a reduction in the number of Atlantic hurricanes during a major El Niño event.
   (ans: TRUE)

3. If a hurricane remains over warm water of sufficient depth, it may survive for several weeks.
   (ans: TRUE)

4. Lows that develop over polar waters during the winter exhibit many of the characteristics of a hurricane and are sometimes referred to as Arctic hurricanes.
   (ans: TRUE)

5. Despite there being many differences in structure, if a weakening hurricane links up with an upper-level trough it may actually become a mid-latitude cyclone.
(ans: TRUE)

6. Statistical models that compare a present hurricane with similar storms in the past have been very successfully used to forecast changes in a hurricane's intensity.
(ans: FALSE)

7. Most hurricanes develop in warm tropical waters at the Equator even though the Coriolis force is zero there.
(ans: FALSE)

8. Because hurricanes are somewhat more frequent there, the yearly list of names adopted for Eastern Pacific hurricanes is somewhat longer than the list for North Atlantic hurricanes.
(ans: TRUE)

9. The terms typhoon and cyclone refer to the initial weaker stages in the development of a hurricane.
(ans: FALSE)

10. The name of a particular memorable or damaging hurricane will not be used again for a period of at least ten years.
(ans: TRUE)

Word Choice Exam Questions

1. Hurricane development is more likely when preexisting upper-level winds are STRONG WEAK . (circle one answer)
(ans: WEAK)

2. Tropical cyclone development is most likely in a region where surface winds CONVERGE DIVERGE. (circle one answer)
(ans: CONVERGE)

3. Hurricanes are WARM COLD core lows. (circle one answer)
(ans: WARM)

4. In a hurricane are the fastest winds and strongest thunderstorms found closer to the CENTER or the outer EDGE of the storm? (circle one answer)
(ans: CENTER)

5. Cloud seeding has been used in attempts to INCREASE DECREASE the diameter of the eye wall and thereby weaken hurricanes. (circle one answer)
(ans: INCREASE)

6. In a hurricane moving northward along the Atlantic coast of the United States, the strongest winds will be on the EAST WEST side. (circle one answer)
(ans: EAST)

7. From 1953 to 1977, the Weather Service used just MALE FEMALE names for hurricanes. (circle one answer)
(ans: FEMALE)

8. In most tropical regions the seasons are marked by differences in TEMPERATURE PRECIPITATION. (circle one answer)
(ans: PRECIPITATION)

9. Does the temperature difference between the ocean and cloud top determine the maximum strength of a storm in the HEAT ENGINE or the ORGANIZED CONVECTION representation of a hurricane. (circle one answer)
    (ans: HEAT ENGINE)

10. The hurricane path shown in the figure at right suggests the storm is moving around a center of HIGH LOW pressure. (circle one answer)
    (ans: HIGH)

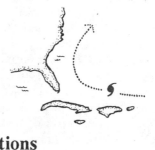

Short Answer Exam Questions

1. Hurricane _____, which crossed south Florida in 1992, is the costliest natural disaster in United States history.
    (ans: ANDREW)

2. More than 6000 people were killed in Texas in 1900 when a hurricane struck _____.
    (ans: GALVESTON)

3. Over 11,000 people were killed in Central America in October, 1998, by the strong winds, huge waves, and torrential rains produced by hurricane _____.
    (ans: MITCH)

4. Considerable damage may be caused by _____ that tend to form in the right front quadrant of an advancing hurricane.
    (ans: TORNADOES)

5. The clear eye in the center of a hurricane is produced by _____ air.
    (ans: SINKING)

6. The eye wall is a ring of intense _____ that surround the center of a hurricane.
    (ans: THUNDERSTORMS)

7. Hurricanes derive their energy from transfer of sensible and _____ heat from warm tropical oceans into the atmosphere.
    (ans: LATENT)

8. The last Atlantic hurricane of 1999 was named Lenny. The name of the first hurricane in 2000 will start with the letter _____.
    (ans: A)

9. The storm surge can be especially damaging when it coincides with _____.
    (ans: HIGH TIDE)

10. Lines on a map showing the direction of wind flow are called _____.
    (ans: STREAMLINES)

Essay Exam Questions

1. In what ways do weather conditions in the tropics and at middle latitudes differ?

2. With sketches show the structure of a mature hurricane as it would appear from the side and from above. Indicate and label the major features.

3. From where do hurricanes derive their energy? What factors tend to weaken hurricanes? Would you expect a hurricane to weaken more quickly if it moved over land or over cooler water?

4. Very heavy rainfall amounts are often recorded when a hurricane or tropical storm moves over land. Why do these storms produce so much rain?

5. List and describe some of the conditions that are favorable to hurricane development. What atmospheric conditions inhibit hurricane formation and growth?

6. Would you expect hurricanes in the Southern Hemisphere to be any different from hurricanes in the Northern Hemisphere?

7. Hurricane season for the tropical North Atlantic and North Pacific oceans normally runs from June through November. Why don't hurricanes form in these locations at other times of the year?

8. Describe a hurricane as completely as you can by giving typical values for the following characteristics: diameter, location and size of the eye, direction of rotation and speed of winds, central pressure, direction and speed of movement, duration. When and where do hurricanes form?

9. Where is the Bermuda high located during the summer and fall? How might the path of a hurricane, moving toward the west from Africa, be affected by the Bermuda High as the hurricane approaches the United States?

10. List some of the other names given to hurricanes in other parts of the world. Where are these different names used?

11. In your opinion do hurricanes pose the greatest threat to the east or west coast of the United States? Explain.

12. Even though more hurricanes form, on average, over the Eastern Pacific than over the tropical North Atlantic, we generally hear less about them. Why do you think this is so?

13. In recent years, the number of deaths caused by hurricanes has decreased, but the cost of hurricane damage has increased. How would you explain this?

14. Why are hurricanes so destructive? List some of the hazards associated with a hurricane.

15. What is a storm surge? How does a storm surge form?

Chapter 12
Air Pollution

Summary

Air pollutants and air pollution meteorology are covered in detail in this chapter. Many concepts introduced earlier in the text, such as atmospheric stability and small scale wind circulation patterns, are relevant to this topic and are integrated into the discussion.

The chapter begins with a brief historical review of air pollution. Many students will be surprised, perhaps, to see that concern over air pollution dates back to the 13th century. Students may also be unaware of the very serious air pollution events that occurred earlier in this century in Europe and the United States. The London smog of 1952, for example, remains today the world's worst air pollution disaster.

Sources and environmental effects of the primary air pollutants, carbon monoxide, sulfur dioxide, nitrogen oxides, particulate matter, and volatile organic compounds are discussed next. Tropospheric ozone, a pollutant and component of photochemical smog, is discussed together with stratospheric ozone in this chapter. The pollutant standards index provides a quantitative, readily understood measure of air quality. We see that while air quality has improved following the passage of clean air legislation, many urban areas still frequently exceed these standards. Weather conditions, local topography, and urban environment can all influence the buildup of air pollutants in particular regions. The chapter concludes with a discussion of acid deposition.

Key Terms

(Listed in approximately the same order they appear in the text. Terms in boldface are emphasized and appear at the end of the chapter in the text.)

air pollutants
fixed sources
mobile sources
primary air pollutants
secondary air pollutants
particulate matter
aerosols
Arctic haze
wet haze
carbon monoxide (CO)
hemoglobin
sulfur dioxide (SO$_2$)
sulfur trioxide (SO$_3$)
sulfuric acid (H$_2$SO$_4$)
**volatile organic
   compounds (VOCs)**
hydrocarbons
carcinogens
nitrogen dioxide (NO$_2$)

nitric oxide (NO)
oxides of nitrogen
smog
photochemical reactions
photochemical smog
Los Angeles-type smog
London-type smog
ozone (O$_3$)
stratospheric ozone
tropospheric ozone
PAN (peroxyacetyl
   nitrate)
photochemical oxidants
chlorofluorocarbons (CFCs)
chlorine
Montreal Protocol
hydrochlorofluorocarbons (HCFCs)
hydrofluorocarbons (HFCs)
ozone hole

National Ozone
   Expedition (NOZE-1)
polar vortex
polar stratospheric clouds
primary ambient air
   quality standards
secondary standards
nonattainment areas
pollutant standards
   index (PSI)
radiation (surface) inversion
subsidence inversion
mixing layer
mixing depth
fanning smoke plume
fumigation
looping smoke plume
atmospheric stagnation
urban heat island

country breeze   dry deposition   **acid deposition**
METROMEX (Metropolitan   wet deposition   **acid fog**
     Meteorological Experiment)   **acid rain**   pH scale

Teaching Suggestions, Demonstrations, and Visual Aids

1.   Heat a small piece of coal using a propane torch in class. The burning coal will often produce a lot of black smoke and a pungent, sulfurous odor. Students will get a better appreciation of how unhealthy conditions must have been during the London smog episodes.

2.   Effective classroom demonstrations of some of the common reactions in air pollution chemistry have been given by J. L. Hollenberg *et al.* (ref: "Demonstrating the Chemistry of Air Pollution," *J. Chem. Educ., 64*, 893-894, 1987).

3.   It is a relatively easy matter to dissolve carbon dioxide gas in water and show, using an acid/base indicator solution, that this turns the water acidic. Bromothymol blue is an indicator that turns yellow in an acid, blue in a base, and green in a neutral solution.

     Fill three beakers with distilled water and add a sufficient quantity of bromothymol blue to each to turn the color of the water a deep green. Add white vinegar to one beaker and ammonia to another. The water in these beakers will turn yellow and a blue, respectively.

     Fill a fourth beaker with distilled water and add a small amount of baking soda to make the water slightly alkaline (in some parts of the country, tap water is already alkaline and can be used). Add some bromothymol blue indicator to the water. Next add a few small pieces of dry ice to a flask with a side spout. Stopper the flask and connect a small piece of flexible tubing to the side arm of the flask. Immerse the other end of the tubing in the beaker containing the water. As the dry ice sublimates, the CO_2 gas will bubble throught the water and slowly make it acidic. The changing color of the indicator solution will show that this conversion is taking place.

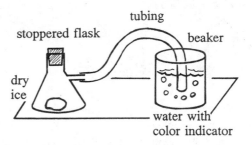

Student Projects

1.   A daily air quality summary is given in many local papers. Have students report on conditions in their location. What emissions are of most concern? What are the primary sources of these emissions? How do the reported values correlate with observed atmospheric conditions, visibility, and synoptic weather conditions?

2.   Have students investigate and report on measures being taken locally to reduce air pollution. This might include carpooling, subsidized bus passes or other use of mass transit, use of oxygenated fuels during certain times of the year, vehicle emissions inspections, and home fire place no-burn nights.

Multiple Choice Exam Questions

1.   The following toxic gas was an important component in London's smoke fogs.
     a. ozone (O_3)
*   b. sulfur dioxide (SO_2)
     c. radon (Rn)
     d. carbon monoxide (CO)

2. The smoke in London smogs came primarily from
   a. exhaust from diesel engines.
   b. trash fires.
   c. factories in Eastern Europe.
   * d. coal combustion.

3. The Great London Smog of 1952 remains today the world's worst air pollution disaster; 4000 deaths were blamed on high levels of
   a. ozone (O_3)
   b. carbon monoxide (CO)
   * c. sulfur dioxide (SO_2)
   d. chlorine (Cl)

4. Which of the following is not true of fine particulate matter (particles less than one micrometer in diameter) in the atmosphere?
   a. particles may remain suspended in the atmosphere for several weeks
   * b. particles are not readily removed from the atmosphere by rain and snow
   c. particles are small enough to penetrate into the lungs
   d. particles can cause a significant reduction in visibility

5. Collectively, particles of soot, smoke, dust and pollen are called
   a. hydrocarbons.
   * b. aerosols.
   c. carcinogens.
   d. haze.

6. Which of the following statements is not true of carbon monoxide (CO)?
   a. replaces oxygen in the blood's hemoglobin
   * b. is removed slowly from the atmosphere
   c. is produced by the incomplete combustion of carbon-containing fuels
   d. roughly half of the CO in the atmosphere is produced by automobiles

7. Which of the following gases will replace oxygen in blood hemoglobin and thereby reduce the transport of oxygen to the brain?
   a. sulfur dioxide (SO_2)
   * b. carbon monoxide (CO)
   c. carbon dioxide (CO_2)
   d. methane (CH_4)

8. Volcanoes are an important natural source of
   a. chlorofluorocarbons.
   b. ozone.
   * c. sulfur dioxide.
   d. carbon monoxide.

9. Photochemical smog is also termed
   a. London-type smog.
   b. subsidence smog.
   c. mixing layer smog.
   d. sea breeze smog.
   * e. Los Angeles-type smog.

10.   Which of the following gases is an example of a volatile organic compound or hydrocarbon?
a. sulfur dioxide
b. carbon dioxide
 * c. methane
d. ozone

11.   Nitrogen dioxide (NO_2) reacts with ___ in the atmosphere to form nitric acid (HNO_3).
a. hydrogen
 * b. water vapor
c. ozone
d. carbon dioxide

12.   A primary component of photochemical smog is
 * a. ozone.
b. carbon monoxide.
c. sulfur dioxide.
d. chlorofluorocarbons.

13.   If the concentration of stratospheric ozone were to decrease, which of the following might also occur?
a. less absorption of ultraviolet radiation in the stratosphere
b. an increase in the number of cases of skin cancer
c. the stratosphere would cool
d. more ultraviolet radiation would be absorbed at the earth's surface
 * e. all of the above

14.   Once released into the atmosphere, chlorofluorocarbons remain for about
a. 10 days.
 * b. 100 years.
c. 1 year.
d. 1 month.

15.   In 1978, the United States banned the non-essential use of chlorofluorocarbons (CFCs). This was because
a. CFCs are a primary component of photochemical smog.
b. CFCs are toxic gases.
 * c. CFCs reduce the ozone concentration in the stratosphere.
d. CFCs react with water vapor to form acid rain.

16.   Polar stratospheric clouds form above Antarctica when ___ in the stratosphere is ___.
a. temperature, high
 * b. temperature, low
c. pressure, high
d. pressure, low

17.   Polar stratospheric clouds play a role in
a. global warming.
 * b. ozone destruction.
c. photochemical smog.
d. acid rain formation.

18.   The term "ozone hole" refers to a ___ decrease in ozone concentration.
a. permanent
 * b. yearly
c. monthly
d. daily

19.   HFCs and HCFCs are
       a. the primary components of photochemical smog.
*   b. replacements for CFCs.
       c. clean-burning fossil fuels.
       d. cancer-causing chemicals produced by automobiles.

20.   You might expect high levels of chlorine monoxide (ClO) to be associated with
       a. volcanic activity.
       b. global warming.
*   c. destruction of stratospheric ozone.
       d. vehicular traffic in urban areas.

21.   A pollutant standards index value of 35 on a particular day would indicate ___ conditions.
*   a. good
       b. unhealthful
       c. extremely hazardous
       d. moderately hazardous

22.   Air becomes unhealthy when the pollutant standards index reaches
       a. 1.
       b. 3.
       c. 10.
*   d. 100.

23.   Overall, the air in Los Angeles is ___ it was 10 years ago.
*   a. less polluted today than
       b. more humid today than
       c. about as polluted today as
       d. significantly denser today than
       e. more polluted today than

       Questions 24 - 26 refer
       to the adjacent diagram.

24.   The mixing depth, shown in
       the diagram, is about how
       many meters thick?
       a. 0
*   b. 100
       c. 200
       d. 400

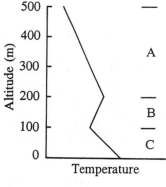

25.   The mixing layer, in the diagram, is found
       a. in layer A.
       b. in layer B.
*   c. in layer C.
       d. above layer A.

26.   In the diagram, the greatest concentration of pollutants would be found
       a. in layer A.
       b. in layer B.
*   c. in layer C.
       d. above layer A.

27. A mixing layer is characterized by
*   a. enhanced vertical air motions.
     b. suppressed vertical air motions.
     c. strong horizontal winds.
     d. high concentrations of pollutants.

28. Which of the following conditions would act to prevent a high concentration buildup of pollutants near the surface?
     a. light surface winds
     b. a strong subsidence inversion
     c. a large, slow-moving anticyclone
*   d. a deep mixing layer

29. Pollution is most severe in urban areas when
     a. a cold upper-level low moves into a region.
     b. a warm front passes through the area.
*   c. a large slow-moving anticyclone moves into an area.
     d. a storm system begins developing to the west.
     e. a cold front passes through the area.

30. Atmospheric stagnation is a condition normally brought on by
     a. thunderstorms.
*   b. slow-moving anticyclones.
     c. overcast skies.
     d. tall buildings in a city.
     e. movement of an upper level trough overhead.

31. Which of the following over a fairly long duration would probably result in polluted conditions?
     a. a radiation inversion
*   b. a subsidence inversion
     c. persistent winds
     d. overcast skies

32. Which of the following contribute(s) to the formation of an urban heat island?
     a. a large part of the incident sunlight in rural areas is used to evaporate water in vegetation and the soil.
     b. heat is released by vehicles in urban areas.
     c. heat is released slowly in cities at night.
*   d. all of the above.

33. On clear, cold winter nights, cities tend to cool ____ than rural areas and have ____ minimum temperatures.
*   a. more slowly, higher
     b. more quickly, higher
     c. more slowly, lower
     d. more quickly, lower

34. A country breeze would probably be associated with
     a. a large high-pressure areas that forms over the city.
     b. a hot and humid summer day in a large city.
     c. a period of heavy rain that falls over a city.
*   d. a strong heat island.

35. A country breeze blows
    a. from the city toward the country at night.
    b. from the city toward the country during the day.
  * c. from the country toward the city at night.
    d. from the country toward the city during the day.

36. A decline in the health of forests in Germany has been attributed to
    a. erosion caused by excessive lumber cutting.
  * b. acid rain.
    c. increased CO_2 concentrations and global warming.
    d. urbanization.

37. The problem of acid rain is probably most severe in which of the following regions?
    a. Gulf Coast
  * b. New England
    c. Desert Southwest
    d. Pacific Northwest
    e. Central Plains

38. Rain with a pH of 5.6 would be considered
  * a. acidic.
    b. alkaline.
    c. neutral.
    d. polluted.
    e. harmful.

39. Erosion of many limestone buildings, fountains and sculptures is being caused largely by
  * a. acid rain.
    b. ozone.
    c. vibrations caused by automobile traffic.
    d. urban heat island.

True False Exam Questions

1. Transportation accounts for nearly 50% (by weight) of the pollution acros the United States.
   (ans: TRUE)

2. Particles with diameters less than 1 micrometer can remain suspended in the atmosphere for several weeks.
   (ans: TRUE)

3. Dry haze scatters more sunlight than wet haze and causes a more noticeably drop in visiblity.
   (ans: FALSE)

4. Carbon monoxide (CO) has a strong pungent odor that warns of its presence before concentrations can build to dangerous levels.
   (ans: FALSE)

5. Carbon monoxide is removed quickly from the atmosphere by microorganisms in the soil.
   (ans: TRUE)

6. The Arctic stratosphere is normally too cold to allow formation of the clouds that help activate ozone-destroying chlorine.
   (ans: FALSE)

7. A radiation inversion will generally persist for a longer period of time than a subsidence inversion.
   (ans: FALSE)

8. A looping smoke plume like that shown at right indicates relatively unstable atmospheric conditions.
   (ans: TRUE)

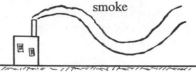

9. A country breeze will carry pollutants into the heart of a city and cause an increase in concentrations.
   (ans: TRUE)

10. Oxides of nitrogen from automobile exhaust appear to be the main cause of acid rain in the Northeastern United States.
    (ans: FALSE)

Word Choice Exam Questions

1. A pollutant that reaches peak concentration everyday between 1:00 and 3:00 in the afternoon is probably a PRIMARY SECONDARY pollutant. (circle one answer)
   (ans: SECONDARY)

2. Is ozone a component of LONDON-TYPE or LOS ANGELES-TYPE smog? (circle one answer)
   (ans: LOS ANGELES-TYPE)

3. You would expect to find the highest tropospheric ozone concentrations on a SUNNY CLOUDY day. (circle one answer)
   (ans: SUNNY)

4. There is currently concern about INCREASING DECREASING concentrations of ozone in the troposphere and INCREASING DECREASING concentrations of ozone in the stratosphere. (choose one word from each pair)
   (ans: INCREASING, DECREASING)

5. The ozone hole refers to a SEASONAL PERMANENT decrease in ozone concentrations in the TROPOSPHERE STRATOSPHERE above the SOUTH NORTH pole. (choose one word from each pair)
   (ans: SEASONAL, STRATOSPHERE, SOUTH)

6. Does the HFC or HCFC family of compounds pose the smallest risk to the earth's ozone layer? (circle one answer)
   (ans: HFC)

7. Do the chlorofluorocarbons (CFCs) in the atmosphere come from NATURAL or MAN-MADE sources? (circle one answer)
   (ans: MAN-MADE)

8. Subsidence inversions are produced by RISING SINKING air motions. (circle one answer)
   (ans: SINKING)

9. The serious air pollution disasters mentioned in the text were associated with stationary centers of HIGH LOW pressure. (circle one answer)
   (ans: HIGH)

10. Would a pH value of 3.2 be considered ACIDIC, NEUTRAL, or BASIC? (circle one answer)
    (ans: ACIDIC)

11. Some studies suggest that cities might modify their local climate and cause   MORE LESS precipitation to fall in the city than in the surrounding countryside. (circle one answer)
(ans: MORE)

Short Answer Exam Questions

1. Precipitation is naturally somewhat acidic (pH 5.0 to 5.6) because it contains dissolved _____.
(ans: CARBON DIOXIDE)

2. Downwind of a coal-fired power generation plant you might expect to find high _____ concentrations which might lead to the formation of acid rain.
(ans: SULFUR DIOXIDE (SO_2))

3. Methane (CH_4) is a common, naturally occurring example of this class of chemical compounds.
(ans: VOLATILE ORGANIC COMPOUNDS (VOCs) or HYDROCARBONS)

4. Photochemical reactions take place in the presence of _____.
(ans: SUNLIGHT)

5. _____ are formed when the two most abundant gases in the atmosphere react during high temperature combustion.
(ans: OXIDES OF NITROGEN)

6. Sherwood Rowland and Mario Molina were awarded the Nobel Prize for their work on _____.
(ans: OZONE DESTRUCTION BY CFCs)

7. The term smog was used for the first time in _____ to describe mixture of smoke and fog common there.
(ans: LONDON)

8. In the late 1970s, the United States banned all nonessential uses of _____ which were at the time widely used as propellants in spray cans.
(ans: CHLOROFLUOROCARBONS (CFCs))

9. While _____ are rapidly being phased out in accordance with international agreements, they are readily available on the black market.
(ans: CHLOROFLUOROCARBONS (CFCs))

10. Cities are generally warmer than the surrounding rural areas. This region of city warmth is referred to as a(n) _____.
(ans: URBAN HEAT ISLAND)

11. The control of _____ is problematic because it is a secondary pollutant and its formation depends on the concentrations of other pollutants such as oxides of nitrogen and hydrocarbons.
(ans: TROPOSPHERIC OZONE)

12. _____ is eroding the foundations of many stone structure, monuments, and statues throughout the world.
(ans: ACID DEPOSITION or ACID RAIN)

Essay Exam Questions

1. List several atmospheric pollutants. What are the most important sources and environmental or health effects of these pollutants?

2.   What atmospheric conditions would you expect to find associated with a major air pollution episode?

3.   A Stage 1 health advisory alert is issued when PSI values for a particular pollutant fall in the range from 200 to 299. Who might be adversely affected by such an event? What measures should these people take to minimize the health risks to them?

4.   Explain why locating industrial facilities on the perimeter of a city might not always prevent air pollution in the city.

5.   What is the urban heat island effect? How could an urban heat island affect atmospheric conditions nearby?

6.   How can topography contribute to pollution in a city or region?

7.   Would you expect to find the same environmental conditions upwind and downwind of a large city? Explain.

8.   What causes acid rain? What are some of the environmental concerns associated with acid rain? Are problems with acid rain confined to a small area or do they extend over a large region?

9.   Describe some of the measures that are being taken to reduce the problem of acid precipitation.

10.   Is the ozone that is found near the earth's surface a primary or a secondary pollutant? When during the day would you expect to find the peak concentrations of ozone? What are some of the environmental concerns associated with ozone?

11.   How does Los Angeles-type smog differ from London-type smog?

12.   How do you think pollutants are removed from the atmosphere? Does this occur quickly or slowly?

13.   Describe some of the ways an industrial facility that is constructed in or near a large urban area could attempt to reduce emissions of air pollutants.

14.   Describe how the use of a tall smoke stack might improve air quality near a large industrial facility.

15.   Would you expect the concentrations of air pollutants to vary significantly during the day in the city where you live? If so, when would you expect to find the highest concentrations of pollutants?

Chapter 13
Global Climate

Summary

This chapter examines the different climatic regions found on the earth. The primary emphasis is on global scale climates, but micro- and macroscale climates are also mentioned briefly. The chapter reviews the factors that affect and determine the climate of a particular region. These climatic controls include seasonal and latitudinal variations in incident sunlight, proximity to land or sea, ocean and wind currents, and topographical effects. Global distributions of mean temperature and annual precipitation amounts are presented and form the basis for climate classification using the Köppen system.

Each of the five major climatic types in the Köppen classification system are discussed in detail. Examples of yearly temperature variations and monthly precipitation amounts are given for a representative location in each group and for the major sub-categories. A tropical climate, for example, is characterized by abundant rainfall and very little seasonal variation in mean temperature. Seasonal changes are much larger at middle latitudes, and several different climate zones can be identified depending on whether summers are warm or cool, dry or moist, and by the severity of the winter. Arid zones are found on the earth in areas dominated by subtropical high pressure systems or in the rain shadow of large mountain ranges.

Key Terms
(Listed in approximately the same order they appear in the text. Terms in boldface are emphasized and appear at the end of the chapter in the text.)

microclimate
mesoclimate
macroclimate
global climate
climatic controls
orographic uplift
rain shadow
Köppen classification system
tropical moist climates (Group A)
tropical rain forest
tropical wet climate (Af)
climograph
leaching
laterite
tropical monsoon climate (Am)
tropical wet-and-dry climate (Aw)

savannah grass
monsoon
dry climates (Group B)
arid climate (BW)
xerophyte
semi-arid climate (BS)
steppe
moist subtropical mid-latitude climates (Group C)
humid subtropical climate (Cfa)
west coast marine climate
marine climate (Cfb)
dry-summer subtropical (Mediterranean) climate (Cs)
coastal Mediterranean climate (Csb)
interior Mediterranean climate (Csa)
chaparral

moist continental climates (Group D)
humid continental climates (Dfa & Dfb)
subpolar climates (Dfc)
humid continental with hot summers (Dfa)
humid continental with long cool summers (Dfb)
taiga
boreal climate
taiga climate
polar climates (Group E)
polar tundra (ET)
permafrost
tundra vegetation
polar ice cap (EF)
highland climates (Group H)

Teaching Suggestions, Demonstrations, and Visual Aids

1.   Initially, the variety of labels used for the major groups and subcategories in the Köppen classification system will be confusing to students. Keep a map, such as Figure 13.6, displayed throughout the discussion and use a specific city or region to illustrate each climatic zone.

        Encourage students to learn the classification groups by understanding the differences between them and the cause of those differences. Show how climate depends on latitude by observing the changes that occur as one moves in a line from the equator toward the North Pole at constant longitude. Then examine how climate is modified as one moves from west to east across the United States at a single middle latitude. Show where features in the global circulation such as the subtropical highs and the ITCZ are located at various times during the year and explain how these affect climate.

2.   Present and discuss representative examples (plots of average temperature and monthly precipitation totals) of each of the important climate types. List one or two of the key characteristics that can be used to distinquish between the different climate classifications. Then present some new data, but do not reveal the location where the data was obtained. Ask the students how these data would be classified. Then ask the students where, within a particular region such as the United States, these data might have been obtained. After a period of discussion, reveal the actual location.

Student Projects

1.   Have students collect and prepare a plot of yearly average temperature data and average monthly precipitation totals for their city. How would their town be classified using the Köppen system?

2.   Have students attempt to locate different macroscale climate regions in the city where they live. The students will have to devise a system to be used to identify and classify different climate zones. Students could, for example, compare average conditions in high- and low-lying areas in their town, average conditions near and far from a body of water, or conditions inside a city with conditions in a rural area nearby. Are there significant differences in macroscale climates in their city? Are any differences reflected in the types of vegetation found at different locations within the city.

3.   Have the students look for different microscale climatic environments. Students could, for example, compare average conditions on the north- and south-facing sides of a large building. Students would have to determine what measurements or observations could be made to identify and classify different microscale environments.

4.   In some locations, students could identify and classify the different climatic zones found at different altitudes on a nearby mountain range. Students could, for example, determine the predominant vegetation types at different levels and attempt to relate this seasonal temperature and precipitation variations.

5.   Students might examine how or whether parameters such as the primary agricultural product in a region, energy consumption, population density or life expectancy depend on climate.

Multiple Choice Exam Questions

1.   Microclimate refers to the
        a. climate of a valley or forest.
        b. climatic conditions inside a house or building.
        c. climatic changes that occur over a short period of time.
   *   d. small climatic region near the ground.
        e. climate of an area about the size of a town.

2.
*
The climate of an area about the size of a town would be described as
a. mesoclimate.
b. macroclimate.
c. microclimate.
d. urban climate.

3.
Which of the following is considered a climatic control?
a. ocean currents
b. intensity of sunshine and its variation with latitude
c. prevailing winds
d. altitude
*
e. all of the above

4.
Which section of the United States is most likely to experience a persistent subsidence inversion during the summer?
*
a. Pacific Coastal regions
b. Central Plains
c. Southern Florida
d. Atlantic Coastal regions
e. Midwest

5.
Which of the following cities would most likely have a dry summer?
a. Chicago, Illinois
b. Denver, Colorado
*
c. Los Angeles, California
d. Baltimore, Maryland
e. Seattle, Washington

6.
A rainshadow desert is normally found
a. in the center of a large surface anticyclone.
b. on the back (western) side of a large thunderstorm.
c. in polar regions where the air is cold and dry.
d. in the center of the ITCZ.
*
e. on the downwind side of a mountain range.

7.
The greatest likelihood of experiencing a dry month of February would be along
a. the equator.
*
b. the west coast of Mexico (latitude 20 °N).
c. the Southern California coast (latitude 35 °N).
d. the Gulf Coast near New Orleans (latitude 30 °N).
e. the coast of southern Alaska (latitude 60 °N).

8.
The rainiest places in the world are usually located
a. downwind from mountain ranges.
b. in the region of the subtropical highs.
*
c. on the windward side of mountains.
d. in the middle of continents.
e. along the western side of continents.

9.
The lowest average temperatures in the world occur in
a. Northwestern Europe.
b. the Arctic.
*
c. the Antarctic.
d. Northern Siberia.

10. Which of the following help explain why the lowest average temperatures in the world are found in Antarctica?
    a. dry air
    b. high altitude
    c. surface reflects incident sunlight
  * d. all of the above

11. The Köppen scheme for classifying climates employs annual and monthly averages of
  * a. temperature and precipitation.
    b. precipitation and stream runoff.
    c. ocean levels and surface pressure.
    d. population density and agricultural output.
    e. sunshine and soil type.

12. Which letter below is not used to represent one of Köppen's climatic types?
    a. A
    b. B
    c. C
  * d. G
    e. H

13. According to Köppen's classification of climates, tropical climates are designated by the letter
  * a. A.
    b. B.
    c. T.
    d. D.
    e. C.

14. In Köppen's system of classifying climates, dry climates are designated by the letter
    a. A.
  * b. B.
    c. C.
    d. D.
    e. E.

15. The earth's rainforests are found in
    a. humid subtropical (Cfa) climates.
  * b. tropical wet (Af) climates.
    c. tropical wet and dry (Aw) climates.
    d. all of the above.

16. Which below is not characteristic of a tropical wet climate (Af)?
    a. greater temperature variation between day and night than between the warmest and coolest months
       of the year
  * b. extremely high afternoon temperatures, usually much higher than those experienced in middle latitudes
    c. abundant rainfall all year long
    d. afternoon showers and high humidity

17. The term monsoon refers to
    a. the short summer rainy season observed in some locations.
    b. a short dry season.
    c. a period of heavy rainfall produced by thunderstorms.
  * d. a seasonal shift in wind circulation.

18.   The climate classification for a region with average monthly temperatures that remain above 64 °F throughout the year and abundant rainfall, except for a short 1 or 2 month dry period, would probably be
       a. tropical wet (Af).
       b. moist subtropical (Cs).
*   c. tropical monsoon (Am).
       d. humid continental (Dfa).

19.   The tropical wet-and-dry climate is influenced mainly by the
       a. polar front and the subtropical highs.
       b. polar front and the ITCZ.
       c. subtropical highs and polar front.
*   d. ITCZ and subtropical highs.
       e. subtropical highs and polar lows.

20.   Savanna grass would most likely be associated with which climate type?
       a. tropical rainforest (Af)
       b. tropical monsoon (Am)
       c. semi-arid (BS)
*   d. tropical wet-and-dry (Aw)

21.   In a tropical wet-and-dry climate, the dry season occurs with the
       a. high sun period (summer).
*   b. low sun period (winter).
       c. close proximity of the ITCZ.
       d. all of the above

22.   In a dry climate
       a. there are no plants.
*   b. potential evaporation and transpiration exceed precipitation.
       c. there is no precipitation.
       d. air temperatures seldom drop below freezing and days are always hot.
       e. winters are short, but cold.

23.   The most abundant climate type over the face of the earth is
       a. moist tropical climates.
*   b. dry climates.
       c. moist subtropical mid-latitude climates.
       d. moist continental climates.
       e. polar climates.

24.   The highest temperatures in the world occur in
       a. tropical moist climates.
       b. subtropical moist climates.
       c. continental moist climates.
       d. continental dry climates.
*   e. subtropical deserts.

25.   Which climate type would normally have the highest afternoon temperatures during the summer?
       a. A
*   b. B
       c. C
       d. D
       e. E

26.   One would most likely see xerophytes in which climatic type?
       a. A
   *   b. B
       c. C
       d. D
       e. E

27.   Which of the following is an example of a xerophyte?
       a. oak tree
       b. banana tree
   *   c. cactus
       d. tundra

28.   Which of the following climatic regions would probably have the <u>largest daily</u> temperature range?
       a. tropical wet climate
   *   b. arid climate
       c. east coast marine climate
       d. mediterranean climate

29.   Deserts that experience low clouds and drizzle tend to be found mainly
       a. in the center of continents.
       b. in the rain shadow of a mountain.
       c. on the eastern side of continents.
   *   d. on the western side of continents.
       e. on small islands near the equator.

30.   One would most likely experience steppe vegetation in a
   *   a. semi-arid climate.
       b. humid subtropical climate.
       c. marine climate.
       d. subpolar climate.
       e. tropical wet-and-dry climate.

31.   Locations at middle latitudes with monthly average temperatures in the winter that are below 64 °F,
       but above 27 ° F have ____ climates.
   *   a. humid subtropical
       b. moist continental
       c. semi arid
       d. steppe

32.   A humid subtropical climate is found in what region of the United States?
       a. Southwest
   *   b. Southeast
       c. Central Plains
       d. Southern California

33.   A city located on the east coast of the United States with hot, muggy summers and mild winters
       (the average temperature of the coldest month is above 27 °F) has a ____ climate.
   *   a. moist subtropical (Cfa) climate
       b. mediterranean (Cs) climate
       c. tropical wet and dry climate (Aw)
       d. moist continental (Dfa)

34.   To be considered a moist continental climate
       a. winter snowfall must exceed summer rainfall.
*   b. monthly average temperatures must fall below 27 °F during the winter.
       c. total rainfall must exceed 60 inches.
       d. a region must be located more than 500 miles from the nearest ocean.

35.   A city on the west coast of the United States with mild winters and a long cool summer would have
       a ___ climate.
*   a. moist subtropical (Cfb)
       b. tropical wet and dry (Aw)
       c. moist continental (Dfa)
       d. semi arid (BS)

36.   According to Köppen's classification of climates, marine climates are observed in the United States mainly
       along
*   a. the Pacific Northwest coast.
       b. coastal areas of the middle Atlantic states.
       c. the coast of New England.
       d. the Gulf Coast.
       e. coastal margins of Southern California.

37.   Mediterranean climates are characterized by
*   a. cool, wet winters and mild to hot, dry summers.
       b. cold, wet winters and hot, humid summers.
       c. cold, relatively dry winters and mild, humid summers.
       d. mild, wet winters and mild, humid summers.
       e. cold, snowy winters and hot, dry summers.

38.   The primary reason for the dry summer subtropical climate in North America is
       a. that storms do not form in summer.
       b. that the air is too cool to produce adequate precipitation.
*   c. the Pacific high moves north in summer.
       d. the ITCZ moves north in summer.
       e. the Bermuda high intensifies and shifts northward in summer.

39.   One would not expect to experience a D-type climate in
       a. Alaska.
       b. New England.
       c. Southern Canada.
*   d. South America.

40.   Most of Canada lies within which climatic type?
       a. A
       b. B
       c. C
*   d. D
       e. E

41.   Which climate type normally has the largest annual range in temperature?
       a. tropical climates
       b. humid-subtropical climates
       c. polar ice cap climates
*   d. subpolar climates
       e. dry climates

42. A taiga forest would be found in which climatic type?
  a. tropical rainforest
  b. ice cap
  c. polar tundra
  d. humid subtropical
* e. subpolar

43. A region with long, very cold winters and average temperatures that exceed
  50 °F only one or two months during the summer would have ____ climate.
* a. a subpolar (Dfc)
  b. a polar tundra (ET)
  c. a polar ice cap (EF)
  d. an alpine (An)

44. Thawing of an upper layer of permafrost would most likely be observed in which climatic type?
  a. polar ice cap
  b. humid continental with warm summers
  c. humid subtropical
* d. polar tundra

45. Average monthly temperatures that exceed 32 °F but remain below 50 °F is characteristic of
  a. the polar ice cap (EF) climate zone.
  b. the subpolar (Dfc) climate zone.
* c. the polar tundra (ET) climate zone.
  d. alpine (An) climate zone.

46. Tree growth is not possible in a region where
  a. annual precipitation is 20 inches or less.
* b. average monthly temperatures never exceed 50 °F.
  c. average monthly temperatures are sometimes less than 32 °F.
  d. evaporation exceeds total annual precipitation.

47. When the average temperature of the warmest month averages 32 °F or below, Köppen classified this
  as a(n) ____ climate.
  a. subpolar
* b. polar ice cap
  c. polar tundra
  d. arctic

48. When the average temperature of the warmest month of a region averages above freezing, but below 50 °F,
  you might expect to observe what type of vegetation there?
  a. savanna grass
* b. tundra
  c. taiga
  d. none - it's too cold for anything to grow

49. The climate of a city situated high in the mountains of the middle latitudes would, according to Köppen,
  be classified as
  a. tundra.
  b. subpolar.
  c. alpine.
* d. highland.

50.   The variety of climatic zones that one observes on a mountain are due primarily to differences in
       a. atmospheric pressure.
       b. relative humdity.
       c. rainfall amounts.
  *   d. temperature.

True/False Exam Questions

1.   So little sunlight reaches the ground in a tropical rain forest that surface vegetation is scarce.
       (ans: TRUE)

2.   In the tropics, day/night temperature changes are often greater than differences between the warmest and
       coldest months of the year.
       (ans: TRUE)

3.   Leaching is a process that enriches rain forest soils.
       (ans: FALSE)

4.   There are a few locations in the world where average annual rainfall totals exceed 400 inches.
       (ans: TRUE)

5.   To be classified a tropical moist climate (Group A) a region's rainfall must be plentiful and fall uniformly
       throughout the year.
       (ans: FALSE)

6.   Some of the driest places on earth are coastal deserts that are adjacent to large bodies of relatively cool
       water.
       (ans: TRUE)

7.   The term xerophyte refers to plants that are able to survive extended periods of below freezing temperatures.
       (ans: FALSE)

8.   Warm, dry winds that occur frequently throughout the year are characteristic of a Mediterranean climate.
       (ans: FALSE)

9.   The average temperature of the warmest month that occurs during the year is used to distinquish between
       moist continental climates (Group D) and polar climates (Group E).
       (ans: TRUE)

10.   Despite the fact that the average monthly temperature never rises above freezing, a variety of plant types
       is able to survive in a polar ice cap climate.
       (ans: FALSE)

11.   The term boreal climate refers to a subpolar climate.
       (ans: TRUE)

12.   The upper meter of soil will thaw out and become swampy and muddy in a region with a polar tundra
       climate.
       (ans: TRUE)

Word Choice Exam Questions

1. Would LONGITUDE or LATITUDE generally have the greatest effect on a region's climate. (circle one answer)
   (ans: LATITUDE)

2. Do the isotherms on a map of mean annual temperatures usually lie in a NORTH-SOUTH or an EAST-WEST orientation? (circle one answer)
   (ans: EAST-WEST)

3. Do the highest mean temperatures occur where there is persistent HIGH or LOW pressure and CLEAR or CLOUDY skies? (choose one word from each pair)
   (ans: HIGH, CLEAR)

4. The Pacific high found off the West Coast of the United States moves NORTH SOUTH in the summer. (circle one answer)
   (ans: NORTH)

5. Is the greatest summer/winter temperature variation found in the INTERIOR of a continent or along a COASTLINE? (circle one answer)
   (ans: INTERIOR)

6. The coldest region on earth is the NORTH SOUTH pole. (circle one answer)
   (ans: SOUTH)

7. Precipitation is ABUNDANT SCARCE in polar regions. (circle one answer)
   (ans: SCARCE)

8. The figure at right suggests that the prevailing winds blow from the WEST EAST. (circle one answer)
   (ans: EAST)

   West   East

9. Sinking air is best established and the driest conditions are found on the EASTERN WESTERN side of a subtropical high pressure center. (circle one answer)
   (ans: EASTERN)

10. Along the West Coast of the United States, the greatest precipitation amounts occur during the WINTER SUMMER. (circle one answer)
    (ans: WINTER)

11. You might expect to find record TEMPERATURES PRECIPITATION in a mountainous region in the tropics. (circle one answer)
    (ans: PRECIPITATION)

12. You would expect to find a xerophyte in a region with a DRY WET climate. (circle one answer)
    (ans: DRY)

Short Answer Exam Questions

1. The region on the leeward side of a mountain range where precipitation is scarce is called a(n) _____.
   (ans: RAINSHADOW)

2.   The Köppen climate classification system is based on annual and monthly averages of _____ and
     _____.
     (ans: TEMPERATURE, PRECIPITATION)

3.   Köppen related _____ to climate because observation stations were scarce in the early 1900s when
     his classification scheme was first published.
     (ans: TYPES of NATIVE VEGETATION)

4.   In a region with a dry climate, _____ exceeds _____.
     (ans: EVAPORATION and/or TRANSPIRATION, PRECIPITATION)

5.   A seasonal reversal of prevailing winds is referred to as a(n) _____.
     (ans: MONSOON)

6.   A Northern Hemisphere location with a tropical wet-and-dry climate will experience its wet season in the
     summer when the _____ migrates to a position north of the equator.
     (ans: INTERTROPICAL CONVERGENCE ZONE (ITCZ))

7.   In a(n) _____ region one can travel through many climate zones in a relatively short distance.
     (ans: MOUNTAINOUS)

8.   Match each of the climate zones at left below with the appropriate temperatures from the list at right.
     Moist subtropical mid-   a. coldest month below -3° C (27° F),
       latitude climate (Group C)_____   warmest month above 10° C (50° F)
     Moist continental   b. warmest month below 18° C (64° F),
       climate (Group D)_____   coldest month above -3° C (27° F).
     Polar climate (Group E)_____   c. warmest month above 18° C (64° F).
                                                      d. warmest month below 10° C (50° F).

     (ans: B, A, D)

9.   In a polar tundra climate, soil is permanently frozen to depths of hundreds of meters. This condition is
     known as _____.
     (ans: PERMAFROST)

10. Fill in the letters used in the Köppen system to identify each of the following climate types.
     Tropical moist climates _____
     Polar climates _____
     Dry climates _____
     (ans: A, E, B)

Essay Exam Questions

1.   In general, would you expect to find more rainfall on the western side or the eastern side of the subtropical
     high pressure centers? How does this affect climatic conditions along the east and west coast of the United
     States?

2.   The hottest places on earth are not found near the equator in tropical wet climates but rather in arid climate
     regions. Why is this true?

3.   Discuss some of the factors that determine where the wettest places in the world are found.

4.   Each of the five major climates groups in the Köppen system are found somewhere in the United States.
     Identify each of the five groups and suggest a likely region in the United States where each climate type
     could be found.

5.   The greatest one-month rainfall total (366 in.) occurred in Cherrapunji, India, in July of 1861. The greatest 24 hour rainfall total (43 in.) in the United States occurred in Alvin, Texas, on July 25, 1979. The greatest 42 minute rainfall total (12 in.) occurred in Holt, Missouri, on June 22, 1947. What meteorological conditions do you think produced these record precipitation amounts?

6.   What meteorological information is the primary basis for climate classification using the Köppen system?

7.   Make a rough sketch of North America and indicate approximately where the following climatic types would be found:

     tropical moist climates   moist subtropical climates
     dry climates   moist continental climates
     polar climates   highland climates

     List the principal characteristics of each climate type and describe the climatic controls that influence the location of each climatic region shown on your map.

8.   What differences exist between tropical wet (Af), tropical monsoon (Am), and tropical wet and dry (Aw) climates? Would you expect to observe any significant differences in types of vegetation in these different climates groups?

9.   A yearly rainfall of 14 inches in a hot climate will support only sparce vegetation. The same total amount of rain in north central Canada would support a conifer forest. Why is this possible?

10.   How is it possible for regions with a desert climate to be found next to an ocean, which you might expect to be an abundant source of moist air?

11.   Yearly rainfall amounts appear to be most variable in regions with small annual amounts of rainfall. Why is this so?

12.   Where is the Mojave desert located? What factors account for the Mojave desert being found there?

13.   Identify and describe the different climatic zones you would observe if you moved from west to east across the middle of the United States?

14.   The coldest month in a moist subtropical climate (C) remains above 27 °F. In a moist continental climate (D), the coldest month drops below 27 °F and the warmest month exceeds 50 °F. The temperature of the warmest month in a polar climate does not exceed 50 °F. What is the significance of the 27 ° F and 50 °F thresholds?

15.   Seattle, Washington (lat. 47.5 °N) has a coastal mediterranean (Csb) climate. New York, New York (41 °N) has a humid subtropical (Cfa) climate. What differences in climate would you expect to find between these two locations?

Chapter 14
Climate Change

Summary

This chapter explores the subject of climate change and begins with a discussion of some of the experimental techniques such as dendrochronology, analysis of O^{18} and O^{16} ratios in ice and marine sediments, and study of geologic formations, which have been used to infer past climatic conditions. A short history of climate on the earth reveals that large changes in the earth's climate have occurred in the past. Students will be surprised, perhaps, to find that the earth was appreciably warmer 65 million years ago; so warm in fact that polar ice caps did not exist. Ice sheets began to reform about 2 million years ago, at the start of the Pleistocene epoch, and advanced as far south as New York as recently as 18,000 to 22,000 years ago. Important changes in climate have occurred during the past 1000 years; for instance, the Little Ice Age between about 1550 and 1850 had important effects on agriculture and living conditions in Europe.

Several of the suggested causes of climate change are examined. Plate tectonics, for example, might explain climate changes that occur on a time scale of millions of years. Shorter term, 10,000 to 100,000 year, variations might be associated with changes in the earth's orbit around the sun. There is evidence, too, that the sun's output may vary with time and that volcanic eruptions can have relatively short term, but significant, effects on climate.

The present concern that anthropogenic emissions of carbon dioxide and other greenhouse gases are causing global warming is examined. While there seems to have been a small increase in global average temperatures during the past century, we see that, because the response of the oceans to warmer temperatures and increasing CO_2 amounts and the effects of clouds are not well understood, there are large uncertainties in the computer model predictions of future changes. Some of the possible consequences of an increase in average surface temperatures are discussed.

Key Terms

(Listed in approximately the same order they appear in the text. Terms in boldface are emphasized and appear at the end of the chapter in the text.)

alpine glaciers	climatic optimum	**theory of plate tectonics**
continental glaciers	medieval climatic optimum	theory of continental
CLIMAP (Climate long-	**Little Ice Age**	drift
range investigation	"year without a	ridge
mapping and prediction)	summer" (1816)	subduction
isotope	**water vapor-temperature**	degassing
dendrochronology	**rise feedback**	**Milankovitch theory**
Pleistocene epoch	**positive feedback**	**eccentricity**
Ice Age	**mechanism**	**precession**
interglacial period	runaway greenhouse effect	**obliquity**
Bering land bridge	**negative feedback**	forcing factor
Younger-Dryas (event)	**mechanism**	aerosols
Holocene epoch	**snow-albedo feedback**	**sulfate aerosols**
mid-Holocene maximum	runaway ice age	nuclear winter

sunspots	conveyor belt (ocean)	radiative forcing
faculae	thermohaline circulation	**desertification**
Maunder minimum	radiative equilibrium	biogeophysical feedback
(solar) magnetic cycle	**radiative forcing agents**	mechanism

Teaching Suggestions, Demonstrations, and Visual Aids

1.   Climate change is an area of active research at present and receives a lot of coverage on television, in newspapers, and in popular magazines. Use current news or articles to motivate or stimulate discussion in class. *Science News* magazine is a good source of up-to-date information on recent research results. At some universities, it may be possible to bring in guest speakers who will describe their research and how it relates to climate change.

Student Projects

1.   Have students obtain climatological data (mean temperature and precipitation amounts), from their city or a city nearby, for as long a period of time as possible. Are there any noticeable periodic variations or long-term trends? Can any observed fluctuations be correlated with recent volcanic eruptions, strong ENSO events, or the sunspot cycle? Where were the weather data obtained? Has urbanization had any effect on the weather data?

It might be possible to obtain a section from a recently cut tree. Then, if a date can be accurately identified with one of the growth rings, try to determine whether the width of the rings is correlated with past mean annual temperatures or yearly rainfall amounts.

2.   Using a book that describes the local geology, have the students prepare a report on the past climate in their region. If possible, photograph or obtain samples from geological structures that were used to infer past conditions.

3.   Several excellent articles have appeared recently that review recent climate-related research and which could serve as the basis for a student report. See, for example: R.J. Charlson and T.M.L. Wigley, "Sulfate Aerosol and Climate Change," *Sci. Am., 270*, 48-57, Feb. 1994; W.S. Broecker, "Chaotic Climate," *Sci. Am., 273*, 62-28, Nov. 1995; D. Schneider, "The Rising Seas," *Sci. Am., 276*, 112-117, Mar. 1997; T.R. Karl, N. Nicholls, J. Gregory, "The Coming Climate," *Sci. Am., 273*, 78-83, May 1997; R.B. Alley and M.L. Bender, "Greenland Ice Cores: Frozen in Time," *Sci. Am., 278*, 80-85, Feb. 1998; K. Taylor, "Rapid Climate Change," *Am.Sci., 87*, 320-327, Jul/Aug 1999.

Multiple Choice Exam Questions

1.   The CLIMAP project was able to reconstruct the earth's ocean surface temperature in the past by examining
   a. deep ocean water.
   b. rock layers on land.
* c. thousands of feet of sediment at the bottom of the ocean.
   d. soils deposited over the North American continent.

2.   Evidence suggests that throughout much of the earth's history, the global climate was
* a. warmer than it is today.
   b. colder than it is today.
   c. about the same temperature as it is today.
   d. more variable than it is today.

3.   Which of the following is not true?
   a. oxygen 16 evaporates more readily from the ocean than oxygen 18
* b. oxygen 16 and oxygen 18 are found in roughly equal amounts in ocean water
   c. the nucleus of oxygen 18 contains two more neutrons than the nucleus of oxygen 16
   d. both oxygen 16 and oxygen 18 are found in the shells of marine organisms

4.   Dendrochronology is the study of
      a. the ice ages.
*   b. the annual growth rings of trees.
      c. the time history of past climatic conditions.
      d. fossil pollen.
      e. lake-bottom sediments.

5.   The higher the ratio of oxygen 18 to oxygen 16 in the shells of organisms that lived in the sea during the
      geologic past, the ___ the climate at that time.
*   a. colder
      b. warmer
      c. wetter
      d. drier

6.   A high concentration of oxygen 16 found in the ice caves of Antarctica and Greenland would
      indicate ___ at the time the ice was formed.
*   a. cold air temperatures
      b. mild winters
      c. intense ultraviolet radiation
      d. the caves were under the ocean

7.   Which of the following has been used to reconstruct past climates?
      a. analysis of pollen in soil deposits and sea bottom sediments
      b. study of documents describing floods, droughts and crop yields
      c. the ratio of oxygen 18 to oxygen 16 in the shells of marine organisms
      d. study of geologic formations
*   e. all of the above

8.   Presently ice sheets and glaciers cover ___ of the earth's surface.
*   a. about 10 percent
      b. less than 1 percent
      c. approximately two thirds
      d. none

9.   During the Pleistocene epoch
      a. continental glaciers continuously covered large parts of North America and Europe.
      b. it was much warmer than now.
*   c. continental glaciers alternately advanced and retreated over large portions of North America and Europe.
      d. tropical vegetation was growing over vast regions of the Central Plains of North America.

10.   Thick sheets of ice advanced over North America as far south as New York as recently as
      a. 1816 ("the year without a summer").
      b. 1550.
*   c. 18,000 to 22,000 years ago.
      d. 2 million years ago, at the beginning of the Pleistocene epoch.

11.   The "year without a summer" occurred in
      a. 1950.
*   b. 1816.
      c. 1735.
      d. 1681.
      e. 1492.

12. During the climatic optimum
*   a. the climate favored the development of certain plants.
   b. average temperatures were colder than at present.
   c. continental ice sheets began to melt.
   d. alpine glaciers began to advance down river valleys.

13. Over the past 100 years or so, it appears that average global temperatures have
*   a. increased slightly.
   b. fluctuated widely but shown no overall change.
   c. decreased slightly.
   d. remained constant.

14. The Viking colony in Greenland perished during
   a. the Pleistocene epoch.
   b. the climatic optimum.
*   c. the Little Ice Age.
   d. the explosion of Mt. Pinatubo.

15. During the Little Ice Age
   a. the climatic optimum occurred.
   b. the Bering land bridge formed.
*   c. alpine glaciers grew in size and advanced.
   d. continental glaciers covered large portions of North America.
   e. sea level lowered by about 280 ft.

16. The "year without a summer" (1816) may have been caused by
   a. soot from coal fires.
*   b. particulate matter and gases from volcanoes.
   c. a dust cloud produced when a meteorite collided with the earth.
   d. deforestation.

17. If the earth were in a cooling trend, which process below would most likely act as a <u>positive</u> feedback mechanism?
*   a. increasing the snow cover around the earth
   b. increasing the water vapor content of the air
   c. decreasing the amount of cloud cover around the globe
   d. increasing the carbon dioxide content of the air

18. If the earth were in a warming trend, which of the processes below would most likely act as a <u>negative</u> feedback mechanism?
   a. increasing the water vapor content of the air
*   b. increasing the snow cover around the earth
   c. decreasing the amount of cloud cover around the globe
   d. increasing the carbon dioxide content of the air

19. Plate tectonics "explains" certain climatic changes by showing that these changes may be related to
   a. mountain building.
   b. the amount of CO_2 and H_2O released into the atmosphere.
   c. the paths taken by ocean currents.
   d. the position of the continents.
*   e. all of the above

20. A positive feedback mechanism
   a. acts to reinforce an initial change.
   b. acts to weaken or oppose an initial change.
   c. will cause a positive change.
   d. will cause a negative change.

21. Which theory explains how glacial material can be observed today near sea level at the equator, even though sea level glaciers probably never existed there?
   a. Milankovitch theory
   * b. theory of plate tectonics
   c. volcanic dust theory
   d. Maunder theory

22. The Milankovitch Theory proposes that climatic changes are due to
   a. variations in the earth's orbit as it travels around the sun.
   b. volcanic eruptions.
   c. changing levels of CO_2 in the earth's atmosphere.
   d. particles suspended in the earth's atmosphere.

23. During a period when the earth's orbital tilt is at a minimum, which would probably <u>not</u> be true?
   a. there should be less seasonal variation between summer and winter
   b. more snow would probably fall during the winter in polar regions
   * c. there would be a lesser likelihood of glaciers at high latitudes
   d. there would be less seasonal variations at middle latitudes

24. Precession of the equinox refers to
   a. changes in the shape of the earth's orbit as the earth revolves around the sun.
   b. changes in the tilt of the earth as it orbits the sun.
   c. changes in the seasons, especially from winter to summer.
   * d. the wobble of the earth on its axis.

25. The Milankovitch theory suggests that climates changes on the earth could be caused by
   a. changes in the shape of the earth's orbit around the sun.
   b. changes in the direction of tilt of the earth's axis.
   c. changes in the amount of tilt of the earth's axis.
   * d. all of the above.

26. Volcanic eruptions that have the greatest impact on global climate appear to be those rich in
   a. nitrogen.
   b. water vapor.
   c. carbon dioxide.
   * d. sulfur.

27. Large volcanic eruptions with an ash veil that enters the stratosphere, tend to ___ at the surface.
   a. increase temperatures
   b. increase precipitation
   * c. decrease temperatures
   d. have no effect

28. It appears that, as the number of sunspots increases, the sun's total energy output
   * a. increases slightly.
   b. decreases slightly.
   c. begins to alternately increase and decrease above average values.
   d. does not change.

29. The Milankovitch cycles in association with other natural factors explain how glaciers may advance and retreat over periods of
   a. hundreds of millions of years.
   b. several million years.
   c. hundreds of thousands of years.
   * d. ten thousand to one hundred thousand years.
   e. hundreds of years.

30. The Maunder Minimum refers to a time when
   a. the earth was in the middle of an ice age.
   b. the tilt of the earth's axis was less than it is now.
   c. the earth was closer to the sun than it is now.
   d. few snowstorms occurred over the United States.
   * e. there were fewer sunspots.

31. Studies reveal that during colder glacial periods, CO_2 levels ___ during warmer interglacial periods.
   a. were higher than
   * b. were lower than
   c. were about the same as
   d. were more variable than

32. For CO_2 to produce a global warming of between 1 °C and 3.5 °C, climatic models predict that the concentration of this gas <u>must</u> also increase in the atmosphere.
   a. chlorofluorocarbons (CFCs)
   b. nitrous oxide (N_2O)
   * c. water vapor (H_2O)
   d. ozone (O_3)

33. An increase in atmospheric CO_2 concentrations will most likely lead to ___ in the troposphere and ___ in the upper atmosphere.
   a. warming, warming
   b. cooling, warming
   * c. warming, cooling
   d. cooling, cooling

34. It is now known that, overall, clouds
   a. have a net warming effect on climate.
   * b. have a net cooling effect on climate.
   c. have no net effect on climate.
   d. are the single most important feature in determining climate.

35. The most recent warming trend experienced over the Northern Hemisphere could be the result of
   a. increasing volcanic eruptions.
   b. light colored particles in the stratosphere.
   * c. increasing levels of greenhouse gases.
   d. a decrease in the energy emitted by the sun.
   e. an observed decrease in snow cover.

36. Everything else being equal, a gradual increase in global CO_2 would most likely bring about
   * a. an increase in surface air temperature.
   b. a marked decrease in plant growth.
   c. a decrease in evaporation from the earth's oceans.
   d. no change in global climate.

37.   Which of the conditions below would most likely produce warming at the earth's surface?
       a. increase the amount of low-level global cloudiness
       b. increase the amount of sulfur-rich particles in the stratosphere
       c. decrease the energy output of the sun
       d. increase the amount of global snow cover
*   e. increase the amount of high-level global cloud cover

38.   Which below is not one of the possible consequences of global warming predicted by climate models?
       a. accumulations of additional snow in Antarctica
       b. a reduction in average precipitation over certain areas
*   c. lowering of sea levels
       d. a cooling of the upper atmosphere
       e. a drop in the rate of ozone destruction in the stratosphere

39.   Climate models predict that if average global temperatures rise, average global precipitation will
*   a. increase.
       b. decrease.
       c. remain the same.
       d. vary from year to year.

40.   Which of the following is not true of the Sahel?
*   a. is mostly a sand-covered desert
       b. is a region of variable rainfall
       c. has experienced great famine
       d. is located in North Africa

41.   A biogeophysical feedback mechanism in the Sahel relates
       a. reduced cloud cover to increasing surface temperatures and an increase in rainfall.
*   b. reduced vegetation to a decrease in surface temperatures and a reduction in rainfall.
       c. an increase in vegetation to an increase in surface temperatures and a reduction in rainfall.
       d. a decrease in vegetation to a lowering of surface albedo and an increase in rainfall.

True/False Exam Questions

1.   Many scientists believe the earth is in a comparatively warm part of an ice age.
       (ans: TRUE)

2.   Glaciers have advanced over large areas of North America and retreated as many as 10 times during the past 2 million years or so. The most recent extension of glaciers, as far south as New York and the Ohio River Valley, occurred approximately 200,000 years ago.
       (ans: FALSE)

3.   Most of the increase in global mean surface temperatures in the past 150 years or so has occured at night.
       (ans: TRUE)

4.   Recent evidence suggests that the variations in the earth's orbit around the sun proposed by Milankovitch actually have very little effect on the earth's climate.
       (ans: FALSE)

5.   Venus is about the same size as the earth but has an atmosphere that is nearly 100 times more dense than that of the earth. Even though Venus is closer to the sun, average surface temperatures on Venus are much colder than on the earth.
       (ans: FALSE)

6. A cloud composed of a large number of small cloud droplets is apparently more reflective than a cloud composed of fewer but larger droplets.
(ans: TRUE)

7. Some of the warmest years in the twentieth century occurred during the 1990s. Large volcanic eruptions such as the 1991 eruption of Mt. Pinatubo in the Philippines, which injected an estimated 20 million tons of sulfur dioxide into the atmosphere, are thought to cause small increases in mean global surface temperatures that can persist for one to three years following the eruption.
(ans: FALSE)

8. Some scientists have suggested that droughts which recur every 20 years or so on the Great Plains of the Unites States may be correlated with the sun's 22-year magnetic cycle.
(ans: TRUE)

9. While carbon dioxide concentrations have been increasing steadily for the past century or so, the concentrations of methane (CH_4), nitrous oxide (N_2O), and other greenhouse gases have been decreasing.
(ans: FALSE)

10. The combined effect of trace greenhouse gases (such as methane (CH_4), nitrous oxide (N_2O), and CFCs) in enhancing the greenhouse effect is about equal to carbon dioxide.
(ans: TRUE)

11. Warm ocean water can't contain as much dissolved carbon dioxide as cool ocean water.
(ans: TRUE)

Word Choice Exam Questions

1. The Bering land bridge was exposed during the most recent GLACIAL INTERGLACIAL period which allowed human and animal migration from Asian to North America. (circle one answer)
(ans: GLACIAL)

2. The Vikings colonized Greenland and explored the coast of North American during a relatively WARM COLD period about ONE TEN thousand years ago. (choose one word from each pair)
(ans: WARM, ONE)

3. Did the Little Ice Age occur during a period of HIGH or LOW sunspot activity? (circle one answer)
(ans: LOW)

4. Global mean surface temperatures appear to have increased slightly during the past 150 years or so. The greatest increase has occurred at POLAR MIDDLE TROPICAL latitudes and over the CONTINENTS OCEANS. (choose one word from each group)
(ans: MIDDLE, CONTINENTS)

5. Would you expect the chain reaction known as a runaway greenhouse effect to result from an unchecked POSITIVE or NEGATIVE feedback process? (circle one answer)
(ans: POSITIVE)

6. The earth circles the sun in a(n) CIRCULAR ELLIPTICAL orbit. (circle one answer)
(ans: ELLIPTICAL)

7. Analysis of bubbles in polar ice cores indicate that periods of warmer-than-average temperatures are accompanied by relatively HIGH LOW atmospheric carbon dioxide concentrations. (circle one answer)
(ans: HIGH)

8. Human activities add aerosols to the atmosphere; the overall effect of these particles on climate appears to be a net COOLING WARMING of surface temperatures. (circle one answer)
    (ans: COOLING)

9. Sulfate aerosols are good REFLECTORS ABSORBERS of sunlight and their effect on climate has been studied extensively in recent years. (circle one answer)
    (ans: REFLECTORS)

10. The nuclear winter scenario envisions an upper level layer of strongly REFLECTING ABSORBING soot particles which would cause the ground to cool by reducing the amount of sunlight able to reach the ground. (circle one answer)
    (ans: ABSORBING)

11. When the conveyor belt ocean circulation stops, winters in Europe are much WARMER COLDER than normal. (circle one answer)
    (ans: COLDER)

Short Answer Exam Questions

1. Human and animal migration from Asia to North America occurred a glacial period 18,000 to 22,000 years ago when low sea levels meant that the _____ was exposed.
    (ans: BERING LAND BRIDGE)

2. Atmospheric concentrations of _____ are expected to increase to about 500 ppm by the year 2100. The predicted 1° to 3.5 °C means global warming of surface air assumes that atmospheric concentrations of _____ will also increase.
    (ans: CARBON DIOXIDE, WATER VAPOR)

3. Two atoms of an element that have the same number of protons but different numbers of neutrons in the atom's nucleus are known as _____.
    (ans: ISOTOPES)

4. The theory of plate tectonics was formerly known as the theory of _____.
    (ans: CONTINENTAL DRIFT)

5. The number and size of sunspots reaches a maximum approximately once every _____ years.
    (ans: 11)

6. In a thermohaline circulation, ocean currents are caused by differences in _____ and
    _____.
    (ans: TEMPERATURE and SALINITY)

7. The Maunder minimum between 1645 and 1715, a period were there were few if any _____ occurred during the coldest part of the Little Ice Age.
    (ans: SUNSPOTS)

8. The Milankovitch theory suggests that glacial and interglacial episodes during the past 2 million years are caused by small changes in _____ and _____.
    (ans: TILT of the EARTH'S AXIS, SHAPE of the EARTH'S ORBIT around the sun)

9. An increase in global average temperatures and humidity might cause an increase in _____ which could promote warming or cooling.
    (ans: GLOBAL CLOUDINESS)

10.   The Intergovernmental Panel on Climate Change (IPCC) concluded that global _____ has risen 10 to 25 cm over the past 100 years and attributed the increase to global warming.
(ans: SEA LEVEL)

Essay Exam Questions

1.   Describe some of the techniques used to infer past climates. About how far back are these different methods able to reconstruct past climatic conditions?

2.   Explain how analysis of glacial and polar ice cores provide important clues about past climate.

3.   Briefly describe the climatic variations that have occurred since the beginning of the Pleistocene epoch to the present day.

4.   Asia and the North American continent have been connected by a land bridge at various times during the past. When was the Bering land bridge most recently exposed? Did this coincide with a warm or cool climatic period?

5.   When did the Little Ice Age occur? Have there been any suggestions of a possible cause of the Little Ice Age?

6.   What are meant by the terms positive and negative feedback mechanisms? Give an example of a process that would be considered a positive feedback mechanism during a period of warming on the earth. Can you think of a negative feedback mechanism?

7.   List and discuss some of the ways that plate tectonics might affect the earth's climate.

8.   Discuss the changes that occur in the earth's orbit and orientation of the earth in its orbit. Over what time scales do these different changes occur?

9.   What combination of the earth's orbital eccentricity, and precession and obliquity of the earth's axis would produce hottest summer temperatures in the Northern Hemisphere?

10.   Explain why we might expect changes in climate on the earth to be correlated with the number of sunspots visible on the sun.

11.   Assume that you have 100 years of continuous temperature records from you local weather service office. Discuss some of the difficulties you might have trying to determine whether average temperatures have increased during this period.

12.   Carbon dioxide concentrations in the atmosphere have been increasing steadily since the beginning of the industrial revolution and may double by the middle of the next century. Why is this of concern?

13.   Does deforestation act to increase or decrease atmospheric carbon dioxide concentrations?

14.   In addition to carbon dioxide, what other gases may contribute to the problem of global warming? Why might global warming lead to an increase in global cloudiness? What possible effects would increased cloudiness have on global warming?

15.   What are some of the possible consequences of global warming?

16.   Where is the Sahel located? Is this a region of scarce, variable or abundant rainfall? Describe the biogeophysical feedback mechanism whereby a reduction in surface vegetation might cause a reduction in precipitation amounts.

Chapter 15
Light, Color, and Atmospheric Optics

Summary

This chapter describes and explains a variety of atmospheric optical phenomena. The chapter begins with a brief review of the physical nature of light and explains our physiological perception of light and color. A first group of optical effects, which are all produced by scattering of light, is then discussed. Air molecules, for example, selectively scatter the shorter wavelengths of sunlight and give a clean sky its deep blue color. Larger aerosol particles scatter different wavelengths more equally, and can turn the sky milky white. White clouds, the blue color of distant mountains, and crepuscular rays are additional examples of light scattering.

A second category of optical phenomena involves refraction and the dispersion of light. Mirages form when light is bent as it propagates through air layers with different densities. An inferior mirage can cause light from the sky to be bent so that it appears to be coming from the ground, and may make a road surface appear wet on a hot dry afternoon. Under unusual circumstances, refraction and dispersion can cause a green flash of light to appear as the sun sets below the horizon. Haloes and sundogs are relatively frequent events and occur when light passes through a high thin cloud layer composed of ice crystals. The formation of primary and secondary rainbows is discussed in some detail. In a primary rainbow, light rays are refracted as they enter a raindrop and are then reflected off the back inside surface of the raindrop. To see a rainbow, you must have the sun behind you, and it must be low in the sky.

A brief discussion of corona and cloud iridescence, which are produced by diffraction, is included at the end of the chapter.

Key Terms
(Listed in approximately the same order they appear in the text. Terms in boldface are emphasized and appear at the end of the chapter in the text.)

rods	white night	**sun pillar**
cones	**green flash**	**rainbow**
reflected light	**mirage**	critical angle
scattered light	shimmering	internal reflection
diffuse light	**inferior (lower) mirage**	primary rainbow
selective scatterer	**superior (upward) mirage**	secondary bow
blue haze	Fata Morgana	**corona**
terpenes	**halo**	**diffraction**
crepuscular rays	tangent arc	**iridescence**
transmitted light	**dispersion (of light)**	glory
refraction (of light)	**sundog (or parhelia)**	brocken bow
scintillation	mock suns	Heiligenschein
twilight		

Teaching Suggestions, Demonstrations, and Visual Aids

The two books by C.F. Bohren, <u>Clouds in a Glass of Beer</u> and <u>What Light Through Yonder Window Breaks</u>, are excellent sources of atmospheric optics demonstrations (see references on pps. 44 and 59 of this manual).

1.   Be sure that students understand the color of an object is determined by the wavelength(s) of light reflected or scattered by the surface of the object and is usually not because the object is emitting light. Place a red filter on the overhead projector (small sheets of gelatin filter material should be available at a local photograpic supplies store). Place a green or blue object in the red light. The object will appear black. Place a white object in the red light and it will appear red.

2.   Many students will not appreciate the difference between reflection and scattering of light. R.M. Price and K.M. Parrish have described an effective demonstration (ref: *Am. J. Phys.*, 50, 473, 1982). Illuminate a smooth piece of aluminum foil with a beam of light. The beam will be reflected by the mirror-like surface. Next crumple the foil into a ball and then straighten and flatten it out. The light will now be scattered off in all directions by the wrinkled surface.

To demonstrate scattering, shine a beam of light (from a laser, a slide projector, or cover the top of an overhead projector with a piece of cardboard with a small circular aperture cut in the middle) through an aquarium or large beaker filled with water. If the water is clean and free of bubbles, the beam of light will be invisible. Next, add a small amount of milk to the water. The beam of light will become clearly discernible. If the light source is white, the scattered light might also have a bluish tint. The fat globules in milk are sometimes small enough to selectively scatter short wavelengths. In this case, place a white screen at the far end of the aquarium to make the transmitted light visible to the class. The transmitted light will have a yellow or orange hue. If more milk is added, the beam of scattered light will broaden and become more diffuse; this is a demonstration of multiple scattering (see chapter 14 in <u>Clouds in a Glass of Beer</u>).

Shine a laser or beam of light across the front of a darkened classroom. Unless the air is unusually dusty, the beam will not be visible. Then clap two chalk board erasers together so that the chalk dust falls into the light beam. The beam will become visible. Or, hold a piece of dry ice above the beam so that the cloud that forms around the dry ice will descend into the light beam. This dense cloud scatters most of the incident light. Very little directly transmitted light will be visible on the opposite wall of the classroom.

3.   Refraction can be demonstrated using a rectangular piece of thick (3/4 or 1 inch) plexiglas. Polish the edges of the plexiglas (suitable materials are often available from the plexiglas distributor). Press the plexiglas against a vertical screen. Using a laser or other narrow beam light source, cause light to shine down on the top edge of the

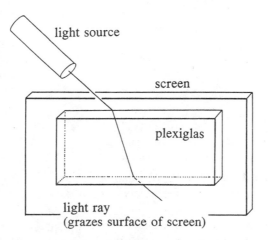

plexiglas at an angle. With care the light source can be oriented so that the light beam just grazes the surface of the screen and its path will be visible. The light beam will bend noticeably as it enters the plexiglas and then again, in the opposite direction as it exits the plexiglas. Vary the angle of the incident beam of light.

A semi-circular piece of plexiglas can be used to show internal reflection as illustrated below. The incident light ray strikes the plexiglas at a right angle and is not refracted. The angle at which the ray strikes the flat edge of the plexiglas can be varied to show internal reflection. (ref: R. Bruman, <u>Exploratorium Cookbook I</u>, 1984; available from the Exploratorium, 3601 Lyon St., San Francisco, CA 94123). A circular piece of plexiglas can be cut on a lathe and used to illustrate the passage of a light ray through a raindrop.

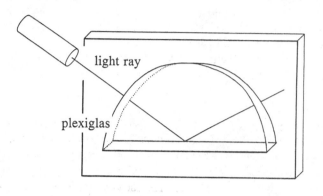

To illustrate the dispersion of light into colors by a raindrop, cover the back half of a spherical glass flask and fill the flask with water. Support the flask vertically with a ring stand and clamp. Project a collimated beam of white light, through a hole in a screen, onto the upper half surface of the flask. The colored light will be visible on the screen. The angle of minimum deviation is also illustrated well by this demonstration. The color and clarity of the rainbow is improved if a smooth metallic coating can be applied to the flask instead of the foil.

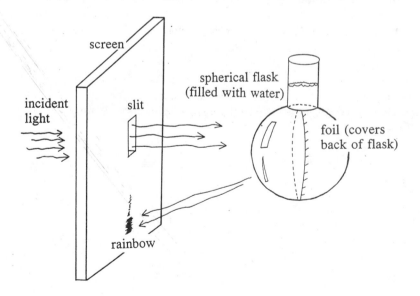

4.   Two articles, "Swimming Pool Optics" by H. Kruglak (ref: *Phys. Teacher,* 440, Oct. 1987) and "How Many Fish are in the Tank?" by P.J. Ouseph (*ibid.*), illustrate refractive effects.

5.   Demonstrate the dispersion of white light into its component colors using an equilateral prism. Cover the overhead with a large piece of cardboard which has a narrow slit cut in the middle. Hold the prism in the narrow beam of light between the projector and the screen. The spectrum will be projected onto the screen.

216

Student Projects

1.   Many of the demonstrations above or others in the two books by Bohren could be performed and explained in class by a student or group of students.

2.   Many phenomena such as halos, sundogs and rainbows occur frequently enough that they can be observed and photographed by students.

3.   Students might investigate additional phenomena not discussed in the chapter, such as polarization. Students could also investigate visibility in their locality and devise a means for estimating visibility (see Chapter 16 in <u>Clouds in a Glass of Beer</u>).

Multiple Choice Exam Questions

1.   White light is ___ of electromagnetic radiation.
   a. a single long wavelength
   b. a single short wavelength
* c. a mixture of all visible wavelengths
   d. a mixture of all types

2.   Imagine that this piece of paper is illuminated with white light and appears red. You see red light because
   a. the paper absorbs red and reflects other visible wavelengths.
   b. the paper emits red light.
* c. the paper reflects red and absorbs other visible wavelengths.
   d. the paper disperses white light.

3.   Beams of light that shine downward through breaks or holes in clouds are called
   a. an inferior mirage.
* b. crepuscular rays.
   c. glorys.
   d. corona.
   e. superior mirage.

4.   On the average, as a cloud grows thicker (taller), which below does <u>not</u> occur?
   a. more sunlight is reflected from the cloud
   b. less sunlight is transmitted through the cloud
* c. less sunlight is absorbed by the cloud
   d. more light is scattered by the cloud

5.   Red sunsets, blue moons, and milky-white skies are <u>mainly</u> the result of
   a. refraction.
   b. dispersion.
   c. reflection.
* d. scattering.
   e. diffraction.

6.   Another name for diffuse light is
* a. scattered light.
   b. refracted light.
   c. dispersion of light.
   d. transmission of light.
   e. scintillation of light.

7. The process that produces crepuscular rays in the atmosphere is
    a. scintillation.
    b. diffraction.
*   c. scattering.
    d. dispersion.
    e. refraction.

8. If the earth did not have an atmosphere, the sky would appear ___ during the day.
    a. white
*   b. black
    c. red
    d. blue

9. Stars are not visible during the day because
*   a. the scattered light coming from the sky is too bright to be able to see the weaker light from stars.
    b. the earth is pointed away from the center of the galaxy.
    c. the light from the stars is absorbed and scattered by the atmosphere and does not reach the ground.
    d. all of the above

10. Which of the following would be true if the earth did not have an atmosphere?
    a. there would be fewer hours of daylight
    b. the sky would always be black
    c. the stars would be visible in the sky during the day
*   d. all of the above

11. On a foggy night, it is often difficult to see the road when the high beam lights are on because of ___ of light by the fog.
    a. absorption
*   b. scattering
    c. transmission
    d. refraction
    e. diffraction

12. Air molecules selectively scatter visible light because
*   a. air molecules are smaller than the wavelength of visible light.
    b. air molecules are much larger than the wavelength of visible light.
    c. air molecules are the same size as the wavelength of visible light.
    d. the electrons that orbit around the outside of the air atoms have a blue color.

13. Clouds are composed of water droplets and ice crystals. Clouds appear white because the ice crystals scatter all the visible wavelengths of sunlight about equally. This is largely due to the ___ of the cloud droplets and crystals.
    a. composition
    b. concentration
*   c. size
    d. shape

14. The sky is blue because air molecules selectively ___ blue light.
*   a. scatter
    b. absorb
    c. diffract
    d. disperse
    e. emit

15. The blue color of the sky is due to
 *   a. selective scattering of visible light by air molecules.
     b. the filtering effect of water vapor in the earth's atmosphere.
     c. reflection of sunlight off the earth's oceans.
     d. transmission of visible light through the ozone layer in the earth's stratosphere.

16. A cloud of relatively large smoke particles that absorb rather than scatter sunlight would appear
 *   a. black
     b. blue
     c. red
     d. white

17. If the earth's atmosphere did not contain any water vapor, the sky would have a ____ color.
     a. white
     b. black
     c. orange
 *   d. blue

18. What color would the sky be if air molecules selectively scattered only the longest wavelengths of visible light?
     a. white
     b. blue
 *   c. red
     d. black

19. Which of the following is capable of producing a red sunrise or sunset?
     a. small suspended salt particles
     b. volcanic ash
     c. small suspended dust particles
 *   d. all of the above

20. If the setting sun appears red, you may conclude that
     a. the sun's surface temperature has cooled somewhat at the end of the day.
 *   b. only the longest waves of visible light are striking your eye.
     c. the next day's weather will be stormy.
     d. you will not be able to see the moon that night.

21. The blue haze often seen in the clean air found in mountainous regions is mainly due to the ____ of light.
     a. refraction
     b. absorption
     c. diffraction
 *   d. scattering

22. When the color of the sky is deep blue, you could conclude that the air is relatively
 *   a. clean.
     b. polluted.
     c. cold.
     d. moist.

23. The sky will begin to turn milky white
     a. when the concentration of ozone begins to reach dangerous levels.
 *   b. when small particles such as dust and salt become suspended in the air.
     c. when the relative humidity decreases below about ten percent.
     d. on an oppresively hot day of the year.

24. When a ray of white light strikes a glass prism it will be dispersed into its component colors as shown at right. Which of the rays shown would have the shortest wavelength?
  a. a
  b. b
  c. c
  d. d
* e. e

25. This can only be seen when the sun is to your back and it is raining in front of you.
  a. sundog
  b. halo
* c. rainbow
  d. sun pillar
  e. corona

26. Secondary rainbows occur when
* a. two internal reflections of light occur in raindrops.
  b. light refracts through ice crystals.
  c. a single internal reflection of light occurs in raindrops.
  d. light refracts through a cloud of large raindrops.
  e. the sun disappears behind a cloud and then reappears.

27. Clouds in the tropics tend to move from east to west. Consequently, which rhyme best describes a rainbow seen in the tropics?
* a. rainbow at the break of dawn/ means, of course, the rain is gone
  b. rainbow at the break of day/ means that the rain is on the way
  c. rainbow with a setting sun/ means that sailors can have some fun
  d. rainbow in the morning/ means that sailors should take warning

28. Which of the following processes must occur in a raindrop to produce a rainbow?
* a. refraction, reflection, and dispersion of sunlight
  b. refraction, reflection, and scattering of sunlight
  c. reflection, scattering, and dispersion of sunlight
  d. transmission, reflection, and dispersion of sunlight
  e. refraction, transmission, and scattering of sunlight

29. At sunset in the middle latitudes, look for a rainbow toward the
  a. north.
  b. south.
* c. east.
  d. west.

30. ____ shows where you would expect to see a red-colored band of light in the secondary rainbow.
  a. Point a
* b. Point b
  c. Point c
  d. Point d

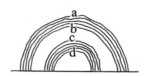

31. Looking in the general direction of the sun you would <u>not</u> be able to see a
    a. corona.
    b. halo.
    c. sundog.
  * d. rainbow.
    e. sun pillar.

32. Which below is <u>not</u> true concerning a secondary rainbow?
    a. it is usually fainter than the primary rainbow
    b. it is seen above the primary rainbow in the sky
    c. the order of its colors is reversed compared to the primary rainbow
  * d. the raindrops which produce the secondary rainbow are larger than the raindrops producing
       the primary bow

33. Which of the following is <u>true</u> about rainbows?
    a. the rainbow will be seen in the west when the sun is setting
    b. rainbows form when rays from the sun are scattered
    c. the brightest rainbows are seen around noon
  * d. to see a rainbow at sunrise, you should look toward the west

34. The bending of light that occurs when it enters and passes <u>through</u> a substance of different density is called
    a. diffraction.
    b. reflection.
  * c. refraction.
    d. scattering.

35. Which of the paths would the light
    ray follow in the figure at right
    when it travels from a less dense
    into a more dense substance?
  * a. bends toward the normal
    b. does not bend
    c. bends away from the normal
    d. is reflected back into the low density material

36. Which of the following phenomena is <u>not</u> produced by refraction?
    a. halos
  * b. crepuscular rays
    c. mirages
    d. sundogs
    e. none of the above

37. Refraction of light by the atmosphere is responsible for
    a. scintillation of starlight.
    b. mirages.
    c. causing the sun to appear to flatten-out on the horizon.
    d. increasing the length of daylight.
  * e. all of the above

38. Because of atmospheric refraction, a star seen near the earth's horizon is actually
    a. slightly higher than it appears.
  * b. slightly lower than it appears.
    c. much dimmer than it appears.
    d. much further away than it appears.

39. When a beam of white light passes through a glass prism, it is separated into its component colors. This is called
   a. diffraction.
   * b. dispersion.
   c. selective scattering.
   d. iridescence.

40. On a summer evening at middle latitudes, twilight adds about how much time to the length of daylight?
   a. 2 minutes
   b. 5 minutes
   * c. 30 minutes
   d. 2 hours

41. This phenomena can sometimes be seen near the upper rim of a setting or rising sun.
   a. sun pillar
   b. the glory
   c. a corona
   * d. the green flash

42. The green flash is largely an example of ___ of light by the earth's atmosphere.
   * a. refraction
   b. reflection
   c. absorption
   d. diffraction

43. Which of the following are caused by the bending of light through ice crystals?
   a. rainbows and halos
   b. halos and the green flash
   * c. halos and sundogs
   d. sundogs and sun pillars
   e. mirages and sundogs

44. A ring of light encircling the sun or moon could be either
   a. a rainbow or a halo.
   b. a halo or a sundog.
   * c. a halo or a corona.
   d. a sundog or a crepuscular ray.

45. Halos are caused by
   a. refraction of light passing through raindrops.
   b. scattering of light by ice crystals.
   * c. refraction of light passing through ice crystals.
   d. diffraction of light by cloud droplets.
   e. reflection of light by ice crystals.

46. As light passes through ice crystals, ___ is bent the least and is, therefore, observed on the ___ of halos or sundogs.
   * a. red, inside
   b. red, outside
   c. blue, inside
   d. blue, outside

47. To see a sundog at sunrise, you should look toward the
    a. north.
    b. south.
    * c. east.
    d. west.

48. To see a sundog, you should look about 22 degrees
    * a. to the right or left of the sun.
    b. above the sun.
    c. below the sun.
    d. all of the above

49. You would most likely see a halo or sundog with which of the following cloud types?
    a. altostratus
    * b. cirrostratus
    c. nimbostratus
    d. cumulus

50. Sunlight reflecting <u>off</u> ice crystals produces
    a. crepuscular rays.
    b. halos.
    * c. sun pillars.
    d. sun dogs.

51. Sun pillars are caused by ___ of light.
    a. dispersion
    b. diffraction
    c. scattering
    d. refraction
    * e. reflection

52. An atmospheric phenomenon that causes objects to appear inverted is called
    a. a superior mirage.
    * b. an inferior mirage.
    c. scintillation.
    d. dispersion.

53. A mirage is caused by
    a. scattering of light by air molecules.
    * b. the bending of light by air of different densities.
    c. a thin layer of moist air near the ground.
    d. reflection of light from a hot surface.

54. Which of the diagrams below correctly depicts the bending of light in an inferior mirage?

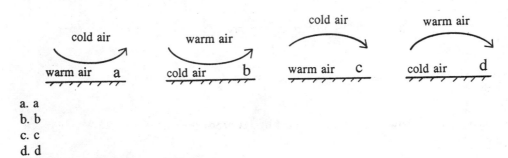

    * a. a
    b. b
    c. c
    d. d

55. A wet-looking road surface on a clear, hot, dry day is an example of
    a. a superior mirage.
    b. scintillation.
    c. diffraction.
    d. condensation.
  * e. none of the above

56. Which of the following would you most likely observe over snow covered ground in the winter?
  * a. superior mirage
    b. sun pillars
    c. crespuscular rays
    d. shimmering

57. Cloud iridescence is caused mainly by
    a. refraction.
    b. reflection.
  * c. diffraction.
    d. dispersion.

True/False Exam Questions

1. The base of a thick cloud will appear dark because most of the light passing through the cloud is absorbed before being transmitted to the base of the cloud.
   (ans: FALSE)

2. Although rare, the sun can appear blue when an abundance of similarly-sized smoke or dust particles selectively scatter red light.
   (ans: TRUE)

3. A sky with a deep blue color indicates high humidity.
   (ans: FALSE)

4. Because of refraction a star appears to be higher in the sky than is actually the case.
   (ans: TRUE)

5. The primary rainbow is produced by raindrops falling below a cloud; the secondary bow is produced by frozen precipitation.
   (ans: FALSE)

6. Light is refracted when it enters a raindrop and refracted again when it leaves the drop.
   (ans: TRUE)

7. Drops of water can refract and disperse white light, ice crystals cannot.
   (ans: FALSE)

8. Mirages can be produced by either a very cold or very hot layer of air next to the ground.
   (ans: TRUE)

9. Mirages can sometimes make distant objects appear taller than is really the case.
   (ans: TRUE)

10. Mirages, haloes, and rainbows are all optical phenomena produced by the refraction of light.
    (ans: TRUE)

Word Choice Exam Questions

1. If you travelled high up into the atmosphere where there is very little air left above you, would you expect the sky to appear DARKER or LIGHTER than at sea level. (circle one answer)
    (ans: DARKER)

2. Is the blue color of the sky due to the fact that air molecules are LARGER than, the SAME size as, or SMALLER than the wavelength of visible light and selectively SCATTER ABSORB short wavelengths of light. (choose one word from each group)
    (ans: SMALLER, SCATTER)

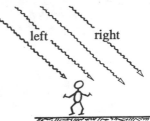

3. Rays of sunlight are shown in the picture at right. To see the blue light scattered by the atmosphere, the observer should look up and toward the RIGHT LEFT. THe person would see the brightest light when looking up and LEFT RIGHT. (choose one word from each pair)
    (ans: RIGHT, LEFT)

4. Because of bending of sunlight by the atmosphere the sun will appear to rise about two minutes EARLIER LATER than would otherwise be the case. (circle one answer)
    (ans: EARLIER)

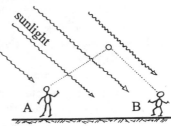

5. Two people in the figure at right are looking at the same point in the sky. Is person A seeing SCATTERED or UNSCATTERED light? (circle one answer)
    (ans: SCATTERED)

6. The sun often appears redder as it sets. Does this mean that, as the sun sets, MORE or LESS blue light is being scattered as the sunlight passes through the atmosphere. (circle one answer)
    (ans: MORE)

7. To see a sundog or halo it is important that the cloud be THICK THIN. Does the cloud need to be composed of ICE crystals or supercooled WATER droplets? (choose one word from each pair)
    (ans: THIN, ICE)

8. Enlarged and normal views of light passing through a raindrop and being separated into colors are shown at right. Ray A would have LONGER SHORTER wavelength than ray B. The rays shown would produce the PRIMARY SECONDARY rainbow. You would see color A at a HIGHER LOWER elevation angle above the horizon than ray B. (choose one word from each pair)
    (ans: SHORTER, PRIMARY, LOWER)

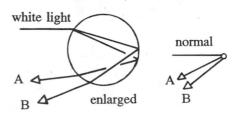

9. To see the secondary rainbow, you should look ABOVE BELOW the primary rainbow. (circle one answer)
    (ans: ABOVE)

10. The two people in the figure at right are looking at a rainshower. Will PERSON A, PERSON B, or BOTH PEOPLE see a rainbow? (circle one answer)
    (ans: PERSON A)

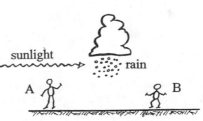

11.   A(n) INFERIOR SUPERIOR mirage will sometimes cause a HOT COLD road surface to appear to be covered with water. (choose one word from each pair)
(ans: INFERIOR, HOT)

Short Answer Exam Questions

1.   Scattering of sunlight by an air molecules is illustrated in the figure at right. Answer the questions with A, B, or C, which refer to the three groups of rays in the figure.
Group _____ is scattered light.
The most intense beam of light would be _____.
There would be more short wavelength light
   than long wavelength light in group _____.
(ans: B, A, B)

2.   Light rays that "bounce" off a surface at the same angle are _____; when the rays are sent off in all directions they are _____.
(ans: REFLECTED, SCATTERED)

3.   What might you infer about particles that scatter sunlight and produce a blue haze?
(ans: PARTICLE SIZE is less than the wavelength of visible light)

4.   When white light passes through a glass prism, it is refracted and split up into different colors. This "selective" refraction is called _____.
(ans: DISPERSION)

5.   Light is refracted or bent when it passes from one transparent material into another with a different _____.
(ans: DENSITY)

6.   If you see that the sky is covered with a thin, high altitude, ice crystal cloud (cirrostratus) one morning, you might expect to be able to observe what two optical phenomena during the day?
(ans: HALO and SUNDOG)

7.   White light passing through a 6-sided ice crystal will be separated into colors just like light shining through a glass prism. In the atmosphere this process would produce a(n) _____.
(ans: HALO or SUNDOG)

8.   When the sun is setting and a thin cirrostratus layer cloud is present, you might see a(n)_____.
(ans: SUNDOG)

9.   A ray of white light can interact with a raindrop in a variety of ways as shown below. Which two correctly illustrate rainbow formation?

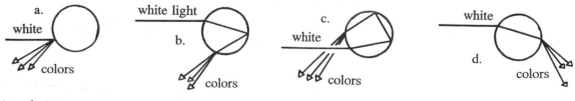

(ans: b,c)

10.   A ring of light surrounding the sun or moon could indicate a(n) _____ or a(n) _____.
(ans: HALO or CORONA)

11. A ring of light around the moon consisting of a alternating bands of light and dark is probably a(n) _____.
(ans: CORONA)

Essay Exam Questions

1. What color would the sky be if the earth's atmosphere were composed entirely of carbon dioxide molecules? Do you think that this is what sometimes causes the sky on Mars to appear red?

2. With a sketch, show why the setting sun will often appear red to an observer on the ground. Why does the sun appear white at noon, and red at sunrise and sunset?

3. Why aren't stars visible in the sky during the day?

4. Why do distant mountains appear blue?

5. Distinquish between the processes of reflection, refraction and scattering of light. Give an example of an atmospheric phenomena produced by each one. Which of these processes produces dispersion?

6. Illustrate with a sketch the refraction and dispersion of light as it passes through a glass prism.

7. Sketch the path that a ray of light follows as it passes through a raindrop and forms a primary rainbow. How is the path of a ray forming the secondary rainbow different?

8. Sketch a rainbow. Your drawing should show the correct positions of the primary and secondary bow and the proper order of colors in each. Where would the sun be in your picture?

9. What phenomena causes a road surface appear to be wet on a hot, clear, dry day? Why does the road appear to be wet? How would the road appear if it really were wet?

10. Using a diagram, if necessary, show why an inferior mirage produces an inverted image.

11. Would you expect to see a halo under clear or cloudy conditions? What does a halo tell you about upper atmospheric conditions?

12. What produces a sundog? Where and at what time of day should you look to try to see a sundog?